P9-DFR-718

Mass Communication
and Political
Information Processing

COMMUNICATION

A series of volumes edited by:
Dolf Zillmann and **Jennings Bryant**

Mass Communication and Political Information Processing

Edited by
Sidney Kraus
Cleveland State University

LAWRENCE ERLBAUM ASSOCIATES, PUBLISHERS
1990   Hillsdale, New Jersey   Hove and London

Copyright © 1990 by Lawrence Erlbaum Associates, Inc.
All rights reserved. No part of the book may be reproduced in
any form, by photostat, microform, retrieval system, or any other
means, without the prior written permission of the publisher.

Lawrence Erlbaum Associates, Inc., Publishers
365 Broadway
Hillsdale, New Jersey 07642

Library of Congress Cataloging-in-Publication Data

Mass communication and political information processing / edited by
  Sidney Kraus.
        p.   cm.
    Papers presented at a symposium on "political informational
  processing" held during a congress entitled "communication and
  cognition—applied epistemology" held Dec. 6–8, 1987, in Gent,
  Belgium.
    ISBN 0–8058–0389–0
    1. Mass media—Political aspects—Congresses.   I. Kraus, Sidney.
  P95.8.M377   1990
  302.23—dc20   89–23516
                                                      CIP

Printed in the United States of America
10 9 8 7 6 5 4 3 2 1

For my daughters-in-law, *Lynn (Pere) Gerou*
and *Lu Ann Schwartzlander-Kraus*,
and my son-in-law, *Kevin Richardson*,
who are all an important part
of my family

Contents

ix

PART II: STRATEGIES AND EFFECTS

PART III: IMAGE-INFORMATION STIMULI

Contributors

Robert Abelman • Department of Communication, Cleveland State University

Stanley J. Baran • Department of Theater Arts, San Jose State University

James R. Beniger • Annenberg School of Communications, University of Southern California

Diane Brigliadoro • Department of Communication, Cleveland State University

Carl Camden • Account Planning Group, Wyse Advetising

Tsan-Kuo Chang • Department of Communication, Cleveland State University

E. De Bens • Department of Communication Science, State University of Gent, Belgium

Gary Jones • Annenberg School of Communications, University of Southern California

Sidney Kraus • Department of Communication, Cleveland State University

Gerald M. Kosicki • School of Journalism, Ohio State University

Gladys Engel Lang • School of Communication and Departments of Sociology and Political Science, University of Washington

Kurt Lang • School of Communication and Department of Sociology, University of Washington

Jack M. McCleod • School of Journalism and Mass Communication, University of Wisconsin-Madison

Harold Mendelsohn • Center for Mass Communication Research and Policy, University of Denver

Frank E. Millar • Department of Communication, University of Wyoming

Dan Nimmo • Department of Communication, University of Oklahoma

Gary R. Pettey • Department of Communication, Cleveland State University

George Sapin • Account Services, Wyse Advertising

Klaus Schoenbach • School of Journalism, Academy for Music and Theater, Hannover, West Germany

Steve Verba • Marketing Decisions Group, Wyse Advertising

Preface

In 1986, organizers of the 20th anniversary celebration of Communication and Cognition proposed a congress entitled: "Communication and Cognition—Applied Epistemology," to be held in Gent, Belgium, December 6–8, 1987. They invited me to participate as a convener of a symposium on "Cognitive Politicology," a title that I subsequently changed to "Political Information Processing."

The rationale for the symposium—unique, innovative papers prepared especially for the symposium—was developed in consultation with many of the scholars whose chapters appear in this volume. A brief, informal organizing session at the International Communication Association's annual meeting in 1986 provided some information about tactics, topics, and participants. Subsequent discussions with these and other investigators revealed current interest in cognitive processing of political information that was approached from an interdisciplinary perspective. It became evident that a variety of research methodologies would be utilized. The topics were generated within broad, nonmutually exclusive categories. We would organize the symposium into three sessions: (a) theoretical constructs; (b) strategies and effects; and (c) image-formation stimuli.

This book is the result of the events just described. Ten studies represented in this volume were presented at Gent. Chapters 7 and 8 were developed after the symposium, and chapters 9, 10, and 12 were either additionally researched with material added, or substantially altered, after presentation.

Sidney Kraus

I | THEORETICAL CONSTRUCTS

1 | Principles of Information Selection in Information Processing: A Preliminary Political Analysis

Dan Nimmo
University of Oklahoma

Students of political behavior have traveled a long distance since first they trod the path of empirical analysis of their subject matter. Whether they have made progress along the road of understanding remains to be seen. It is clear, however, that they have resided in many hostelries on the journey. One of the earliest was that of now almost forgotten innkeeper Stuart Rice (1928), whose hospitality provided the view that political behavior is the manifestation of political attitudes—attitudes that filter objects in the individual's social world; lie along a liberal–conservative continuum; and would be normally distributed were it not for disturbing factors such as persuasive messages that make abnormality typical. Other resting points along the way included the shelters of the early voting studies with their emphases on the limited effects of campaigns on attitudinal conversion (Berelson, Lazarsfeld, & McPhee, 1954; Lazarsfeld, Berelson, & Gaudet, 1944); the post-World War II Yale-based, experimental studies of attitude change (e.g., Hovland, Janis, & Kelly, 1953); and the recently furnished lodgings of uses and gratifications (Katz, Gurevitch, & Haas, 1973; Rosengren, Wenner, & Palmgreen, 1985); the spiral of silence (Noelle-Neumann, 1980); agenda setting (McCombs, 1981) and media refraction (Lang & Lang, 1983)—to name but a few of the more elegant.

One of the more contemporary dwellings offering both theory and findings—or bed and breakfast—for scholars of political behavior is identified by the sign outside its door that reads: information processing. As so much of current literature indicates, it attracts both overnight and permanent guests. For example, Bennett (1981) cataloged and reviewed the condition of existing lodges; Conover and Feldman (1984) resided long enough to suggest how

3

people organize their political world via information-processing schema; Kraus and Perloff (1985) offer an information-processing guide to the role of the mass media in political behavior; and, other scholars have checked in to describe the utility of using schema approaches to understand how voters assess presidential candidates (Miller, Wattenberg, & Malanchuk, 1986).

It goes without saying that to discuss political information processing presumes that individuals possess some minimal levels of political information to process in the first place. It is the purpose of this stay in the hostel of information processing to address that question, namely, how individuals select sources that provide the bases for political information processing, particularly their news media sources. This involves, first, a description of a general framework for addressing the question; second, an account of an intensive analysis to illustrate the use of that framework; and, third, a few suggestions for where to turn next.

CHOOSING INFORMATION SOURCES: CHOICES PRIOR TO PROCESSING

Typically, studies of people's sources of political information ask individuals what media they rely on most for political information—newspapers, news-magazines, radio, television, and so on. Or, they ask which particular news journals they read, broadcasts they listen to, or televised newscasts they watch. Agenda-setting studies proceed to analyze the content of particular media, assess which items and issues are emphasized most, then correlate those rankings with the problems that surveyed respondents find most pressing. Early election studies examined the effects of editorial slant on voting choices. One of the most notable efforts to apply explicit information-processing notions to the question of political information sources employed a procedure similar to that of agenda-setting analyses. Thus, for example, Graber (1984) coded a full year's content of the chief newspaper source for the 21 respondents in her in-depth study of how people "tame the information tide" by processing the news. In addition, she also analyzed the content of samples of two other newspapers, the three national TV networks' nightly news programs, and two of the networks' local newscasts. Then, comparing news content emphases with what her respondents learned of political issues, candidates, and other matters, she was able to conclude that the news media "make major contributions to schema formation and development by providing the public with partially preprocessed information in various domains of knowledge and by signalling the relative importance of stories" (p. 213).

What remains unexamined in these agenda-setting, information-processing, and other studies is how people choose their sources of news before they ever process it. As Bennett (1981) argued, this is a matter of key importance.

He noted that "perhaps the most universal and politically important distinction to be drawn about political information is the manner in which it is
controlled." For, "the actor who controls the selection and symbolization of
critical information in a political conflict may possess a decisive measure of
control over key political considerations" (p. 95). Here, Bennett is speaking
primarily of control by sources over the information flow to define issues,
enhance credibility, set rules and procedures, undermine the opposition, and
regulate the scope of involvement by interests not originally a party to the
conflict in question.

But there are at least two ways wherein the control over the selection
and symbolization of information, to use Bennett's concepts, resides in the
recipients of that information themselves. One of these was spelled out clearly
in Robert Lane's (1972) discussion of "the Good Citizen." There, Lane
described what he labeled the *strategy of news intake*. The citizen in everyday
life, he argued, is confronted with the problem of responding to changed
situations through notices that come without any requirement of searching
for them. But when that citizen is faced with the task of searching "for
information and guidance" relevant to "citizenry pursuit of self-interest," then
he or she "must develop a strategy that maximizes a number of values and
minimizes cost" (p. 310). Lane asked: "What kind of strategy?"

The cost–benefit relationships in acquiring information by following the
news are multiple: Some people find news intrinsically interesting, followed
for its own sake, and requiring no additional action; the costs of doing so are
opportunity costs. News deemed rewarding because it is instrumental implies
weighing the costs of attaining it against its practical value. Yet other news
is about events so distant and abstract that any relationship to the citizen's
self-interest is problematic; hence, costs of information gain are high, benefits
low. Given the variability of the cost-reward ratio in acquiring information
Lane offered his "simple formula" for calculation:

$$\text{Ratio of cost to gain in following news} = \frac{\text{Cost of following and understanding the news} + \text{Cost of changing one's situation based on impact of event on self} + \text{Cost of any indicated effort to alter history}}{\text{Probable gain or loss implied by event in the news} + \text{Probability that the event will mature so that the indicated gain or loss will take place}}$$

Although the formula is simple, as Lane indicated, the calculations are
complex. One reason is that it is difficult to attach, as is necessary, a degree
(or weight) of certainty for each probability. And, understanding information
implies a conceptual framework for doing so, each of which is unique to the

individual. Moreover, perceptions of the personal impact of distant events and of one's ability to change things depend on psychic dispositions. Yet, in spite of these complexities—and making use of them—people scan the media, each using one's own "public affairs index" that serves as a guide for what to select, what to ignore in estimating costs and direct or instrumental rewards.

Lane's analysis thus deals with why and how people decide to follow the news at all, a necessary prior condition to processing whatever information they derive from it. It is a decision that gives the citizen at least one form of control over the information process so that control is not monopolized by information sources. There is also another decision yielding citizen control (i.e., the choice over which specific news media to turn to for information if the prior calculus suggests a positive cost–benefit ratio in following news). And, it is a choice that in its own way works to lower those costs in the cost–reward calculation.

DOWNS' FRAMEWORK OF INFORMATION-SELECTION PRINCIPLES

In his classic work, *An Economic Theory of Democracy*, Anthony Downs (1957) considered in detail the costs involved in acquiring information on which voters may make rational decisions. Information gathering plays a prominent role in his multistep outline of rationally deciding how to vote. Information gathering carries a cost, namely, the deflection of scarce resources—in this case, particularly the scarce resource of time used to acquire, assimilate, and weigh alternatives. One way to reduce that cost is to transfer it (i.e., to delegate much of the cost of acquiring raw data, assimilating it, and weighing it) to someone else. In a passage that presages Lane's thoughts on information control, Downs noted that "obviously, whoever" carries out the information-gathering tasks for a person "has a potentially enormous influence upon decisions" (p. 211) even if the delegated agent does not directly make those decisions.

How, then, does one go about delegating the time-consuming efforts of information gathering; how does one choose the source of the political information that will be processed? Downs said that "information is necessarily gathered by means of certain *principles of selection*: rules employed to determine what to make use of and what not to" (p. 212). But the individual does not formulate such principles, then apply them in scanning all potential sources of information to be processed. No, according to Downs, "since the resources any citizen can devote to paying for and assimilating data are limited" one finds oneself "in a situation of economic choice: from among those many sources of information, he must select only a few to tap" (pp. 212–213). This is done by turning to information sources whose selection principles are in accord with one's own.

When citizens rely on others to report events to them, rationality decrees that they select those reporters who provide them with versions of events that closely approximate the versions they would formulate themselves were they expert on-the-spot witnesses. To accomplish this, they must choose reporters whose selection principles are as nearly identical with their own as possible. Then the reporters' inevitable biases will aid their decision-making rather than hinder it. (Downs, 1957, p. 213)

How, then, do citizens choose their own selection principles rationally? Downs' response is that one's selection principles are rational if applying them provides information that is useful in making the decisions that will help produce the social state one prefers. Because people obviously prefer differing social states, no single set of selection principles suits everyone. They will differ from individual to individual depending on the values one wishes to attain in life. Having chosen those principles on the basis of one's values, the next step, according to Downs, is to find out "what reporting agencies also have those principles," rely on them for information, and from time to time check to see that the agencies have not deviated from those selection principles.

Downs thus provided a framework for addressing the question of what news sources provide the political information that citizens process if they find it beneficial to follow news and to process information. First, the individual estimates a preferred social state on the basis of desired ends. Second, the individual formulates selection principles in accordance with that preferred social state. Third, the individual turns to information sources that she or he deems as holding similar principles of selection.

A PRELIMINARY APPLICATION
OF DOWNS' FRAMEWORK

Downs indicated that selection principles are largely unique to each individual. To examine them and their application as prior to information processing, one must therefore study individuals. Simply put, intensive rather than extensive investigating methods are required. Fortunately, as Brown (1974, 1980, 1986) and others have demonstrated, Q-methodology is of particular utility in operationalizing a framework for political subjectivity such as that suggested by Downs' discussion of principles of information selection. Accordingly, this preliminary analysis employs Q-method and its techniques.

In Q-method, individuals qua individuals (i.e., a small, purposively selected sample of people called a P-sample) are asked to model in operant fashion their subjective states of mind regarding specific objects, persons, settings, and the like. They do so through a forced-choice, rank-ordering of statements, views, opinions, or other symbolic representations of subjective appraisals. There are key elements in Downs' framework that lend themselves particularly well to such an approach, namely, the modeling of individuals' principles of information selection as derived from each one's preferred social state; the modeling of individuals' perceptions of the selection principles employed by specific news media as derived from individual appraisals of the preferred social state reflected in those media; and the match between individual selection principles and the media those individuals utilize as sources of political information.

The items rank-ordered by persons in the P-sample constitute the Q-sample, a selection of stimuli from a possible population (called a *concourse*) of stimuli relevant to the question at hand. For purposes of this preliminary inquiry into the application of principles of information selection the Q-sample consists of an adaptation of Milton Rokeach's (1967; Rokeach & Parker, 1970) Value Survey. The Rokeach Value Survey consists of two sets of 18 terminal and 18 instrumental values. Terminal values are those "preferred end states that people strive for" and include such items as "a comfortable life," "an exciting life," and "salvation." Instrumental values are "preferred modes of behavior." "Logical," "loving," and "polite" are examples (Rokeach & Parker, 1970, p. 98). Taken together, they constitute in this study the "preferred social state" that Downs argued enters into the process of formulating principles of information selection.

For Rokeach (1979) the normal procedure for investigating personal values was to ask large, representative samples of individuals to rank-order separately the sets of terminal and instrumental values as "guiding principles in your daily life." In this study, however, the two sets of values have been combined; moreover, two terminal values ("a participatory life" and "a challenging life") and two instrumental values ("skill" and "influence") have been added to Rokeach's set to form a Q-sample of $N = 40$ value statements. And, in keeping with Rokeach's Value Survey, short, parenthetical comments were attached to each value. For example, "a comfortable life" in the Value Survey contains the parenthetical descriptor "a prosperous life"; or "ambitious" is followed by "hard-working, aspiring" in parentheses. (See Table 1.1 for a complete listing of each item of the Q-sample.)

In keeping with the logic of Q-methodology and with the intent of this preliminary inquiry the Q-sample was administered to a small, purposive sample of individuals. The rationale for selecting the P-sample was as follows. Implicit in Downs' framework is the notion that individuals formulate their own selection principles and formulate an image of the selection principles adhered to by specific media "experimentally" (Downs, 1957, p. 214). There is a trial and error process that occurs. The longer a person experiments (i.e., the more experience one has in constructing selection principles and sampling the principles of specific media), the closer we might expect the match to be

TABLE 1.1
**Q-Sample of Guiding Values Operant in Information
Selection Principles**

Terminal Values	Instrumental Values
A Challenging Life (facing up to problems and dealing with them)	Ambitious (hard-working, aspiring)
A Comfortable Life (a prosperous life)	Broadminded (open-minded)
An Exciting Life (a stimulating, active life)	Capable (competent, effective)
A Sense of Accomplishment (making a lasting contribution)	Cheerful (lighthearted, joyful)
A World of Peace (free of war and conflict)	Clean (neat, tidy, orderly)
A World of Beauty (beauty of nature and the arts)	Courageous (standing up for your own beliefs)
Equality (brotherhood, equal opportunity for all)	Forgiving (willing to pardon others)
Family Security (take care of loved ones)	Helpful (working for the welfare of others)
Freedom (independence, free choice)	Honest (sincere, truthful)
Happiness (being content)	Imaginative (daring, creative)
Inner Harmony (freedom from inner conflict)	Influence (being able to advise others what to do)
Mature Love (sexual and spiritual intimacy)	Independent (self-reliant, self-sufficient)
National Security (protection from attack)	Intellectual (intelligent, reflective)
Participatory Life (being in charge of one's own destiny, but working for welfare of others)	Logical (consistent, rational)
Pleasure (an enjoyable, leisurely life)	Loving (affectionate, tender)
Salvation (saved, eternal life)	Obedient (dutiful, respectful)
Self-Respect (self-esteem, feeling good about yourself)	Polite (courteous, well-mannered)
Social Recognition (respect, admiration)	Responsible (dependable, reliable)
True Friendship (close companionship)	Self-Controlled (restrained, self-disciplined)
Wisdom (a mature understanding of life)	Skill (knowing what to do to get things done)

between (a) a person's selection principles and (b) that person's image of the selection principles of his or her preferred information source among several sampled information sources.

Hence, in selecting the P-sample for this study there was an explicit effort to balance two types of political experience. First, a set of five "political neophytes" was selected. These were individuals who had never before voted in a U.S. election but would be eligible to do so for the first time in the 1988 presidential contest. Second, the sample consisted of five additional "political sophisticates" whose ascriptive criteria included voting in several elections (for example, a minimum of two presidential elections), expressions of persistent interest in and/or direct involvement in politics, and continuous monitoring of political information.

As with all such samples in Q-methodology there is no claim that the findings could or should be generalized to larger populations of political neophytes, sophisticates, or citizens generally. With that caution in mind, brief descriptions of the members of the two groups are appropriate. Each of the neophytes is a college student—one freshman, three sophomores, and one junior. Two are female, three are males. One respondent has not determined a college major (designated in Table 1.2 as MW); three are in business (CE, AF, SN); the remaining student is in education and is also a redshirted football player (MB).

The set of political sophisticates is more heterogeneous. Two have extensive experience in statewide electoral politics (each in separate states). One of those holds a law degree, practiced law for a lengthy period, then was in the oil business for several years (PS). The other is a lifelong politician—currently administrative assistant to a U.S. congressman, formerly aide to a U.S. senator, involved in two presidential elections at a high level, and taking part in election campaigns every 2 years since 1964 (GD). A third respondent was involved in campaign politics in Chicago, was a college teacher, and is currently completing a doctorate degree in communication (BH). A fourth respondent has worked in a variety of administrative and planning positions, is a director of research administration, and holds advanced degrees in political science (JT). The fifth sophisticate has an undergraduate degree in political science, worked in sales and sales management for several years, was involved in programs dealing with Native Americans, and is currently administrative coordinator of a major political commercial archive (KW).

To determine preferred information sources, each of the 10 respondents was first reminded that "the race for the presidency in 1988 is already underway." And, "we are in the pre-primary phase, primaries and caucuses occur next year, with the nominations in the summer, the election in November." Each was then asked which of the listed news sources he or she would "follow most regularly." The first set of options was television, newsmagazines, and newspapers. Then, within the selected medium each respondent was asked whether the information source would be for TV, ABC, NBC, or CBS; for newsmagazines, *Time*, *Newsweek*, or *U.S. News & World Report*; for newspapers, *USA Today* or "your local newspaper."

One of the advantages of Q-methodology is that as a mode of intensive analysis (Brown, 1981) it permits a single individual, or small set of individuals, to model their subjective orientations to a variety of objects under a variety of conditions. With the focus of this research on the selection principles of political neophytes and of political sophisticates, and the degree to which those principles match perceived principles of information sources, it was possible to exploit this attribute of Q-method by asking each of the 10 respondents to rank-order items in the Q-sample under a variety of sort conditions. Hence, each respondent was first given the following instruction:

Each of us in our lives has some set of principles or values which guide our actions. Here is a deck of cards. Each card lists a value that people find important in their daily lives and in the life of this nation. Your task is to arrange these values (cards) in order of their importance to YOU as principles you would like to have guide your life with other people.

The Q-sorting format appeared as follows:

	Most Important										Least Important
Number of items	1	2	3	4	6	8	6	4	3	2	1
Score	+5	+4	+3	+2	+1	0	−1	−2	−3	−4	−5

This initial sort constitutes each person's "self-sort," or modeling, of the principles of information selection of that individual. Following appropriate intervals to insure that respondents would not recall details of the self-sort (or any subsequent sort) each individual was instructed as follows in each of eight additional sorting sessions:

Now in 1988 assume that you would be able, through your decision as to whom to support for President of the U.S., to move toward realizing and achieving the values that you want to guide your life. In deciding which candidate to support for president you may want to find out more about each of those persons seeking office. To do that you might turn to several places for information about the candidates. One source of such information might be _____. Consider _____ for a few moments. How would you arrange the values listed on this deck of cards as you think each is important to _____ as a guide to how that source goes about informing people about politics?

Each of the additional sorting sessions then asked the respondent, in order, to sort on each of the following information sources (always employing the same Q-sample and sorting format as in the self-sort): ABC "World News Tonight," NBC "Nightly News," CBS "Evening News," *Time* magazine, *Newsweek* magazine, *U.S. News & World Report* magazine, *USA Today*, and "your local newspaper." Thus, each of the 10 persons in the P-sample sorted the 40 items in the Q-sample nine separate times.

Models of Information-Selection Principles

The emphasis of this study is on each of the 10 persons in the P-sample as an individual with the principal questions being, first, what are the information-selection principles for each; second, how well do these principles match those the individual perceives each information source as practicing; and, third, how close is the match of each person's principles with those held by one's preferred information source? That being the case, each person's nine separate Q-sorts were correlated with one another and the derived correlation matrix factor analyzed.

However, prior to comparing each individual's principles of information selection that his or her views of media principles it is appropriate to take a general look at the principles of neophytes and sophisticates. For this purpose all of the 10 self-sorts were correlated and factor analyzed. Given the focus on neophytes and sophisticates, two factors were extracted and subjected to varimax rotation, with a resulting eigenvalue of .96 for the second factor. The factors explain 80% of trace and 37% of total variance.

In Q-methodology such a factor analysis produces two groups, or clusters, of individuals each of which consists of individuals who have rank-ordered the 40 items in approximately the same ways during their self-sorts. Hence, the factor analysis reveals two sets of persons, each sharing the same principles of information selection. In this instance, the first set consists of six persons, five of whom are the five ascriptive political sophisticates; and the sixth is a female, sophomore business major (AF). The other cluster consists of the remaining political neophytes. Given the composition of the two groups one can, with a single exception, speak of neophyte and sophisticate principles of information selection. The single exception (AF) has a partial explanation. This respondent spent a year in Australia as an exchange student, became interested in Australian politics, and continued her political involvement upon her return to the United States. In this respect, at least, she stands apart from the other neophytes and shares common ground with the sophisticates regarding the salience of politics.

The two Q-factors (i.e., clusters of respondents) are correlated .26, indicating that they are largely distinct. That distinction is apparent in examining the factor scores of items that characterize each factor at the negative and positive ends of the original sorting continuum. Persons loading on both factors ranked "obedient" (dutiful, respectful) as least important (-5) as values guiding their lives. However, whereas sophisticates ranked "salvation" and "influence" as the next least important values (-4), neophytes typically selected "social recognition" and "self-controlled" as least important (-4). A more marked contrast appears in considering values ranked as most important. Sophisticates select "honest," ($+5$), "wisdom" and "freedom" ($+4$). Neophytes rank "family security" ($+5$), "happiness," and "a comfortable life" ($+4$). Individual values that most clearly distinguish between the two groups are "national security," "a comfortable life," and "family security" (ranked as among the least important to sophisticates but most important to neophytes) and "honest," "participatory life," and "equality"—considered most important by sophisticates, least by neophytes.

It is noteworthy that in assessing the information-selection principles of selected news sources the neophyte–sophisticate groupings do not emerge as clearly. For each news source the 10 Q-sorts of respondents on that source were correlated and factor analyzed, with a minimum eigenvalue of .90 accepted for factoring. Cross-individual comparisons regarding the "local" newspaper are complicated by the fact that the specification of that newspaper varies from person to person, that is, the *Dallas Morning News* (JT), the *Daily Oklahoman* (GD), and so on. Turning instead to *USA Today*, two factors emerge, five persons in each; there is a neophyte factor (MB, CE, AF, MW) that also includes one sophisticate (GD). This group concurs that *USA Today* emphasizes values of national security, freedom, and social recognition as most important; salvation, a world of beauty, and mature love as least. The second group is comprised of the remaining four sophisticates plus one neophyte (SN). With this group, the newspaper emphasizes as most important the values of excitement, comfort, and pleasure; as least the values of salvation, wisdom, and logic.

But if one turns to each of the three TV news sources only one factor emerged in each instance, thus indicating that there was consensus among both neophytes and sophisticates regarding the key selection principles of each network. Employing factor scores as indicators one obtains the following thumbnail sketches of the perceived values emphasized by each network as most, then least important:

ABC: national security, intellect, and influence as most; mature loving, love, and a world of beauty as least.

NBC: influence, skill, and capability as most; salvation, mature love, and loving as least.

CBS: national security, logical, and responsibility as most; salvation, mature love, and loving as least.

Perceptions of newsmagazines present yet a different picture. *Time* and *U.S. News* generate single factors. National security, influence, and a world of peace are the leading values respondents perceive the former as emphasizing as most important; mature love, salvation, and loving as least. This latter magazine respondents view as emphasizing national security, capability, and responsibility most; loving, mature love, and salvation least. *Newsweek*, however, is another matter. Two factors, explaining 42% of variance and 94% of trace, emerge ($r = .29$). One is clearly a neophyte factor (loading CE, AF, MB, and MW); for this group, the newsmagazine emphasizes national security, intellect, and broadminded values; but places least importance on beauty, cheerfulness, and a challenging life. By contrast, political sophisticates (and the neophyte SN) constitute a group that perceive *Newsweek* as emphasizing ambition, influence, and excitement; deemphasizing salvation, love, and mature love.

What is apparent from these sketches of each news source as perceived by members of the P-sample is that neophyte and sophisticate groups sometimes emerge, sometimes do not. When they do, however, neither neophytes nor sophisticates view information sources as applying selection principles in keeping with their own as distinct groups. But what does one find if the focus is on particular individuals that comprise each group?

Comparing Personal and Perceived Media-Selection Principles

Consider now each of the five political neophytes in turn, then each of the sophisticates. The findings of initial interest are provided in Table 1.2. As one might hypothesize from Downs' framework, the correlation between each neophyte's principles of information selection (as indicated by the rank-ordering in one's self-sort) and any of the information sources provided as options is modest. With the exception of SN, a junior majoring in economics, correlations between individual self-sorts and media sorts consistently hover in the 0–.20 range—given the verbal label of "slight, almost negligible" in many instances (Guilford, 1956). And, SN's correlation of selection principles with those she perceives the media as employing remain relatively low. Noteworthy as well, and perhaps to be expected from Downs' theorizing, almost as many of the slight correlations for neophytes reported in Table 1.2 are negative as positive.

Inspection of Table 1.2 reveals that, as Downs' view might prophesy, the self-sorts of sophisticates are more highly correlated with their perceptions of media-selection principles than is the case with the neophytes. But the match is scarcely that much closer. The findings can hardly be taken as evidence that the selection principles of sophisticates, *as modeled through this Q-sample*, are more closely associated with their perceptions of those of information sources generally than are those between neophytes' principles and perceptions of media.

TABLE 1.2
Correlations of Individual Self-Sorts as Indicators of Principles
of Information Selection with Perceptions
of Information-Source Principles

Persons	ABC	NBC	CBS	Time	News-week	U.S. News	USA Today	Local
Neophytes								
MB	−.09*	−.16	.11	.17	.08	.08	.12	−.12
CE	−.14	−.03*	−.18	.04	.03	.01	−.03	.14
AF	−.07*	−.19	−.11	−.17	−.08	−.12	−.16	−.31
SN	.25	.18*	.25	.15	.31	.26	.27	.16
MW	−.02	.05	.05	−.12	.13	−.23*	.06	.02
Sophisticates								
GD	.06	.04	−.15	.22	.17*	.17	−.15	−.54
BH	.02	.50*	.38	.08	.00	−.23	.18	.03
PS	−.32	−.03	.45*	−.29	−.04	.21	.16	−.26
JT	.43	.16	.38	−.13	.24	−.03	−.38	.47*
KW	−.14	−.05	.11*	−.08	−.08	−.13	−.04	−.14

*Designated by respondent as preferred information source in 1988

The key findings in Table 1.2 lie not with the correlations of individual's principles of information selection with their perceptions of how those principles are applied by each news source. Rather, what is at issue in considering the Downsian framework is whether or not there is "creation of a system of information" (i.e., one that provides for each person data that are "chosen by means of selection principles in accord with his own" and "comprehensive enough to enable him to make the decisions he faces," 1957, p. 213). The data at hand do not offer a means for addressing the criterion of comprehensiveness. They do, however, address the question of whether individuals choose information sources with selection principles in accordance with their own.

As expected from Downs' reasoning, political neophytes do not choose information sources sharing selection principles with the individual. As Table 1.2 indicates the correlation between each neophyte's selection principles, as measured by the self Q-sort, and that of the person's *preferred information source* is—in four instances—negative, and in every instance low or negligible. Viewed from Downs' reasoning the neophyte's "sampling of the reporting of several different information sources" has not been conducted for a sufficient time to permit the crucial political assessment, namely, derivation and application of "selection principles which consistently lead him to make decisions with outcomes closest to his favorite social state" (p. 214). A "rational choice mechanism" has not been developed.

Persons with long and broad political experience are in a different situation. And, if the data in Table 1.2 are any indication, political sophisticates not only develop selection principles distinct from those of neophytes, they do use them to choose which of several news sources they are most likely to monitor for political information. Consider the cases of BH, PS, and JT. The match, as indicated by the correlations, between preferred values and preferred news sources (NBC, CBS, and the *Dallas Morning News*) is substantial. In the case of KW the correlation is slight, yet is the highest positive. GD's case is slightly different, but only marginally so. Newsmagazines are his preferred information source with respect to the 1988 presidential election; he made no distinction between the three listed as options (correlations between GD's three newsmagazine sorts ranged from .60–.80). Hence, the relationship between political experience, the development of selection principles, and the selection of news sources on the basis of those principles conforms to Downsian assumptions.

THE PROMISE OF DOWNS' FORMULATIONS

A Q-analysis of this nature is not, nor is it intended to be, conclusive. It does suggest that two ascriptive sets of individuals representing different levels of political experience, neophytes and sophisticates, do model selected values as "principles that guide your life" in separate, distinct ways in keeping with ascriptive designations. Moreover, these selection principles are but poorly correlated with those perceived to be utilized by selected information sources in general. But in the case of sophisticates, selection principles are sufficiently correlated with those perceived to be applied by *preferred* information sources to warrant additional inquiry into Downs' notions of political information processing.

One point that is key in the Downsian framework is that tasks of formulating selection principles, sampling the selection principles of news sources, and selecting information sources by matching one's own principles with those of chosen media are tasks that persons carry out in ways that are subjectively and individually unique for each person, source, and condition involved. Samples of items, persons, and conditions may vary (and should do so in ensuing analyses), but results from this preliminary analysis indicate that at least one way to explore these processes unique to individuals is through intensive analysis such as that conducted here.

Also vital to the Downsian framework is the view that there are at least two tasks of information processing that must take place prior to the actual processing of political information itself. One is the task of selecting information to be processed. Prior to that, however, is the rational choice of information-selection principles that will serve each person well in orienting to the political universe. That orientation involves assessing the value of making correct versus incorrect decisions, of determining the relevance of information to any decision that is made, and of estimating the marginal costs of acquiring information. If Downs is correct, it is through the development of principles of information selection that people reduce the travail of such assessments and estimates. Given the sequential priority of that task, it is certainly appropriate that future studies of political information processing at least take Downs seriously and examine how individuals as individuals undertake it.

REFERENCES

Bennett, W. L. (1981). Perception and cognition: An information-processing framework for politics. In S. Long (Ed.), *The handbook of political behavior* (Vol. 1, pp. 69–193). New York: Plenum.

Berelson, B. R., Lazarsfeld, P. F., & McPhee, W. N. (1954). *Voting.* Chicago: University of Chicago Press.

Brown, S. R. (1974). Intensive analysis in political research. *Political Methodology, 1,* 1–26.

Brown, S. R. (1980). *Political subjectivity.* New Haven, CT: Yale University Press.

Brown, S. R. (1981). Intensive analysis. In D. Nimmo & K. R. Sanders (Eds.), *The handbook of political communication* (pp. 627–649). Beverly Hills, CA: Sage.

Brown, S. R. (1986). Q technique and method. In W. D. Berry & M. S. Lewis-Beck (Eds.), *New tools for social scientists* (pp. 57–76). Beverly Hills, CA: Sage.

Conover, P. J., & Feldman, S. (1984). How people organize the political world: A schematic model. *American Journal of Political Science, 28,* 93–126.

Downs, A. (1957). *An economic theory of democracy.* New York: Harper & Row.

Graber, D. (1984). *Processing the news.* New York: Longman.

Guilford, J. P. (1956). *Fundamental statistics in psychology and education.* New York: McGraw-Hill.

Hovland, C. I., Janis, I. L., & Kelly, H. H. (1953). *Communication and persuasion.* New Haven, CT: Yale University Press.

Katz, E., Gurevitch, M., & Haas, H. (1973). On the use of the mass media for important things. *American Sociological Review, 38,* 164–181.

Kraus, S., & Perloff, R. M. (Eds.). (1985). *Mass media and political thought.* Beverly Hills, CA: Sage.

Lane, R. E. (1972). *Political life.* New York: The Free Press.

Lang, G. E., & Lang, K. (1983). *The battle for public opinion.* New York: Columbia University Press.

Lazarsfeld, P. F., Berelson, B. R., & Gaudet, H. (1944). *The people's choice.* New York: Duell Sloan.

McCombs, M. E. (1981). The agenda-setting approach. In D. Nimmo & K. Sanders (Eds.), *The handbook of political communication* (pp. 121–141). Beverly Hills, CA: Sage.

Miller, A. H., Wattenberg, M. F., & Malanchuk, O. (1986). Schematic assessments of presidential candidates. *American Political Science Review, 80,* 522–540.

Noelle-Neumann, E. (1980). *Die schweigespirale* [The spiral of silence]. Munich: R. Piper.

Rice, S. A. (1928). *Quantitative methods in politics.* New York: Knopf.

Rokeach, M. (1967). *Value survey.* Sunnyvale, CA: Halgreen Tests.

Rokeach, M. (1979). Value theory and communication research. In D. Nimmo (Ed.), *Communication yearbook 3.* New Brunswick, NJ: Transaction.

Rokeach, M., & Parker, S. (1970). Values as social indicators of poverty and race relations in America. *The Annals of the American Academy of Political and Social Science, 388,* 97–111.

Rosengren, K. E., Wenner, L. A., & Palmgreen, P. (Eds.). (1985). *Media gratifications research.* Beverly Hills, CA: Sage.

2 | Collective Memory and the News*

Kurt Lang
Gladys Engel Lang
University of Washington

In addressing the esoteric topic of collective memory, we are in fact joining two research traditions and applying them to the study of public opinion. The first of these subsumes the study of events in relation to which public opinion forms, crystallizes, and sometimes becomes polarized; the second, the study of the collective memories that represent the more enduring precipitate of these events distilled by time. The difference between the two is partly a matter of approach and partly a matter of substance.

The relationship between an event and that same event as news has been a long-standing interest of ours. We first explored the subject in our study of MacArthur Day in 1951 and have continued to pursue it since, most ambitiously in our inquiry into the events that made up the Watergate scandal and forced the resignation of Richard Nixon (Lang & Lang, 1953). In these and other inquiries we have been guided by a simple, and perhaps obvious, postulate: What is conveyed to the public via the news media can never replicate the event as experienced by the participants actually present at the scene of the action.

This initial interest of ours has expanded over the years to encompass the mediation of events not only across space but over time as well. Thus, we inferred that the media coverage given to MacArthur upon his return from Korea had built up into what we called a "landslide" effect, a perception of overwhelmingly pro-military and anti-Truman sentiment to a level where it intimidated, even if it did not altogether stifle, the voices inclined toward

*Thomas J. Johnson and Peggy E. Roberts assisted with the preparation of this chapter.

dissent. Perceptions of where the weight of opinion is shifting influence many situations, such as responses to the televised Carter–Ford debate, which we also studied. The differences between immediate responses and those obtained after a week's lapse indicated, although they could not conclusively demonstrate, a gradual redefinition of the original viewing experience toward greater conformity with the dominant viewpoint as conveyed by media reports (Lang & Lang, 1979). Suggestive as such leads may be, data from the study of an event as it happens cannot catch the influence of that event as reworked in collective memory.

Recognizing this difficulty, we began more recently to concentrate on the time element on what survives as memory. For some time now, we have been working on a study of the reputations of painter-etchers, a group of artists who favored a genre that has since gone out of fashion. These reputations too, we insist, are public images—in this case, of persons rather than of events. What aroused our curiosity about this kind of image production were some very apparent disparities between evidence of the recognition some of these artists had achieved in their lifetime and the posthumous survival of that reputation. What could account for the demise of the once well recognized? And, conversely, what had made the reputations of others last and, in some instances, translate into fame through the ages to give them the immortality reserved for the few "greats"? To answer such questions we must study how reputations are mediated. After all, once an artist has died, the responsibility for preserving the work on which the claim to fame must rest unavoidably falls on others, who must bring it to the attention of posterity (Lang & Lang, 1986; see also Lang & Lang, in press). Persons with great accomplishments in other spheres of activity are similarly dependent on mediation if accounts of their feats (events) are to remain known by future generations.

Although the present is forever merging into the past, one can hardly study the two in the same way. Looking at an ongoing event as it is happening by "firehouse research" differs from a study of this same event by way of a retrospective "look back" on it. The firehouse approach is akin to the taking of a snap shot—meant to catch the significant moment between what has already transpired and an impending future. People do indeed make such connections. They affect how the event is perceived and what meanings will be read into it. But in the long run, it is the bystander public, most of them nonparticipants, who have only read about the event or watched it over television, that counts. The attention they pay to the event endows it with new meaning, often to a point where the participants no longer recognize their own experience. The retrospective "looking back" on events has to contend with this ever changing consciousness of a shared historical past.

COLLECTIVE MEMORY

What we call, following Halbwachs (1980), the collective memory of an event is an image bequeathed to posterity. How any event remains a living experience has to be understood as an ongoing process, of which the negotiation between participants and those who report the event is only a beginning. What we think of as the historical "reality" undergoes a similar process of construction and reconstruction. In the words of R. G. Collingwood (1946), every generation more or less writes its own history.

We would like to draw three categorical distinctions between the actual event and the collective memory of that event. These have to do with its time frame, the way it is experienced, and the production versus the reproduction of the event:

1. The actual event exists in a definite time frame. It has an identifiable beginning and end, unaltered by any connection that participants may make between any current happening and other past, present, and possibly future event. By contrast, the collective memory (or folk image) of that event lacks obvious boundaries. New elements are constantly assimilated and anything no longer of use is discarded in the continuous revision.

2. The event is directly experienced and retained as a personal recollection, whereas the knowledge of that event by other contemporaries not present and by those yet to be born comes only through communication.

3. The event is produced by participants; the reality that survives the event is a reproduction with whatever "inaccuracies" this entails. Even personal recollections are modified as experiences are shared and information from other sources is brought to bear on them.

In other words, the collective memory of events is refashioned and assimilated into the present.

In this connection we introduce an important conceptual distinction about the past that is available to contemporaries. At one extreme is *historical knowledge*, representing that part of the past historians have been able to unearth; at the other, the stock of widely shared "memories," the *collective memory*, of which people are expected to be conscious. Even historical knowledge, although undeniably the more erudite of the two, has a less than absolute claim to objectivity through the judicious use of source material. Nevertheless, just exactly what did happen once upon a time or only yesterday, no one will ever know for sure. This does not prevent most of us, including journalists, from having recourse to the images and ideas about the past that are in the public domain. This kind of folk knowledge, based largely on the daily flow of news—including occasional challenges by public figures plugging their own revisionist views—does not always accord with the latest and best historical evidence.

Just as we distinguish between these two kinds of "pasts," so we can also distinguish between two roughly analogous kinds of images of the future: *futurology* as the counterpart of history and the public *agenda* as the counterpart of collective memory. *Futurology*, as used here, encompasses a variety of intellectual constructions ranging from scientifically based projections about such matters as population growth, world resources, and climatic changes to the statement of goals for the year 2000, and even to the utopian dreams formulated as "scientific" socialism. History and futurology are similarly erudite but they diverge from the present in opposite directions. Neither has more than a remote influence on how most people think about the present. Few people really react to either, except insofar as a particular version is incorporated in a myth to justify some program of concrete political action.

With the image incorporated in a myth (in the Sorelian sense), we approach an equally compelling analogy between collective memory as the living image of the past and the special kind of future indicated by the term *agenda*. That term has enjoyed such a vogue among communication researchers and yet is used so loosely to refer to nearly any topic that touches the popular imagination or enters the conversations of some group. Few take the trouble to distinguish topics that refer to the future from topics that refer to the past. We need to restore the original clarity to the concept of public agenda by restricting its use to issues or problems that mandate some resolution or response, and by reviving the concept of collective memory to refer to the public awareness of a common past.

Agenda means, quite literally, the things to be done—usually by some institution or organized body. When some public, large or small, recognizes the need for some decision or action, then, but only then, is the term *agenda* really appropriate. A political agenda focuses discourse on particular issues. Subjects irrelevant to these issues are thereby ruled out. Collective memories serve somewhat the same function and can be considered, to this extent, the functional equivalent of an agenda. And, to push the analogy a step farther, equivalents of the specific institutional agendas are to be found in the memories that organizations store both in their files and in the minds of their members. The difference lies in the orientations embodied in each: An agenda looks ahead toward the future; the collective memory toward the past.

This blurring of the time dimension has probably kept us from dealing more explicitly with memory as a social force. Although all of us recognize, at least implicitly, the force of history, this fundamental understanding has rarely been translated into a study of the media and, in particular, of their influence on what is kept alive or revived. A paper by Michael Schudson (1986) is one of the obvious exceptions, when he pointed out, that what is proferred as "news" covers more than events that are current or fall within the preceding 24 hours. Even cursory perusal reveals many references to events no longer new and, according to widely espoused criteria, not news in the narrow journalistic sense. It is this past and future that, together, frame the reports we receive as current events. Just what part of the past and what kind of future are brought into play depends on what editors and journalists believe legitimately belongs within the public domain, on journalistic conventions, and on personal ideology.

Most generally, references to the past in reputedly up-to-date news are used as semantic markers—to make connections, to fit an event into a category, and to suggest inferences. One makes sense of current events from the vantage point of experiences, including the experience of a common past. At the minimum, the references to previous events serve as pegs on which to hang a breaking story whose significance no one may as yet fully understand. All in all, the past is invoked for four different purposes—to delimit an era; as a yard stick; for analogies; and for the shorthand explanation or lessons it can provide.

Some major events are mentioned time and again in the news but only as convenient dividers with hardly a reference to the experience. Except for the occasional commemoration to revive patriotic sentiment, World War II seems to serve primarily to define the limits of the memory span of most people alive today. Anything previous belongs to another era. A more recent era is seen to have ended with the resignation of Richard M. Nixon and conveniently labeled as "post-Watergate," as if some major political realignment had taken place, or as if the years since August 1974 had been characterized by a new set of attitudes. Memories of other events are identified by their placement in a decade, like the 1960s, which are still imaged as dominated by political activism. But posterity has some leeway in such labeling. The 1950s can, with equal justification, be described as the "Eisenhower years," the period of the "cold war," or the first decade of post-war affluence.

Past events also provide yardsticks for gauging the magnitude and impact of current events. Thus, the margin of an electoral victory, of a stock market decline, of the level of unemployment, or of the death toll in a disaster will be assessed in comparison with a past that only a few will remember but that the reports brings back to mind. The significance or seriousness of a current event comes to hinge on exceeding or coming close to matching an earlier high or low.

An explicit analogy with a previous event or personality establishes an even stronger connection. Supposedly familiar images of the past are invoked when one likens the antics of a Quadaffi to those of Hitler or describes a national leader as another George Washington, an inventor as a second Thomas Edison, or a singer as a new Caruso.

References to the past often go beyond personalities and their motives to function as short-hand explanations. The simplest case does not go beyond linking a news item to some sequence of earlier events without specifying any causal connection, but models to follow or to avoid are often implied. The experience of Munich, where Neville Chamberlain conceded Czechoslovakia to the Nazis, or the more recent trauma of Vietnam are evoked to justify certain policy positions. When such memories blend with anticipations of the future, as they often do, they frame the issue that enters into the public agenda; they may influence the agendas of institutional bodies as well. The lessons implicit in such explanations are difficult to overlook.

To take up again the thread of our basic argument: social scientists have been inclined to take the importance of collective memories for granted, but not to concern themselves with either their origin or their influence. Social scientists prefer hard facts derived from their better understood and more fully developed indicators of position in social structure, of ideology, and of situational pressures. They avoid having to deal with elusive mental images of past events, and they have willingly ceded this subject to historians and literary scholars (e.g., Fussell, 1975), whose interpretations, usually cast in a narrative format, have been less than fully acceptable. The explanatory power of memory, if used at all by social scientists, is called on only as a last resort, after the limits of other explanations have been reached. Yet, what people remember may be crucial when it comes to explaining both the mentality of an era as well as the cleavages between generations. Solid evidence on the role of collective memory, although difficult to come by, could help us better understand how the past spills over into the present.

FIRST EXPLORATIONS

The remainder of this chapter describes an exploratory study of the connection between the timing of events that once were big news and the content of collective memories. It draws on responses to a questionnaire distributed in several classes at the University of Washington in March 1986 and, through these students, to their parents, with each student-respondent asked to have a parent complete and return the same questionnaire. The rationale behind such a procedure was to secure similar responses from two generations of comparable socioeconomic status. Unfortunately, many students did not live at home and others failed for one reason or other to return the parental questionnaire, so that we ended with a sample heavily skewed toward those under 30. Nor can we claim that even the students are fully representative of their age group. This does not, however, invalidate the utility of the limited analysis we performed as a first exploration of the subject at hand.

A major part of the questionnaire consisted of a list of 39 events. The earliest, including the Berlin air lift and the perjury trial of Alger Hiss, date from the late 1940s in the era of the first "cold war." The most recent included the bomb attack on the Marine barracks in Lebanon and the American invasion of Grenada. Respondents were asked to indicate for each of these and similar events, whether they retained a "vivid recollection" or, if they did not, whether they "knew about" the event.[1]

These responses, admittedly crude indicators, give us a handle on a complex phenomenon. The difference between a vivid recollection and knowledge echoes in some respects the distinction William James made between "acquaintance with" and "knowledge about." Anything vividly remembered has to have been "lived through," no matter how much reworked in response to subsequent social influences. Even those who experienced the actual event at a distance, which is to say via the news media, actually "lived through" the event. Their memory is grounded on actual experience of a kind somewhere between the two categories so sharply differentiated by James. The distinction has become increasingly blurred by the vivid images television carries of the event as, for example, during the days following the assassination of John F. Kennedy when millions of people joined in the mourning. Whether the experience is direct or mediated via the news media, those who lived through and reacted to an event like the Kennedy assassination were apt to retain some personal memory not available to those for whom it was all hearsay after the facts.

In designing the study, it was clear to us that most students no longer had any personal memory of events prior to Watergate. The youngest among our respondents—those born after 1965 and 20 or younger at the time of the study—would at best have been in the lower primary grades when the Watergate controversy began. Quite understandably, they also knew very little about the early-vintage Nixon with his sure instinct for the jugular, and what they knew could only have been picked up second hand, from hearsay or reading, although a few reels for occasional replay have been preserved. Given the age distribution of the sample, memories of Watergate presented themselves as a strategic cutting point for exploring images of the past. Therefore, we deliberately overloaded our list with events about Watergate and with earlier episodes associated with Richard Nixon and clearly outside the memory span of anyone under 21.

The proportions who said they knew about (shared in the collective memory) and those with vivid (personal) memories of each event are shown in the first two columns of Table 2.1, where the events are arranged in chronological order. The figures in the third column represent the total number with any familiarity with the event, whether from personal experience or mediated through elders, school, or the mass media.

---

[1]A similar set of questions was used with some success in Lang and Lang (1978) and Roberts and Lang (1985).

TABLE 2.1
Memory of and Knowledge About Events (in percent)

	(1) Knew About	(2) Vivid Memory	(1)+(2)
Berlin air lift	37.8	12.4	50.2
Helen Gahaghan Douglas defeat by Nixon	15.3	3.7	19.0
Alger Hiss perjury trial	28.0	3.9	31.9
Nixon's "Checkers" speech	28.6	4.6	33.2
1st Sputnik launching	58.6	25.1	73.7
Nixon's kitchen debate with Khrushchev	29.0	4.7	33.7
U-2 spy plane shot down over Russia	49.0	14.4	63.4
Kennedy–Nixon TV debates	57.8	13.7	71.5
Bay of Pigs invasion	67.6	13.6	81.2
Nixon loses California governor's race	34.4	10.3	44.7
Civil Rights march to Selma, Alabama	22.7	9.0	31.7
Poor People's March on Washington	34.3	10.3	44.7
Riot in Watts District of L.A.	42.5	18.6	61.2
Six-day Israeli–Arab War	36.1	12.7	48.8
Lyndon Johnson "I will not run again"	26.4	12.5	39.0
Martin Luther King assassination	64.6	24.4	89.0
Czechoslovakia invaded by Soviet Union	38.6	12.0	50.7
Woodstock Music Festival	61.7	16.8	86.4
Clashes at 1968 Democratic Convention	23.7	13.1	36.8
Secret bombing of Cambodia	42.4	14.4	46.8
Kent State shootings	54.2	22.0	76.3
Nixon's trip to China	44.4	31.5	75.9
Watergate break-in	49.3	35.3	84.6
Senate Watergate hearings	46.3	33.2	79.5
Agnew resigns as vice-president	36.4	20.5	46.9
Cox fired as special Watergate prosecutor*	19.7	9.7	29.3
House hearings on impeachment	38.5	35.3	73.7
Nixon resignation speech	37.8	41.5	79.3
Saigon falls to North Vietnamese	39.7	16.8	56.4
Nixon's TV interview by David Frost	21.5	25.6	47.1
Movie *All the President's Men*	43.6	37.8	81.4
Begin/Sadat meeting in Jerusalem	47.6	32.5	80.2
Oil embargo	19.8	68.3	88.1
Three-Mile Island accident	21.5	71.0	92.5
Iran holds American hostage	12.4	80.2	92.5
Marine barracks in Lebanon bombed	22.2	54.7	76.9
Grenada invaded by American troops	17.3	71.7	89.0

*Identified as "Saturday Night Massacre," many respondents failed to make the association. It is therefore omitted from any subsequent tabulation.

The first and most obvious thing to emerge from the table is how much of the content of the collective memory is based not on vivid recollections of the past but on what has since been communicated to people.

Second, and perhaps equally obvious, both personal memory of an event and knowledge about it are affected by the passage of time. Few people had any direct knowledge whatsoever of most of the more remote events. The mix changes as "knowledge acquired since" tends to displace memories based on experience. More and more people merely know about the remote past.

Third, besides their temporal relation to the present, events differ also in their initial impact. Early impressions of all but the truly momentous events erode without something to preserve the experience or revive the memory. These two factors—differential impact and reinforcement—are the cause of deviations from the perfect chronological sequence one might otherwise expect. Thus, decidedly more respondents remembered the first launching of Sputnik, the Russian satellite, which took place in 1957, than remembered a number of later events and more people knew what it was about. Evidence of this technological breakthrough by the Russians had indeed had a dramatic and galvanizing effect. The event still overshadows, at least within the consciousness of this age group, events connected with the civil rights struggle that, through their continued saturation coverage, stirred the nation over much of a decade. No less dramatic, although in quite a different way, was the televised address in which Nixon announced his resignation of the presidency; it still stands out in the personal memory of many and has become a part of the American collective memory. The taking of Saigon by North Vietnamese troops, which followed the resignation by some months, and the fully televised meeting between the leaders of Israel and Egypt a full 4 years later cannot compete with it.

Fourth, to the extent that it is based on personal memory, one would expect consciousness of the past to be distinctly stratified along age lines. The older the group, the longer its memory span. Meanwhile, all contemporaries would be accumulating new memories at roughly the same rate. Those born later would always have a smaller memory stock, so that the historical consciousness of different age groups should approximate a cumulative pattern, with later events added to, rather than selectively displacing, the stock of memories already acquired by each group. Yet elders communicate to the young. Any mediation across generations will erode the age-determined cumulative pattern. Shared memories merge into a common historical consciousness.

We conducted a rough empirical test by taking 12 of the more major events out of the total of 39 to see whether the hypothesized stratification of vivid recollections would be replicated for knowledge about these same events. The first question was whether the personal recollections respondents had of events fitted the pattern of a Guttman-type scalogram, a scale that incorporates the assumption that the earliest event remembered determined (in the statistical sense) that all later events be remembered as well. The second question was whether the distribution of knowledge about these events would reveal a similar pattern. If direct recollection has no influence on what is remembered from the relevant past, the age groups would have roughly similar knowledge.

The results of the test were less than conclusive. The personal-memory scale ("vividly remember") had a reproducibility coefficient of .92, which is acceptable, and a scalability coefficient of .56, which falls somewhat below the .6 minimum. Memory is clearly selective; some events have greater initial impact and not everything experienced is revived by subsequent events. For the collective-memory scale ("know" plus "remember") both coefficients are still lower—reproducibility down to .85 and scalability down to .45. The difference between the two scales is consistent with our expectation. Memories mediated across generations reduce the influence of age in favor of other influences from the milieu in which people move. But the effect of personal memories does not disappear.

Repeated reminders, based on their continued relevance, established some events—even for those too young to have personally shared them—in the collective memory. This is what would appear to have made so many of the young conscious of an event like Sputnik, which many could not have remembered. The 74% who knew about this remote event comes close to the proportion who knew about the far more recent Watergate events (taken together). To be sure, the break-in that gives its name to the protracted controversy but was little noted when it first occurred was known, if not actually remembered, by near 85% of the sample. Yet some who knew about other Watergate events apparently knew nothing about the incident that precipitated the controversy. Overall, specific Watergate events still draw more attention than the fall of Saigon in 1975, possibly because of their initial impact but more likely because more people continue to allude to them in discussions of politics. Woodstock, the historic music festival that took place in summer of 1968, is another deviant case. The documentary of the event was released in 1970 as a full-length feature film that played on the usual movie circuit. Although only a few of the under-30 respondents actually remembered the festival, nearly as many of them as among the older group had come to know of it. The special relevance Woodstock undoubtedly has for the young was reinforced by the availability of visual replays. The different age groups knew about Woodstock in nearly identical proportions.

In spite of these blurrings, the influence of age on knowledge of the past is never completely wiped out. It shows up most clearly for the events related to the civil rights struggles and other controversies of the 1960s. Being old enough to have lived through these events made a difference. The one highly significant exception was the assassination of Martin Luther King, knowledge of which was not age-determined. Although half the sample was not even of school age when King was killed, the fact that the two age groups were equally aware of it is an effect of publicity. The establishment of King's birthday as a national holiday and commemoration by the media have done much to disseminate knowledge of this civil rights leader. Age, however, remains the determining factor for such related events as the March on Washington and the setting for King's momentous "I have a dream" speech that was all but lost in the innumerable radio and TV replays. Few among the young people questioned even knew about the march. There was even less knowledge among the young of President Lyndon B. Johnson's "I will not be a candidate" speech, only a few weeks before King fell victim to an assassin's bullet, and far less for the ugly confrontations connected with the Democratic national convention later that same year.

To summarize, events enter the collective memory through two different but complementary processes. One produces memories through the direct impact of the experience. With time, and as these personal recollections fade, the second takes over. The more remote the event the more will memory of it be based on mediation. Only a few of the major events, reinforced by secondary communications, survive. The knowledge that the then yet-unborn have about them is not just a product of history books. Mass media have an at least equally great effect on how such events are remembered. In the next section, we examine the extent to which personal memory in the form of vivid recollections, no matter how much refashioned, still plays a role with respect to Watergate and other events connected with the career of Richard M. Nixon.

REMEMBERING RICHARD NIXON

The age distribution of the sample, overloaded as it was with people of college age, made Watergate a natural focus for contrasting the memories of political generations. Were we witnessing the opening of a knowledge gap as fewer people retained direct recollections of just what Watergate was all about?

Personal recollections of the Watergate saga have indeed been fading to a point where the new cohorts entering the political arena today will have been completely cut off from any direct experience with these events. Of the over-30-year-olds (born before 1957), 81% retained a "vivid" recollection of Nixon's resignation, 78% of the Senate Watergate hearings, 71% of Agnew's resignation as vice-president, and 70% of the impeachment hearings. It is of some interest that as many members of the older generation should have remembered when Agnew resigned as remembered the presumably more dramatic Senate Watergate hearings. This was not true for the young, only 9% of whom remembered the vice-president's fall from grace; the proportion who actually remembered the "midnight massacre" (a codeword for Nixon's summary dismissal of Special Watergate Prosecutor Archibald Cox, along with those who refused to order the firing) was a mere 4%. More detailed examination of these personal memories points to those born between 1962 and 1966 as a "Watergate generation" initiated into the political world by these events. Memories of these events, when experienced during childhood, is understandably fragmentary. No more than a handful of those born after 1966 had more than the haziest recollections of these traumatic developments.

Although Watergate was still close to many respondents, including those too young to more than "know about" these events, this was not true of the only somewhat less controversial events in Nixon's pre-presidential political career. Far fewer were at all familiar with these things than with Watergate, and the number who actually remembered the early vintage Nixon was smaller still and, not surprisingly, confined to the over-30 generation. It was through his performances in earlier campaigns that Nixon had gained notoriety. In one, he had resorted to such highly questionable campaign tactics as labeling his Democratic opponent, Helen Gahaghan Douglas, a Communist and suc- ceeded in taking away her California Senate seat. Two years later, he had convinced Eisenhower, with his now famous "Checkers" speech (the nation- ally televised response to revelations of a secret fund donated by wealthy California backers for "personal" use), not to remove him from the national ticket. He had successfully exploited his role in bringing Alger Hiss to trial and tried a similar coup by engaging Khrushchev before Russian television in the so-called kitchen debate. His performance in another set of televised debates with Kennedy, and his less-than-gracious concession of the race for the California governorship in 1962, did not exactly rebound to his benefit, but they, too, were part of the image with which he had launched the 1968 campaign for the presidency.

The best known of these earlier events, not surprisingly, proved to be the televised debates with Kennedy (see Table 2.2). Excerpts from these debates have been replayed many times in connection with coverage of subsequent

TABLE 2.2
Percent Who "Knew About" by Age

	30 and Over	Under 30
Campaign against Helen Gahaghan Douglas	46	14
Trial of Alger Hiss	63	25
"Checkers" speech	54	28
Kitchen debate with Khrushchev	47	27
Kennedy–Nixon debates	90	68
Concession in California governor's race	75	38
Secret bombing of Cambodia	85	51
Nixon's trip to open China	95	73

presidential debates against which the dramatic quality of subsequent encounters is forever being measured. Those old enough will remember how in that first meeting Kennedy, still a neophyte, stood up to the more seasoned politician to prove that he was indeed presidential timber, or at least a more formidable opponent than many had been led to believe (Kraus, 1962). Yet even the small degree to which the younger age groups were familiar with these debates graphically illustrates the extent to which collective memory is more than the sum of personal recollections. Although the image left by the original experience will continue to fade, the event survives together with its video recording. Televised replays have the capacity to single out some events for reinforcement.

Frequent references to Watergate combined with occasional replays, as during the Iran-Contra hearings, have helped shape the lore surrounding these events. The positive association between knowledge about them and high exposure to news and, especially, regular newspaper reading supports our contention about the influence of media on memory. For some, the only vivid personal memory of Watergate was the feature film *All the President's Men*, based on Woodward and Bernstein's account. Other events have been periodically revived by the press when they seemed relevant as, for example, during the coverage of the Iran-Contra affair with its many ready comparisons with Watergate (this "story" did not break until after we had finished collecting these data).

Memory jolts from events in the news tend to reduce but not to eradicate age differences on these events. But here, too, the revival has been selective. Thus, the image of Nixon, the statesman, still gives strong competition to the Nixon forced to relinquish the presidency in order to escape impeachment and near-certain conviction by the Senate for having abused the powers of the office he occupied, and for other violations of the law during his term. The statesman image has been supported by memories of the foreign policy achievements during his administration, especially by the resumption of normal diplomatic relations with China. This was dramatized by a much televised presidential trip to Beijing in 1972, at a time when there was as yet no final settlement in Vietnam and that war was still very much in the news. So great had been the fanfare, first about the trip and then about the opening of China, that significantly more respondents knew about this event than knew about Nixon's much disputed secret and illegal bombing of Cambodia, a matter that surfaced time and again during the televised proceedings on impeachment several years later. It does appear that these video segments of the ceremonial China trip—later re-run in political documentaries and political commercials—solidified the image of that diplomatic success. The memory of it still overshadows the illegal bombing that the House Judiciary Committee debated but rejected as ground for impeachment. Without reinforcing video displays, the bombing was soon forgotten as the war wound down. The image of Nixon the statesman has survived rather well the more dismal recollections about his role in Watergate.

As the last step in this exploration of collective memory, we looked at the relationship between personal recollections of specific incidents in the career of Richard Nixon and the opinions people held of the ex-president as gauged by agreement or disagreement with a number of statements about Nixon—whether history will judge him to have been "one of the great American presidents;" whether "there should be a place for him in public life;" whether he "would to almost anything to win an election;" whether his "actions regarding Watergate were serious enough to warrant his resignation;" and so forth. These statements were interspersed with similar ones about Presidents Gerald Ford, Jimmy Carter, and Ronald Reagan.

Selected for this part of the analysis were nine events spanning the length of Nixon's career as a national political figure. We used personal recollections rather than knowledge of these events because the latter are affected too much by the milieu in which one spends one's life and by what is learned only indirectly from various sources. These influences are likely to contaminate, if not overshadow, the effect of actual memory. We are on firmer ground when attributing causal priority to "vivid memories."

Accordingly, we found those with personal recollections of the early Nixon consistently more opinionated about the man, favoring the "strongly agree" or "strongly disagree" options to the less assertive alternatives on the political items. This suggests, if nothing more, that some issues over which older generations may still be polarized have less relevance for those too young to have been involved. The past mediated across generations as history does not always suffice to keep an issue alive.

As to the content of opinions, the responses of those with vivid personal recollections about the less savory aspects of Nixon's career, which is to say the older respondents, favored the "strongly" anti-Nixon categories. More people with these recollections continue to feel even today that "resignation was justified," that Nixon really "abused" the power of his office, that he should not have been pardoned, and that there was no place for him in the future public life of the nation.

For a more detailed examination of these recollections, we grouped the events that referred to Nixon into three sets, each representative of a phase in the career of Richard Nixon. The first four, in terms of time, exemplify a Nixon who had cast himself as a patriot locked in battle with enemies, usually communists and their allies in the news media. The most recent of these was Nixon's press conference the night after the 1962 gubernatorial election in California, when he railed against the media. He promised not to be around any longer to be "kicked around" by the media. The other events in this phase were the campaign against Helen Gahaghan Douglas (1948), the Hiss trial (1949), and the Kennedy–Nixon debates (1960). In the second phase of his career Nixon had sought to build an image as foreign policy expert. This effort comes through in the way he tried to cash in on his so-called "kitchen debate" with Khrushchev (1959) as evidence of his tough-mindedness and ability to "stand up to the Russians," and by the pinnacle of his foreign policy achievement highlighted through the 1972 trip to China. The third phase marked Nixon's fall from power. We used three big media events, all of them Watergate related: the televised Senate Watergate Committee hearings of 1973, the televised impeachment deliberations of the House Judiciary Committee in July 1974, and the televised speech just days later, in which he told the country that he was about to resign.

The number of events vividly remembered from each phase serves as a gross indicator of what has stuck in people's mind about the different Nixons: the politician who went for the jugular, the tough-minded statesman in quest of peace, and the president brought down by Watergate. To simplify the presentation and provide a better overview, we dichotomized memory of each of these phases into those unable to recollect any of these events versus those who remembered at least one. The results are shown in Table 2.3 in the form of net percentage differences between negative and positive responses but taking no account of the strength of the expressed opinion either pro or con. Small net differences should obviously be ignored.

What again stands out is that vivid recollections of Watergate events were strongly related to opposition to the pardon Nixon was so hastily granted contrary to a promise previously given by President Ford. The blanket pardon still seems to rankle; many remember only too well that Nixon resigned for only one reason; to escape a Senate trial in which he would almost certainly have been convicted. Opposition had another deeper foundation in what people remembered about the early Nixon. Where such memories survive,

TABLE 2.3
Net Measure* of Opinion by Recollections

	Watergate	Statesman	Early Nixon
Resignation	−10	− 2	− 6
Abuse of presidential power	−16	− 4	0
Pardon by Ford	−54	−12	−30
Future place in public life	− 4	− 6	− 4
Tough-minded re Russians	+16	−14	−10
Promoter of world peace	+20	+ 4	+12
Remembered as great president	−10	0	+ 6
Will do anything to win	−26	−32	−32
Conniving and unscrupulous	−38	−52	−58
Unqualified as president	−22	−38	−38
"Not a crook"	−16	−12	−14

* + means favorable Nixon; − unfavorable.

anti-Nixon feelings are not much tempered, if at all, by his much heralded foreign policy successes, which even those with long memories were prone to concede. Those with vivid memories of the early Nixon were more suspicious of his proclaimed innocence on Watergate. Because they remembered how far Nixon had been willing to go in order to win a political contest, they were more likely to experience the House Judiciary Committee as little more than a vindication of long-held views. The memory span does make a difference.

On the other hand, among persons whose personal memories go back no farther than Nixon's foreign policy successes, the statesman image remains surprisingly untarnished by Watergate. Many of those just old enough to have been spellbound by the Watergate spectaculars without remembering anything of the earlier years have not abandoned the image of Nixon as a man who, for all his faults, had been able to handle the Russians as few others could. These and other memories of Nixon as the tireless promoter of world peace have survived the proven derelictions that brought on his downfall. Watergate has made some inroads but certainly not dispelled this still positive image.

The strongest and most consistent effect of all memories, but particularly of those that go back to the early Nixon, is on the judgment of his character and qualifications. Many who remember the role Nixon had carved out for himself 10 or more years prior to Watergate still cling to the image of Nixon the unscrupulous and conniving politician ready to do whatever had to be done in order to win. Deserved or not, the reputation Nixon had earned himself in his early career still affect how some people feel about him today, especially after Watergate revived some aspects of the almost forgotten image. The relationships shown in Table 2.3 seem to bear this out with one notable exception: the image of Nixon as the promoter of world peace, which is positively associated with memories from each of the three eras. But for those with longer memories, the statesman image is less likely to spill over and affect evaluations of his character. This explains also the strong feelings among this group that he should not have been pardoned.

The image left by Vietnam and Watergate has received some, but hardly overly strong, reinforcement in recent news items. Memories of these could change in response to the more recent revelations of underhanded arms trading for hostages and of other means of circumventing the will of Congress. They at least have the potential to inject once again into the news Nixon's responsibility for having prolonged the war in Vietnam beyond any necessity. However, one would need better data than those available for this exploratory exercise to generalize with some confidence about long-term effects or predict which of the various direct and mediated memories, on which the several Nixon images are based, is apt to prevail; influences other than memory are always at work. What we can say is that, despite the sharing of memories through a continuing process of mediation (socialization), the members of different age groups do not draw on the same reservoir of personal experiences and that, to this extent, they stand in a different relation to the collective memory. Persons over 60 today may sometimes forget that the majority of adults today are too young to have any recollection of the Great Depression of the 1930s and that the number who remember World War II or even the Eisenhower era is inevitably dwindling. How long will it be before Watergate becomes only mediated history?

This chapter has presented an argument, together with some supporting evidence, that how people recall the past is a matter of some consequence. By disaggregating agenda from collective memory, it has also tried to improve the clarity of these two concepts. Memory, as we have looked at it, is made up of two component parts: a set of more or less vivid personal recollections and a stock of images of the past that, insofar as they continue to be mediated, will lose little of their importance with the passage of time. If there is a conclusion, it is that researchers need to pay more attention both to the content of these memories, what shapes them, and how they govern the conduct of different generations than they have up to now.

REFERENCES

Collingwood, R. G. (1946). *The idea of history.* Oxford: Clarendon Press.

Fussell, P. (1975). *The great war and modern memory.* New York: Oxford University Press.

Halbwachs, M. (1980). *The collective memory.* New York: Harper Colophon.

Kraus, S. (1962). *The great debates.* Bloomington, IN: Indiana University Press.

Lang, G. E., & Lang, K. (1979). Immediate and mediated responses: First debate. In S. Kraus (Ed.), *The great debates: Carter vs. Ford* (pp. 298–313). Bloomington, IN: Indiana University Press.

Lang, G. E., & Lang, K. (1983). *The battle for public opinion: The president, the press, and the polls during Watergate.* New York: Columbia University Press.

Lang, G. E., & Lang, K. (1988). *Recognition and renown: The survival of artistic reputation.* American Journal of Sociology, 94, 79–109.

Lang, G. E., & Lang, K. (in press). *Etched in memory: The building and survival of artistic reputation.* Chapel Hill, NC: University of North Carolina Press.

Lang, K., & Lang, G. E. (1953). The unique perspective of television and its effect; a pilot study. *American Sociological Review, 18,* 3–12.

Lang, K., & Lang, G. E. (1978). Experiences and ideology: The influence of the sixties on an intellectual elite. In L. Kriesberg (Ed.), *Research in social movements, conflicts, and change* (Vol. 1, pp. 197–230). Greenwich, CT: JAI Press.

Roberts, C. W., & Lang, K. (1985). Generations and ideological change: Some observations. *Public Opinion Quarterly, 49,* 460–473.

Schudson, M. (1986). *What time means in a news story* (occasional paper no. 4). New York, N.Y. Gannett Center for Media Studies.

3 | Mind, Affect, and Action: Construction Theory and the Media Effects Dialectic

Harold Mendelsohn
University of Denver

From the days of Aristotle onwards the discussions of how the mass media affect their audiences have been grounded in two opposing images of humankind. . .the one teleological—homo mechanicus; the other, teleonomic—homo sapiens-volens.

Throughout history one or the other image has served as the major model for the proper study of "effects"—depending, interestingly, on the states of the political structures and the technologies of the time. Homo mechanicus suited autocratic rule and the industrial epoch quite well. Rational democracy and the advent of the computer-generated information "revolution" has given new impetus to the homo sapiens-volens paradigm.

The two images have been constituted into a scientific dialectic over time. At one epoch or another each point of view has dominated the major scientific hypotheses posed; the methods by which data were to be gathered; and the conclusions and social policy recommendations to be considered.

In our time, the dialectic has been comprised of "behavioristic" versus "structural–functionalist" theories and research methods. Among behaviorists the "effects" of exposure to the media are considered to be direct, automatic, uniform, and universal. In contrast, functionalists see "effects" as being highly limited and variable in their meanderings through the complex predispositional, cognitive, and mediating barriers that are set up by individuals in order to construct meaning and to protect the personality. The influences of media exposure on behavior are considered to be far more contributory than causal.

In this century up until World War II the strict stimulus–response behavioristic approach dominated research on the effects of mass media exposure. Immediately prior to the war and in the years closely following it a powerful challenge to the shortcomings of the direct effects paradigm was launched by "phenomenistic" sociologists of the structural–function school under the limited effects banner.

By the time the 1960s and 1970s focused attention on television a reaction to the limited effects model was posed by a newly emerging set of social-learning principles within which "imitation" was considered to comprise a satisfactory explanation for the direct effects position. One simply does as one observes, Bandura and his adherents (Bandura, Ross, & Ross, 1963) proclaimed.

As explanation, imitation turned out to be both unnecessary and insuffi-cient. Once again, behaviorism had proved itself to be inadequate to the task of discerning whether and how media exposure and effect are interrelated. Behaviorism's latest failure to support the allegations of the direct effects camp has been giving way to the newly reinvigorated cognition thrust among constructivist psychologists. Researchers in the information-processing mode have once again projected "limited effects" as antithetical to the failed "direct effects" paradigm.

To be human is to be able to construct meaning from the signs and symbols that make up our worlds and govern all our private and social actions. The processes through which humans derive meaning are manifold. To this day, most remain enshrouded in mystery.

Communication has been identified as the principal means by which we attempt both to transmit and to construct meaning via language. *Language* is composed of culturally rooted signs and symbols that may be easily understood and even acted upon in one particular set of circumstances; and yet, be totally incomprehensible and nonactivating in another situation.

To a very important degree, we are slowly returning to a rather fundamental principle: Humans act according to what they know and understand (or misunderstand) and not necessarily according to what they simply see or hear.

"Of the three elements in speech making—speaker, subject and person addressed," wrote Aristotle in *Rhetoric*, "it is the last component—the audi-ence—that determines the end and object of the speech."

And so the agenda for the modern study of communications effects was set early on. Surely, source and message were important in determining whether communication can be effective or not. But unless the message recipient was observed to have been moved to act as intended, the effects of messages could not be determined by examining content alone. Above all, the study of effects must be person-bound. Content plus its targeted recipients in a unique communications or "transactional" situation.

A person-anchored mass communications effects theory calls for adherence to three fundamental assumptions that together comprise the foundation stone of the behavioral sciences. They are: (a) that there is order in human action;

(b) that human behavior is characterized by regularity and scientific lawfulness; and above all (c) that human behavior is not predetermined.

From the very beginning, the determination of whether audiences were to be influenced by philosophy, narrative, poetry, or drama was governed by concerns about the duality of man's nature in its capacity to reflect both "good" and "evil" quite simultaneously. What has puzzled observers of the human condition throughout history has been the ability of the human organism to act in inconsistent, paradoxical ways—to manifest, for example, both passion and intellectual detachment; cruelty and compassion; violence and empathy; sensibility and intolerance; and stupidity and wisdom.

Always the human organism has been considered to be essentially fragile and easily corrupted—as being peculiarly vulnerable to outside forces that can sway individuals as if by some magical powers to actions that are incongruent with their personal interests and the public interests of society as a whole. Whether it be the ancient Greeks or the Hebrews and Christians of biblical times; 17th- and 18th-century European rational philosophers or the American behaviorist psychologists of the current epoch, the major percept of man interacting with the environment has been a mechanistic one. Man's behavior, it has been asserted repeatedly, is basically comprised of set responses to both internal and external "stimuli" that happen to touch them off. Confronted with negative messages audiences will automatically behave in negative ways as a direct consequence. Evil begets evil.

Homo mechanicus has been a predominant psychological image of man that appeared early on as explanation for how communication "worked" in influencing behavior. Because communication had the potentiality for either good or evil, Plato, it will be recalled, would guarantee the triumph of good in his ideal state by banishing the diversionary, emotion-arousing poets (including Homer).

Plato was particularly concerned that innocent youth not be led astray from the contemplative to the affective ways of life. In fact, Plato's plan to rid his Republic of the poets reflected ancient Greek anxieties regarding the ultimate outcome of the perpetual conflict between the rational (i.e., philosophy) and the emotional (i.e., poetry) as each supposedly affected the human personality.

Given the choice between the cognitive and the affective, the philosophers of ancient Greece came down strongly on the side of "reason" as the key instrument for attaining the good, harmonious, self-sufficient life.

Plato's ideal state calls for the total rejection of "passions" and "appetites" (i.e., "Eros") in favor of pursuing the rational contemplative ways of the detached philosopher. The "media" of the time were considered dangerous in their unmatched power to sway the crowd with affect rather than in their ability to enhance their audiences' lives with reason.

The familiar modern assertion that non-didactic political fare—with its focus on affect (i.e., conflict, scandal, and violence)—by itself causes audiences to behave in socially deviant ways has its roots in the very beginnings of Western civilization.

The images that have emerged over time basically paint the "media" of communication as overwhelmingly powerful in their ability to arouse, titillate, excite, and please—to bowl audiences over. . .particularly, "innocent audiences." In other words, the "media" are all-powerful; man is pathetically weak and can do nothing but succumb each time he or she encounters "messages" of any color or stripe regardless of whether such messages are understood or are of any use to their recipients.

It has taken literally centuries of debate and research to turn the model around to considering man to be overwhelmingly powerful in his interactions with the "media," and the media to be uniquely impotent in actually *causing* their audiences to misbehave.

After all it was not until mid-20th century that structural–functionalist Elihu Katz (Katz, Gurevitch, & Haas, 1973) was able to proclaim unequivocally that, "people bend the media to their needs more readily than the media overpower them" (p. 164).

Katz's succinct reversal of the ancient direct effects equation reflects the key theorem of the contemporary limited effects geometry.

Throughout history the direct effects thesis has been favored alike by both prince and peasant; author and reader; clergyman and congregant; teacher and student; scholar and layman; parent and offspring. Note that to this day the "direct effects" paradigm offers a ready-made convenient "explanation" for the failures of both individuals and society to achieve perfection.

The persistent image of man, the wooden, robot-like "responder," originated in ancient times, but it emerged full-blown from the early years of the Industrial Revolution's focus on "mechanics" and the simplistic input–output systems that made simple machines run.

At the same time, European society of the 18th and 19th centuries was witnessing gargantuan disruptions in its political, economic, religious, and social structures. Specifically, the final break-up of the divinely inspired monarchial power to govern was followed by an entirely new method of governance. No longer was governance to reflect the will of God alone. Instead, governance would stem from "public opinion," from the knowledge-based will of the rational common man—from *Homo sapiens*. The *Homo sapiens* image was anathema to the anti-democrats and Royalists whose perception of the common man was unflattering in all regards. The common man is ignorant, they argued; he is governed by emotion, not reason; he is child-like—three attributes that make the ordinary "citizen" highly vulnerable to the manipulations of unscrupulous demagogues. Demagogues command, and the mobs obey.

Abetted by the crowd and imitation theories of Le Bon and Tarde and by the mass society theories of Tonnies, Simmel, and Marx as well as by the early associational conditioning experiments of Wundt and Pavlov, the *Homo Mechanicus* image the Royalists used to equate democracy with mob behavior not only survived, but it flowered into a dominant model for ascertaining the effects of communications, particularly of "mass" communications to this very time. The European picture of "mass man" that came into being in the late 19th century was essentially one of an atomized, ignorant individual who was governed by biological drives over which he or she had little control. Mass man, unfettered by his gemeinschaft ties of old, was particularly vulnerable to external manipulation by gesellschaft media which had joined in a bourgeois conspiracy to deny the anomic mass audience the political "truth." Interestingly, this image of weakling man fighting a losing battle against the all-powerful communications media is still quite popular among today's idealogues of both the left and the right. If the disciples of Karl Marx and adherents of the Ronald Reagan right agree on one thing it is in their shared fundamental belief that the "media" of the western world are constantly conspiring to undermine approved and favored institutions and value systems.

Unlike the Europeans, the Americans founding sociologists, particularly those of the Chicago school—Mead, Cooley, Thomas, Znaniecki were not so much concerned with the seizure and control of political and economic power by the "masses" as they were with the establishment of consensual reciprocities between the governing and the governed. In this view, informed public opinion was seen as the fundamental guideline for democratic political authority. Rather than being exploitative and disruptive, the potentialities of the media were considered to be primarily enlightening and integrative. Thus, from the start, American sociologists were mainly concerned with the two-way horizontal flow of communications—not the percolation downwards process. Their attention focused on what goes on between the people and their leaders in the active reciprocal exchange of ideas, values, beliefs, and opinions, *Homo sapiens* was displacing the mechanical image, and it actually became a dominant image for a short time. The vehicle for both producing and reaching *Homo sapiens* was communication. From interactive exchanges between knowledgeable individual citizens' opinions and the opinions of leaders it was believed that consensus regarding the integration of democratic society emerges. American sociology thus shifted focus from ideologies in broad political and economic contexts to a new social–psychological emphasis on individual values, beliefs, attitudes, and opinions—how they originate, how they are expressed, how they can be harnessed for both the individual and the common good—all within a societal milieu. Ultimately the structural functionalist and transactional orientations to mass communications effects grew out of the American constructivist sociological tradition—an orientation that seeks to understand individual actions—not only per se, but individuals acting in a social context as well. Man was beginning to be perceived as being considerably more complex and powerful than heretofore.

The relationship between "stimulus" and "response," observed the early sociological constructivists, is neither direct nor automatic. Interactions between individual and the environment are never static or linear; nor are they fixed. Instead, the individual and the environment are in constant flux—each acting upon another reciprocally via cognitive and fantasy processes that help us to imagine, comprehend, define, analyze, and interpret varieties of inputs—including media content—that help to reinforce old "realities" and to construct new ones on occasion.

Both, *cognition* and *affect* are equally necessary for message recipients to either attend to them or not.

Unlike the mechanistic image of man as an automaton responder that was being projected by the early S–R behaviorists and European sociologists, the American constructivist sociologists saw human beings as essentially "minded" in their active and creative approaches to the environmental forces that may impinge upon them. "Mindedness" requires message recipients to treat "stimuli" as problems to be understood and solved rather than as overpowering shots from a cannon against which no defense but surrender was possible.

Before we can act on information originating in the mass media, we not only must be aware of it, but above all, we must "process" that information in order to construct meaning from it, the constructivist sociologists were urging.

Sociological constructivism was instrumental in the development of limited effects theory following World War II, and it has served as a powerful challenge to behavioristic interpretation of mass media effects from the start.

The linkages that joined the symbolic-interactionism of Blumler to the social action theories of Parsons, to the structural function theories of Merton to the use-gratifications-multi-step information flow constructs of Lazarsfeld, culminated in the phenomenistic limited effects paradigm that was put forth so succinctly by Klapper in the 1960s. Klapper's principle, "Mass communications *ordinarily* does not serve as a necessary and sufficient cause of audience effects, but rather functions among and through a nexus of mediating factors and influences" (p. 8), capsulated a wide range of empiricism that led to the dominance of limited effects theory in the decades between 1950 and 1970.

The "limited effects" paradigm is deeply embedded in the "theory of action" which was first promulgated as a rationale for basing new 18th- and 19th-century democratic governance on public opinion and popular will. Social observers like Adam Smith, Rousseau, Mills, and Hobbes viewed man as essentially freed from predestination.

There is considerably more to life, they opined, than simply waiting around for some external "stimulus" (i.e., command) to automatically elicit a mysterious hidden "response" over which we as individuals had no control whatever.

To the contrary, thinking mankind was capable of *acting* from his or her capacities for reasoning, discerning, and above all, *selecting* from alternatives those options that best suited individual "needs," "expectations," and "motivations." The sociological action theorists of modern times noted that most external "stimuli," particularly those in the form of "messages"—far from eliciting universal automatic responses, were either avoided, ignored or modified to suit the objectives of those addressed. In their encounters with the media the cognitive, personality, and social status attributes of the individual were seen to serve as gatekeeping filters through which all incoming mass media messages must pass. In sorting out those messages that are of interest and use to the individual message targets can either facilitate, distort, change, or stop any communication that is designed to alter its audiences' attitudes, beliefs, values, or behavior.

Combining theories of cognition, motivation and action produced a new synthesized image of humankind—*Homo sapiens-volens* . . . the individual as a minded, motivated actor in a communications situation.

Where the pulley and belt machines of the Industrial Revolution provided the analog imagery for the behaviorists' *Homo mechanicus*, the "information revolution" beginning with the 1950's "systems" and "cybernetics" approaches to building computers—electronic "thinking machines"—served as new reinforcements for *Homo sapiens*—man the "minded" organism.

Late in the 1950s psychologists of the Herbert Simon and George Miller schools of thought, together with linguists like Naom Chomsky (1965) and cyberneticists like Wiener, (1950) launched what we now recognize to be the "cognitive revolution." Essentially the focus of the new cognitive theorists turned to how the human organism acquired information and knowledge and what it did in processing the information so acquired in order to "construct" meaning for taking action. Overt, "objective" responses to external "stimuli" were essentially irrelevant as variables for study, they averred. The shift in focus from the "overt" to the "covert" was accompanied by yet another reorientation from a behavioristic emphasis on "performance" to renewed cognitive emphasis on knowing and understanding as reflected in "competence."

The computer as analog for "mind" promised a high pay off for the development of an empirically based "science of the mind." From the latter day cognitive school we have found that for all intents and purposes mental acts that govern behavior are as real as the observable physical actions they spark. But how to "measure" thinking and understanding and the rules that guide them?

"Constructivism" in its contemporary emergence from G. H. Mead's (1934) emphasis on the world of "reality" existing only in the meanings we *construct* from symbols has begun to pave a way out from this dilemma.

The emergence of a new computer—based cognitive *Homo sapiens* image has made a profound impact on the thinking of mass communications effects scholars who had been growing ever-more frustrated with the dead ends that behavioristic research had persistently led them into.

In contrast to the deterministic behavioral psychologies of the past which viewed man as purely a mechanical passive reactor to external stimuli like information and entertainment, the new "cognitive" psychological models reinforced structural-functionalist interpretation of fundamentally active and purposive; that is to say, as being primarily *motivated* to understand symbols and their relevance to action taking.

As motivated organisms we not only can select courses of action according to our needs for meaning (these selections take on the form of "decisions"), but we can also anticipate the consequences of our decisions. As a result, we process information not in accordance necessarily with the intent of the communicator; but rather, with regard to how we, the audience, "construct" the world as fitting in with our personal needs, values, expectancies, aspirations, knowledge, and experiences.

And so we are faced with an historical dialectic of thesis (direct effects)–antitheses (limited effects) as applicable to the study of "effects" from the time of the Ancient Greeks to today.

Whether a true synthesis of the diametrically opposed behaviorist–phenomenistic paradigms can ever be accomplished is open to serious question, given the differentiation between the two in their basic images of humankind.

Carl Hovland (1959) attempted just such a melding at the onset of the Age of Television. He failed.

Considerably more promising is the possibility of a new synthesis to be made up of the two schools of psychological and sociological constructivism that share a similarly active image of humankind—individuals as minded and motivated social beings; *interacting* with communications environments purposively, and *reacting* to the same selectively and knowingly in accord with one's status in society.

As a consequence of the new synthesis, one thing is certain . . . no longer will we be bound to view the recipients of mass mediated political information as either victims or patients.

REFERENCES

Bandura, A., Ross, D., & Ross, S. A. (1963). Imitation of film mediated aggressive models. *Journal of Abnormal and Social Psychology, 67*, 575–582.

Chomsky, N. (1965). *Aspects of the theory of syntax.* Cambridge, MA: MIT Press.

Hovland, C. (1959). Reconciling conflicting results from experimental and survey studies of attitude change. *American Psychologist, 14*(1), 8–17.

Katz, E., Gurevitch, M., & Haas, H. (1973). On the uses of the mass media for important things. *American Sociological Review, 38,* 164–181.

Klapper, J. T. (1960). *The effects of mass communications.* Glencoe, IL: The Free Press.

Mead, G. H. (1934). *Mind self and society.* Chicago, IL: University of Chicago Press.

Wiener, N. (1950). *The human use of human beings: Cybernetics and society.* Boston, MA: Houghton Mifflin.

4 Exploring a Relational Perspective to Political Information Processing

Frank E. Millar
University of Wyoming

All social systems are necessarily communication systems (Luhmann, 1986); conversely, all communication systems are necessarily social systems (Duncan, 1968). Further, every social system processes information and the information digested functions to regulate the "distance" between its members (Kantor & Lehr, 1975). Assuming that the "fundamental concept of social science is Power" (Russell, 1938, p. 12) and that politics is about defining, distributing, and justifying power dynamics, then every social system is also political. I assume, therefore, that *political information processing* refers to investigations of the messages-in-circuitry that regulate the "distances" between members of human systems.

The perspective I have utilized in studying social systems has been called "relational communication" (Millar & Rogers, 1976, 1987; Parks, 1977) because it attempts to delineate emergent systemic properties as manifested in communicative processes. From this point of view, a cursory examination of the political information-processing literature (Kraus & Perloff, 1985; Nimmo & Sanders, 1981) suggests two major sources of disagreement about the development of viable communication theories. One, the individual has been identified as both the unit of action and the unit of explanation. When the individual is both the unit of action and explanation, then he or she is necessarily conceived of as an isolatable, independent object that digests information in ways unaffected by the communication networks within which he or she is embedded. Such a conceptualization does not treat people as social beings. Two, this literature appears to exclusively focus on the content information of conventionally defined political campaigns rather than on the distance regulation function of information processing. Such a focus cannot treat power as a relational property.

These two observations of the political information-processing literature suggest that an individual is "victimized" by stimuli in his or her informational environment (Fisher, 1978). Victimization in turn, precludes analyses of relational level properties because the individual is conceived of as a nonparticipant in the victim–victimizer cycle of sociopolitical dynamics. This preclusion, I submit, denies the social (interdependent) and symbolic (intersubjective) nature of human systems by reducing the social group to the summative heap of its members. This reductionistic bias, in turn, serves to propagate "person-blame" explanations of social interactions that function to legitimize an existing social Order by excluding the socialness of communicative dynamics. The "fundamental attribution error" (Sillars, 1982) appears to characterize approaches to political information processing.

The above assertions are explicitly denied from a relational perspective. This denial is grounded in an epistemological framework different from that which apparently underpins political communication research. This chapter, then, briefly describes the epistemological underpinnings of a relational perspective and offers the dramatistic metaphors of comedy and tragedy as useful ones for framing theoretical questions about political dynamics. If "good talk is always exploratory" (Duncan, 1968, p. 43), then the purpose of this chapter is to explore the relevancy of the developing relational perspective to the study of political information processing.

METATHEORETICAL ASSUMPTIONS

A relational perspective is part of the "interactional view" (Watzlawick, Beavin, & Jackson, 1967; Watzlawick & Weakland, 1977; Wilder, 1979). Wilder-Mott (1982) characterized the interactional view as resting on the three epistemological premises of (a) systemic description, (b) pragmatism, and (c) verbal realism. These presuppositions, in turn, are derived from Bateson's (1972, 1979) "cybernetic epistemology" which itself is embedded in the "cybernetic revolution" (Maruyama, 1975) presently occurring in Western science and philosophy.

Cybernetic Underpinning

The relevance of the "cybernetic revolution" to the social science of communication can be illustrated by reviewing and extending Krippendorf's (1984) discussion of ontological and epistemological commitments to observation.[1]

---

[1]Krippendorf (1984) defined *ontology* as that "branch of philosophy that is concerned with the nature of reality or what exists independent of observation" (p. 22), whereas *epistemology*

The application of cybernetic thought "onto itself is producing a shift in the scientific paradigm from ontology to epistemology" (Krippendorf, 1984, p. 22). This metatheoretical shift in emphasis fundamentally alters thinking about communication in five distinct ways.

First, ontological commitments "assign scientific observers the role of discoverers of facts that are unalterably outside themselves" (p. 27). Scientific observations are required to be "objective"—that is, independent of observers and their symbolic expressions. In this way, ontological commitments emphasize that analytical truth is of more theoretic import than synthetic utility, that explanation is the primary goal of science. Such an emphasis readily muddles the distinctions between ideology and theory. In contrast, epistemological commitments assign scientific observers "the role of co-creators of facts" (p. 27). This emphasis asserts that observations of social systems must include the observer. Any observation is composed of the gross elements termed *event, signal,* and *observer* by Bronowski (1978b) and, therefore, predictive utility, not explanatory ideology, is the "bottom line" of science.

Second, when ontological commitments are emphasized, communication is viewed as some kind of stimulus "contained" in some material message or channel or medium that is "transmitted" to others so that communication is done to others. This view necessarily posits a "one-way" conception of communication with its accompanying "conduit metaphor" (Reddy, 1979) approach to the study of symbolic languages.[2] This conception reflects the

---

refers to that "branch of philosophy that is concerned with knowledge, not with what exists" (p. 23). Further, "cybernetic epistemology has become more specific, emphasizing 'processes by which we come to know,' perhaps at the expense of its products or what it is that becomes known" (1984, p. 23). The "processes by which we come to know" are, of course, communication processes. Other presuppositions of a cybernetic epistemology emphasizing how we come to know are itemized by Bateson (1979) in discussing the "communicational characteristics" that "all minds must share" (p. 27).

[2]Reddy (1979) used *conduit metaphor* as a label for a logic that frames discussions about language. The four core expressions of this way of thinking about language are: "(1) language functions like a conduit, *transferring* thoughts bodily from one person to another; (2) in writing and speaking, people *insert* their thoughts or feelings *in* the words; (3) words accomplish the transfer by *containing* the thoughts or feelings and *conveying* them to others; and (4) in listening and reading, people *extract* the thoughts once again from the words" (p. 290, italics added). Conduit metaphor thinking about human language and communication implies the "bizarre assumption that words can have 'insides' and 'outsides'. After all, if thoughts can be 'inserted' there must be space 'inside' wherein the meaning can reside" (p. 288). From the conduit metaphor point of view, what requires explanation in human relationships is the "failure to communicate" (p. 295) for mutual understanding is expected and prescribed as long as words, and hence meanings, are carefully packaged and unwrapped. The longevity of this way of thinking about human interactions stems from the self-sealing nature of its explanations about the inevitable "failures to communicate"—they are the speaker's or listener's fault. The conduit metaphor logic is also maintained by several common English words and phrases that perpetuate and validate this logic in self-validating ways. For example, in addition to those just emphasized, words like 'transmit,' 'decode,' 'encode,' 'carry,' 'translate,' and phrases like "get your idea across," "give me an idea," "put your thoughts into words," and "don't give away your feelings" all imply that words

"mechanistic" and "psychological" perspectives of human communication (Fisher, 1978) and cannot view communication "as a process that makes the whole behave differently from the sum of its parts" (Krippendorf, 1984, p. 30). In contrast, when an epistemological emphasis is accepted, communication is thought of as that participatory process within which and through which social realities are constructed, maintained, and changed. Communication becomes that "relational construction" (p. 29) explaining the "dynamics of interaction and dependency" (p. 30) characterizing social systems that include their own observers.

Third, this shift also results in differing ethical implications. Whereas ontological premises require that observers be detached from their observations and are thereby made "intellectually superior to the object they describe" (p. 23), epistemological emphases embed participant–observers in their work making them responsible for their observations and the subsequent consequences of those observations.

A fourth result of this shift in emphasis is a different conception of message, the primitive term of *communication*. Rather than conceived of as some material "thing" done unto others, a message is now thought of as that intrinsically multilayered (stratified) construction created by the observer when formulating differences between perceptions. In this view, a message might be defined as a synchronic transformation of difference (Millar & Bavelas, 1985); it is conceived of as a difference between perceptions where perception is the active specification (hence inferential construction) of an external event and not the passive reception (hence objective arrival) of one. A possible formalization of this conception of message is shown in Table 4.1.

As a difference, a message itself is a relationship describable by inferring some matrix of distinctions repetitively used in construction; it is not a substantive thing to be described in exclusively matter–energy terms. The function of this matrix of distinctions for the individual member of the social system is the production of predictions about how to behave in interactions with others.[3] The function of messages for the interacting system is the

---

are "filled" with meanings that are "carried" across interactors "in" words. A moment's reflection witnesses, however, that such thinking about language is patent nonsense—though such a logic is useful for upholding the legitimacy of the existing social Order. Simply, conduit metaphor thinking about language and communication "objectifies meaning in a misleading and dehumanizing fashion" (Reddy, 1979, p. 308).

[3]Note that a lack of difference between perceptions is itself a comparison between perceptions and is, therefore, a message. In this sense, the absence of a difference is also "news" that may or may not result in alterations of the observer's behavior. This conception also assumes that individuals are "autopoietic" (Maturana, 1980). Maturana recounts that the term 'autopoiesis' was invented from the words 'autonomy'—the "central feature of the organization of the living" (1980, p. xvii)—and 'poiesis', a Greek word meaning creation or production and the basis for the English word 'poetic'. Thus, autopoiesis refers to the autonomous creation of perceptions by an organism where perception is to be understood *not* "as a grasping of external reality, but rather

TABLE 4.1
Formal Definition of Message

Let:

        P = a perception

and

        $P_{i, j, \ldots n}$ =   a particular perception in a sequence of perceptions

and

        ⌐   =   "in context of"

So:

        P_i ⌐   =   the ith perception in its spatial and/or temporal context

and

        P_i ⌐ $- P_j$ ⌐   =   the difference between successive perceptions (each in its context)

Therefore:

        Message = $\overline{P_i}$ ⌐ $- \overline{P_j}$ ⌐   =   the difference (in its spatial and/or temporal context) between two perceptions

validation and regulation of the "distance" between participant–observers along the control, trust and intimacy dimensions of social relationships (Millar & Rogers, 1987).

A final shift from ontological to epistemological commitments to observation is that only epistemological premises are capable of "characterizing the self-referential nature of social systems" (Krippendorf, 1984, p. 35). This distinction is the most important theoretically because the self-referential feature of human communication systems was explicitly denied by ontological commitments—a denial that effectively precluded the serious study of society, of sociopolitical dynamics.

The Problem of Self-Reference

The problem of self-referential statements is one that "dogs" all formal systems of thought (Bronowski, 1978a) and has lead to the "loss of certainty" in logic and mathematics (Kline, 1980). Self-referential statements were prohibited by the theory of logical types in order to preserve the sacredness of analytical

---

as the specification of one" (p. xv). Maturana emphasized that in order to understand the operations of the nervous system he had to "close off the nervous system," but within this closed network "no distinction was possible between hallucination and perception" (p. xv). Thus, in order to understand perception, he had to "open up" the nervous system so that external reality served a "triggering role in the release of the internally-determined activity of the nervous system" (p. xv). For humans, such triggers are more usefully thought of as learned, cognitive habits than as external causes of information processing.

truth. However, the theory of types was an unsuccessful attempt to deal with self-reference because it (a) proffered a picture theory of language—thereby de-emphasizing epistemological commitments; (b) assumed that "external reality exhibits discrete levels of organization free from loops"—thereby emphasizing ontological commitments; and (c) asserted the practical advisory that symbolic expressions that confuse discrete hierarchical levels of organization "out-there" are destructive of clear representations "in-here" among communicators (Cronen, Johnson, & Lannamann, 1982, p. 94).

A picture theory of language is now widely rejected and is being replaced with conceptions like Reddy's (1979) "toolmaker's paradigm" and Lakoff and Johnson's (1980) "experientialist myth." Neither material nor social reality appears to be organized into discontinuous, lineal hierarchies that can be described by a closed deductive language; both appear to consist of self-organizing loops that manifest "orders of recursiveness" (Bateson, 1979). If the observer cannot be separated from the act of observation (Bohm, 1980; French & Kennedy, 1985; Heisenberg, 1958; von Weizsacker, 1980), then no "objective" boundary between the "out-there" and the "in-here" can be unequivocally drawn; "objectivity" becomes a matter of consensual validation rather than an ontological prerequisite for scientific observations.

The self-referential nature of informal language use results in the human ability to see ourselves as if we were objects isolatable from ongoing communication processes. This ability stems directly from the invention of the Negative—"negation is the very essence of language" (Burke, 1966, p. 457). Although Burke's (1966) definition of *humanness*[4] included the phrase "inventor of the negative," he quickly amended this by suggesting that "it might be more accurate to say that language and the negative 'invented' man" (p. 9). The negative is not the name for a thing, but a principle, an idea, a second-order "rule of relations" (Wilden, 1980, p. 185) that has no strictly physical existence whatsoever. In "positive" nature, things are what they are; they are not what they are not (e.g., there can be no disbelievers in nature, no heretics, no nonvoters).

The ability to see ourselves as objects also results in the "paradoxical quality" (Krippendorf, 1984) or "problematic twistiness" (Hofstadter, 1985) of self-referential statements. (All paradoxes are self-referential but not all

---

[4]Burke's (1966) definition of humanness states that:
"Man is
    the symbol-using (symbol-making, symbol-misusing)
    animal
    inventor of the negative (or moralized by the negative)
    separate from his natural condition by instruments of
    his own making
    goaded by the spirit of hierarchy (or moved by the
    sense of order)
    and rotten with perfection" (p. 16).

self-referential assertions are paradoxical. For example, both class M and class N in Russell's famous paradox are self-referential but only class N is paradoxical.) A general label for a symbolic system (e.g., a sentence, an ideology, a theory) that "twists back on itself and closes a loop . . . is reflexivity" (Hofstadter, 1985, p. 6). As Mead (1934) emphasized, reflexivity is a necessary condition for becoming socialized, for becoming a member of a sociopolitical community in communication. "Reflexiveness . . . is the essential condition, within the social process, for the development of mind" (p. 134) or consciousness. However, it is "absurd" to conceive of mind exclusively "from the standpoint of the individual human organism"; rather, mind and its proper subset consciousness must be regarded as "arising and developing within . . . the matrix of social interactions" (Mead, 1934, p. 133).[5]

An individual can be said to be "in" society when the lawlike assertions grounded in the Negatives proselytized by that society are "in" the individual. The way people become members of a human, social system is, therefore, the internalization of that community's language system. All the problems of consciousness and conscience arise from our ability to see ourselves as if we were objects separate from our environs while simultaneously bound within them.[6]

---

[5]"A cybernetic thesis ('thesis' in the sense that we have experienced little to the contrary) suggests that 'the nervous system is organized or organizes itself such that it computes a stable reality' (von Foerster, 1974, p. 53). This 'reality' is located neither inside nor outside the observing organism but resides in the ongoing process of drawing distinctions and formulating relations. In this process, 'facts' may come into being" (Krippendorf, 1984, pp. 27–28). The neurological aspects of this inherently neural-social interaction of autopoietic systems is avoided in this essay. For recent discussions of these neural-social characteristics see Pribram (1986) and Delbruck (1986).

[6]According to von Weizsacker (1980), the original meaning of the Latin verb *informe* was "to form" or "to fashion." Its present meaning is "to fashion in the mind" or "to represent to oneself". He interprets the noun *informatio* to mean "the bringing of matter into form, or form into matter" (p. 38). Information, then, is any molded "form," or "structure," or "pattern" that can refer to "all kinds of objects and events perceivable to the senses" (p. 39). Thus, the contents of consciousness are information where information is to be understood as "linguistic in nature" (von Weizsacker, 1980, p. 39). Through language we humans name our perceptions which are the emergent result of nervous system activity triggered by external events. Our ability to name these complex interactions, however, readily leads to the assertion that language simply records or pictures external events and, thereby, we project our immanent constructions by denying that we are necessarily part of the perceptions and messages created. To say that "information is linguistic in nature" is to assert that it is necessarily structured in and by some symbolic system, that the contents of one's mind are fashioned in one's mind with the meta-tool of language. Thus, information is constructed in and through symbolic languages that are their own context (Burke, 1966; Wilden, 1980), a context that is problematically associated with the ecological relations within which the "structure" was constructed. This essay assumes, therefore, that a consciousness is structured like a language, that unconsciousness is structured like a communication system, and that the crossing of the consciousness-unconsciousness bar is structured by language (Wilden, 1980).

All "laws" are "essentially negative" (Burke, 1966, p. 11). This is true whether we are talking about the "Thou-can-not" prescriptions of science or the "Thou-shall-not" prescriptions of human societies. Whereas scientific "laws" describe which interactions with the environment will not work, sociopolitical "laws" define those social interactions that should not occur. Both types of prescriptions constrain choice. Both types are necessary for functional, felicitous social relationships. Both types describe relational redundancies observable in interactions, and both are used to make predictions about subsequent acts in situations embedded in the ongoing process of interacting. Finally, both types are quickly turned into "quasi-positives" (Burke, 1966) specifying what a person can or should do although strictly speaking, both types only describe what cannot or should not be done. Even though both prescriptions can become "quasi-positives," logically and developmentally, the moralistic negatives of "right" and "wrong" precede the scientific negatives of "true" and "false"—"the negative *Command* is prior to the *Propositional* negative" (Burke, 1966, p. 454).

These "quasi-positives" become the basis for a society's conception of the Perfect proselytized by that society's "consensus narrative" (Carey, 1988). The "perfection principle" (Burke, 1966) is intrinsic to symbolic languages based on the Negative. The "negative is an idea" and, therefore, "there can be no image of it" for in "imagery there is no negative" (Burke, 1966, p. 430). The *idea* of eliminating the Negative is the Perfect. The "perfect" performance is thought of as that enactment that is free of error (scientific prescriptions) or free of guilt and sin (moralistic prescriptions).

As an idea, the Perfect, like the Negative, has no material existence whatsoever. Importantly, and in contrast to ecological cybernetic systems, there appears to be "no principle of control intrinsic" to symbol systems that counteracts the tendency to follow ideas to their "perfect" extreme (Burke, 1966, p. 19). Each human society specifies its own definition of the perfect social Order. Any empirical enactment, however, always involves some deviation from the perfect even though observations of it are "close enough" (i.e., sufficient lack of sin) to be called "outstanding" or "competent" for the sociopolitical purposes at hand.

Every historical human society is grounded in a series of ideas of various degrees of generality (Bateson, 1972) so that "mind is a necessary explanatory principle" (Bateson, 1977, p. 239) in relational communication even while mind or "consciousness can be explained only through communication" (Duncan, 1968, p. 45). The internalization of these general ideas and the prescribed performances associated with them perpetuates that society for itself by itself through constraining the actions and cognitions of its members. In this way, "society" creates its members and its members recreate "society."[7] The general ideas are both "in" repetitive social practices and "beyond" those practices; they are both legitimized (i.e., "lawfully" established) by enacted practices and legitimize (i.e., sanction and authorize) those enactments. Each is ground for the other as figure. Human culture, therefore, is inherently self-referential, and its stability is a function of self-validating metatheoretical commitments, self-regulating behavioral patterns, and self-sealing cognitive schemas. These reflexive characteristics are observable in the repetitive interactions and consensus narratives performed by society's members. The legitimation patterns of social practices and cognitions about them are the domain and focus of political information processing from a relational point of view.

Two general metaphors for describing the sets of ideas unfolded in social practices and narratives are comedy and tragedy. Comedy and tragedy both resonate with the other and require the other for meaning; therefore, a certain kind of "competition" exists between them. This "competition" is analogous to that manifested between the metaphoric and metonymical poles of language processes (Jakobson, 1971) and between the complementary and symmetrical poles of message patterns (Bateson, 1979). If reliable measures of these dramatistic metaphors are constructed, their frequency ratios are expected to indicate the "personality" or "climate" or "culture" of the society studied. Further, gross inequalities in these ratios—indicating the predominance of one type over the other—are expected to index that society's typical "pathology". Conversely, comparative equality in the frequency ratios of comic and tragic performances is assumed to be "stabilizing" for that social system. If reliable indicators of these metaphors, however gross, could be developed, both the "stability" and "change" of a society's interactions can be assessed by comparing relative frequencies over time. The comedy–tragedy pair presumes that every historical society is legitimized by "transcendental" ideas that are *immanent* in the redundant messages-in-circuitry constituting the communicative relationships that make up that society. Simply, "sociopolitical ideologies are created" (Duncan, 1968, p. 33) and recreated in habituated communication relationships.

COMEDY AND TRAGEDY

Social drama is a drama of legitimation, the attempt to legitimize authority by persuading those involved that such order is "necessary" to the survival of the community. (Duncan, 1968, p. 49)

. . . politics is dramatic ritual. . . . In fact, denying the ritualized nature of politics

---

[7]"In the beginning was the Word" and the issue ever since has been Whose word is The word. As members of social systems, we are taught early and thoroughly that who is more important

is itself part of the ritual. "Truth, not artifice" and "issues, not images" are themselves important chants and central themes in the political dramas. (Meyrowitz, 1985, p. 277)

The previous discussion of epistemological commitments to observation and the problem of self-reference was intended to evidence that humans live "by those propositions whose validity is a function of their belief in them" (Bateson, 1951, p. 212). Similarly, Becker (1975) asserted that "man is an animal who has to live in a lie in order to live at all" (p. 122); he argued that because "all secular societies are lies" (comic dramas of legitimation) and "all religious integrations are mystifications" (tragic dramas of legitimization), every historical society rests on either a "hopeful mystification or a determined lie" (p. 124). The dramatistic terms of *comedy* and *tragedy* are useful metaphors for thinking about both the relational form and informational content of the mystifications and lies characterizing the social dramas within which people participate. Participation allows humans to identify with one another in order to differentiate themselves from one another and, therefore, we co-create Ourselves and Them.

The writings of Duncan (1968) have most influenced my own thoughts on comedy and tragedy. Every social Order is instantiated in some kind of hierarchy (bureaucratic, charismatic, theocratic) that differentiates humans into "ranks, classes, and status groups" while simultaneously unifying humans in "appeals to principles of order" upon which their ranking is based and within which their ranking is legitimated (Duncan, 1968, p. 51). Given the necessity of such appeals, every "hierarchy functions through persuasion, which takes the form of courtship in social relationships" (p. 53) so that "courtship" is the "rhetoric of hierarchy" (p. 54) in sociopolitical dramas. "Superiors must persuade inferiors to accept" their dominant position just as "inferiors must persuade superiors to accept them as loyal followers" (p. 53). But people also persuade one another to interact as "equals" by agreeing to abide by relational rules that they themselves have constructed and can therefore change by themselves for themselves. In a necessarily short-hand way, Table 4.2 summarizes Duncan's conceptualizations of these two general

---

than what or where. Socialization involves inculcating the habit that the authority describing what's "real" is to be given more weight in constructing meanings (tragic, ontological emphasis) than is the falsifiable prediction of what's described (comic, epistemological emphasis). As members of social systems, we believe because we believe we're supposed to believe the authority who would not be the authority if not believed. A social system not so characterized is difficult, if not impossible, to envision. The danger of this inculcated habit, of course, is that individuals will consistently foresake their human ability to say 'no' to the authority. The more unreservedly we say 'yes' and deny our right to say 'no', and vice-versa, the more dehumanized we become and the more we are victimized by our own ideals.

TABLE 4.2
Duncan's (1968) Characteristics of Comedy and Tragedy

Comic Dramas	Tragic Dramas
Based on the principle of reason in society (p. 60); reason is born in conversations that depend on conversants remaining bound by their mutually agreed upon conversational constraints (p. 37).	Based on the principle of victimage (p.59); "victimage is the means by which people purge themselves of fear and guilt in their relations with each other" (p. 39).
Comedy thrives on sanctioned doubt which is a method of inquiry (p. 62); doubt is a way of creating truth (p. 226) and mystification must be submitted to rational inquiry (p. 81).	Tragedy thrives on mystery which sustains the faith (p. 60); mystery creates a "higher" value that dignifies and glorifies our life by casting a "halo of eternity about the temporal" (p. 234).
Dramatic form in which people bring into consciousness the many incongruities between the ends desired and means used to achieve them (p. 60) and, thereby, undermines mystery in society.	Dramatic form that excludes from consciousness the many ends-means incongruities by opening up the mind to the supernatural above and "beyond" reason and, thereby, undermines reason in society (p. 127).
Teaches that whatever separates humans from each other is evil (p.60).	Teaches that whatever separates humans from our gods is evil (p.60).
Social appeal is based on reason and sanctioned doubt (p. 60); doubt is essential to social integration (p. 36) for it unites people in agreed upon rules of their own making (p. 38); it is not a sin to challenge rules (p. 90) for rules are contingent upon agreement and we learn to relate as equals by acting together under rules we've created (p. 58).	Social appeal is based on guilt and fear (p. 59); guilt originates in disobeying the "commandments" believed necessary for social order (p. 135), while fear arises from being ex-communicated from our gods (p. 144); the final appeal of tragedy is expressed in a "great leap into a supernatural" (p. 126) with whom we must relate if our lives are to have meaning.
The ultimate "good" in society is a social one which can only be reached if humans communicate freely with one another as peers, as equals; "social euphoria" is born in laughter which deepens our social bonds (p 61); the "ideal type" of equality is friendship (p. 56) for a friend is the most important self in our own development as an individual (p. 58).	Offers societal members "vicarious atonement" through the suffering and death of sacrificial victims (p. 59); function of atonement is re-establishment of communication with authorities believed necessary for social order (p. 144); public punishment, like punishment of self, is a purgation of guilt (p. 59) caused by disobedience (p. 140); social euphoria is obtained in communion with the transcental It sustaining social order.

(Continued)

TABLE 4.2

(continued)

Comic Dramas	*Tragic Dramas*
Punishes pride against fellow humans, the hubris that places one above others (p. 60); comedy censures those who separate humans from one another (p. 127); comic rituals depict victims who are "laughed out of court" because they rejected reasonable ways of living together (p. 126).	Punishes pride against the gods, the hubris that places a human equal to or above the commandment-givers (p. 60); tragedy destroys those who separate humans from their gods (p. 127); tragic victims must suffer and die because they've disobeyed the ultimate principles believed necessary for social order (p. 126).
The comic victim keeps people in touch with the world, is a means of communicating with each other as humans (p. 24); comic victims suffer but this victimage is intended to bring them back into the group once they've learned their errors (p. 126).	The tragic victim keeps us in touch with supernatural powers, is a means of communicating with our gods who may be "beyond" communication (p. 24); tragic victims must suffer and die because they are beyond hope and in their destruction lies our salvation (p. 54).
Comic gods remind us that vices are often brought about by an excess of virtue (p. 175); in laughing at ourselves we "purify" ourselves as social beings (p. 176).	Tragic gods remind us that virtue is only attained in subordination to the ultimate principles of Order and in bowing to the will of our superiors (p. 53); vice is not believing in the "right" of our superior to command in the name of some sacred principle (p. 54).
Teaches that humans must be urged to criticize for reason lies in criticism (p. 26).	Teaches that humans must be urged to believe, for we must believe in order to act (p. 26).

Both dramatistic forms assume that belief in absolute authority is born in communication. Both comedy and tragedy sustain authority because the "drama of community is the drama of authority," is a "struggle over beliefs about how to create order in human relationships" (p. 64). Since reason is the final arbiter of human differences in comedy, comic forms emphasize the communal nature of society which establishes its own authority, legitimacy. Conversely, since tragedy utilizes a supernatural agent as the final arbiter of differences, tragic dramas emphasize communion with the trancental It who is beyond society yet sustained in society by legitimizing the Order of that society. Both comic and tragic authorities not only expect obedience and disobedience, but actually name them and thereby create them (p. 139). Thus order and disorder are reciprocally defined (p. 64), originate in (p. 130) and are sustained by habituated communication relationships.

ways of legitimizing and instantiating the social relations constituting any given social Order.

One strength of Duncan's argument is the insistence on descriptions of both cognitive meanings and enacted rituals, of interpretations and interactional dynamics. Either type of data without the other is insufficient to adequately model the self-referential characteristics of sociopolitical processes. The messages-in-circuitry, constituting and regulating a society from within itself, are the primary data of empirical investigations of a society's political information processing patterns. Any historical social Order is maintained and changed through habituated "distance regulation" (Kantor & Lehr, 1975) patterns that function to unfold the "principles of order" believed necessary for the survival of that community's identity.

Social scientists are familiar with the notion of praxis—an instrumental, practical exchange that momentarily binds participants together around a common object for the accomplishment of their separate goals. However, a self-referential dramatic point of view would also emphasize interpretive constructs that bind people in the common idea of themselves. One such construct is Laing's (1967) notion of nexus. Laing used the term *nexus* to describe the intersubjective cognitive bonds that hold a group together for itself to itself by itself. His focus was on describing what it means to be a member of a social system from the member's point of view rather than from a nonparticipant, "objective" perspective. From a participant–observer point of view, a group is "not a social object out there in space" but the "quite extraordinary being formed by each person's synthesis of the same multiplicity into We, and each person's synthesis of the multiplicity of syntheses" (Laing, 1967, p. 85). The phrase "multiplicity of syntheses" refers to the multiple levels of perception indicated by the Interpersonal Perception Method (Laing, Phillipson, & Lee, 1966), a most under-utilized method for statically describing the degrees and levels of "consensus" amongst societal members (Scheff, 1967).

The nexus is ubiquitous; it is "everywhere in each person, and is nowhere else than in each" (Laing, 1967, p. 87). The "highest ethic of the nexus is reciprocal concern" where "each person is concerned with what the other thinks, feels, does" so that "every action of mine is always the concern of the other members of the group" (p. 89). Anybody is everybody else's business so that everyone feels constrained by self's concern for others' concern for self and by self's concern for others. Any defection from this ubiquitous matrix of obligated concerns is punishable (victimage) by nexus ethics and the worst punishment devised is exile or "excommunication" (p. 87)—loss of contact with our gods.

Every member of the group is "expected to be controlled and to control the others" (p. 89). However, these mutually constraining patterns are deemed benevolent and loving for actions "done to please, to make happy, to show one's gratitude to the other" are the "highest form of action" by nexus standards (p. 89). Nonetheless, benevolence is contingent upon the acting out of the socially prescribed relational "distances" for the stability of the nexus is sustained through the malevolence "done by the members of the group on each other" (p. 89). We are kept "in" the group by not "rocking the relational boat" which is reflexively defined, steered and legitimated by the group.

The nexus exists because it is believed in and believed that others also believe in its existence. Without this habituated pattern of intersubjective cognitions, we would cease to be and hence I would cease to be. Who am I without you telling me who I am and me telling you who you are? Don't tell me We are not, for then I am not. I know I am because of the terror you generate in me by telling me We are not. Don't falsify our lies or demystify our mystifications for without them, who are We? In other words, membership in a human social system is inherently double binding (Sluzki & Ransom, 1976; Wilber, 1977; Wilden, 1980) in the sense that independent individuality is bestowed on the individual by his or her community that simultaneously denies and denies the denial that his or her individuality is dependent on Us to grant and legitimize—and so We are.

The relevance of the nexus construct to macropolitical analyses is that every social, symbolic system is characterized by these ubiquitous, reciprocal interiorizations the content of which are our general ideas defining the Perfect. No group can sustain itself solely on praxal exchanges between independent actors for the group per se could not know itself to itself if the actors viewed themselves as independent beings unconstrained by the sentiments of others. Every human social system (e.g., family, corporation, nation-state) exists because it is believed to exist by those whose messages-in-circuitry make it a self-sustaining, self-perpetuating "reality." Social groups are abstractions, are nominalizations, are ideas that have no concrete, material existence whatsoever. They must be unfolded in repetitive interaction patterns. Land exists; coal, gold, uranium, silver exist; roads, monuments, buildings exist; water, trees, shrubs, flowers exist; but groups like the University of Wyoming, the community of communication and cognition scholars, the Republican Party, the Catholic Church, and the United States exist because members say they exist and because we say we exist, we do.

We Say.   Social reality is *talked.* It exists nowhere else but in the enacted dramas within which participant–observers create and recreate the group's existence. Without these dramatic rituals (e.g., Thanksgiving dinners, political campaigns, inaugural addresses, graduation ceremonies, cheering on our hockey teams, scholarly conventions, Congressional hearings, etc.) the group simply evaporates through nonperformance. A group can withstand deviants, dissenters, scandals, heretics—actually deviance and heresy are more important than deviants and heretics because the legitimizing process is logically and developmentally prior to its momentary products—but the group cannot withstand indifference. In-difference, the lack of differentiation and hence the lack of unity and identity.

Politics has always been and must always be primarily concerned with "images," with dramatizations that provide experiential memories of our ideas about ourselves and our principles of order which bind *us* together in ways demonstrably distinguishable from *them*. "Political reality rests in political images" (Meyrowitz, 1985, p. 278). First, substantive "issues" of sufficient magnitude to activate the nexal properties of a nation's populace (e.g., war, depression, etc.) occur infrequently—fortunately—and rarely in time for the next election. Most citizens, most of the time, are only concerned with the affairs of their smaller, more intimate groupings. However, the nation, in order to be a nation, must have a reservoir of sentiments that can be activated for system-wide purposes (e.g., defense against external and internal "enemies").

Second, any public office is inherently "liturgical in nature" (Meyrowitz, 1985, p. 278). If these offices were not so judged, then culture—the more common name for nexal characteristics—could not be sacred. As Eco (1984) points out, "even in the handling of practical things . . . a kind of theology is required" (p. 242). Every group attempts to legitimize its practices and pronouncements with honorable, sacred, holy ideas. Simply, "social order depends on consecration through communication" (Duncan, 1968, p. 23). If culture was not viewed as sacred, then culture could not fulfill its purpose as the denial of death (Becker, 1973). "We the people . . ."; "The American people will not stand for . . ."; "The women of our great land want . . ."; "Power to the People!" "No taxation without representation!" are all habituated phrases and slogans that keep the reservoir of sentiments sufficiently full for members to think of themselves as a nation unto itself.

Third, substantive issues are invariably complex including multiple variables recursively related (e.g., acid rain, depletion of the ozone layer, budget deficits, the limits of the public's right to know, the Iran-Contra scandal, etc.). Descriptions of such issues are not readily reduced to simple, unilateral, causal explanations where *a* scapegoat (the president, Gulf Oil Company, male chauvinists, the Miami News-Herald, Colonel Oliver North, etc.) can be held to blame. Given political offices are "liturgical in nature," talk from these offices must espouse fairly simple, but vivid "images." The liturgy always chants the benefits of the necessary principles of order defining the social system to and for its members. "Good" and "bad" guys are the content of the "liturgy" (e.g., televised political commercials). Intellectual activities are primarily solitary and isolating. Emotional activities are public and socializing. Intellect does not play well in liturgical performances.

At least in America, if not the world (a worldwide satellite news network is expected in the early 1990s), communication technologies are changing the nature of political rituals. These changes are decidedly comic in emphasis as Meyrowitz's (1985) analyses well illustrate. Due to television in particular, the means–ends discrepancies between chants of the idealized Perfect and interactions in the problematic present, are increasingly difficult to disregard. In Duncan's (1968) words, "thanks to modern communication, it is no longer possible to hide our failure in ignorance or false illusions" (p. 28). Mystery demands exaggeration. Exaggeration requires concealment of the techniques of mystification. Television is unveiling these techniques.

Second, "high status" has always been and must always be buttressed by the "nonreciprocal flow of information" between superior and inferior positions (Meyrowitz, 1985, p. 168). However, "through television, 'the people' now have more access to the personal expressive behaviors of leaders than leaders have to the personal behaviors of the people" (p. 168). The people see too much of their political leaders too often. High status figures are losing the ability to limit access to information about themselves and their performances. Anybody can become everyone else's business with today's communication technologies. As we see our superiors sweat under poignant questions, offer slips of the tongue, trip when taking the podium, appear confused when expressing hesitant responses, and fail to accurately report the "facts," our willingness to accept them as superiors by acting out the steps of deference appropriate to the superior–inferior dance is lessened. The inferiors' "right" to choose differently is heightened while the superior's "right" to command is simultaneously weakened. In general, the electronic media are undermining the hierarchy believed necessary for implementing our sacred principles of social Order.

Third, the image displayed on American mass media of leaders and aspiring leaders is "clearly one of human beings, rather than of gods" (Meyrowitz, 1985, p. 283). Leaders and aspiring leaders in the courtship drama are being "stripped of their aura and are being brought closer to the level of the average person" (p. 270). A social system cannot have both disclosure of its leaders' humanness and maintain sufficient "mystification necessary for an image of greatness" (p. 276). The binding capacity of the idea of "greatness" deteriorates in proportion to the relational distance between superiors and inferiors; its unifying ability dissipates "as the image of distant leaders comes to resemble an encounter with an intimate acquaintance" (p. 273). The comic desire to be "close" to our leaders "competes" with the tragic components necessary for defining "great" leaders. The technological capacity of the media to instantaneously put us "in touch" with our leaders, therefore, undermines their "greatness."

In summary, a comic resonance characterizes modern communication technologies. This same vibration is echoed by 20th-century science as the shift to epistemological over ontological commitments illustrated, and as "fundamentalists" of whatever ilk continuously bemoan. Politics is about the validation and regulation of the comic and tragic principles believed necessary for the survival of the social system. These principles are both formed in and formed by the relational distances characterizing a social system's dramatic performances. These sociopolitical enactments are inherently reflexive.

Ontological commitments and tragic dramas asserted and reinforced the descriptively closed, sacred scripts of a society as True, as Divine, as the only way to act, think, feel in order to attain the Perfect. A tragic orientation is grounded in the premise that "law is imposed by fear, whose true name is fear of God" (Eco, 1984, p. 578). Epistemological commitments and comic dramas open up habituated patterns of thought and behavior to doubt, skepticism, and criticism. Predictive utility and experiential felicity are humbly offered as the criteria for assessing social relationships. Whereas a tragic orientation views the world as a set of answers, a comic orientation posits that the world must be comprehended as a series of questions. In tragedy, both questions and answers are qualitative. In comedy, the questions are qualitative, whereas momentary answers are quantitative.

The principles of order sustaining any sociopolitical system are repetitively recreated and relegitimated by us, by those who are affected by and who affect these principles. We are our own legitimizers.

The study of political information processing from a relational perspective is focused on the legitimation dramas within which *right* and *wrong* performances are reflexively defined. Of course, what constitutes "right" and "wrong" social relationships will change in time so that the study of politics is inevitably about changes in stabilizing patterns and stability in changing conditions. In contrast to Meyrowitz (1985), therefore, the issue is not whether a social group "must *either* re-establish distance and mystification *or* redefine downward many formerly high status roles" (p. 169, italics added). Rather, the theoretical question is *how* any human social system can "balance" these "competing" properties that simultaneously unify and divide its members. The metaphors of comedy and tragedy embedded in a cybernetic epistemology are useful for investigating such questions about our relational oscillations as manifested in communication processes.

REFERENCES

Bateson, G. (1951). Conventions of communication: Where validity depends upon belief. In J. Ruesch & G. Bateson (Eds.), *Communication: The social matrix of psychiatry* (pp. 212–227). New York: Norton.

Bateson, G. (1972). *Steps to an ecology of mind.* New York: Ballantine.

Bateson, G. (1977). Afterword. In J. Brockman (Ed.), *About Bateson* (pp. 235–247). New York: Dutton.

Bateson, G. (1979). *Mind and nature: A necessary unity.* New York: Dutton.

Becker, E. (1973). *Denial of death.* New York: The Free Press.

Becker, E. (1975). *Escape from evil.* New York: The Free Press.

Bohm, D. (1980). *Wholeness and the implicate order.* London: Routledge & Kegan Paul.

Bronowski, J. (1978a). *The origins of knowledge and imagination.* New Haven, CT: Yale University Press.

Bronowski, J. (1978b). *The common sense of science.* Cambridge, MA: Harvard University Press.

Burke, K. (1966). *Language as symbolic action: Essays on life, literature, and method.* Berkeley, CA: University of California Press.

Carey, J. W. (1988). Editor's introduction: Taking culture seriously. In J. W. Carey (Ed.), *Media, myths, and narratives: Television and the press* (p. 8–18). Newbury Park, CA: Sage.

Cronen, V. E., Johnson, K. M., & Lannamann, J. W. (1982). Paradoxes, double binds, and reflexive loops: An alternative theoretical perspective. *Family Process, 21,* 91–112.

Delbruck, M. (1986). *Mind from matter? An essay on evolutionary epistemology.* Palo Alto, CA: Blackwell Scientific Publications.

Duncan, H. D. (1968). *Symbols in society.* London: Oxford University Press.

Eco, U. (1984). *The name of the rose* (W. Weaver, Trans.). New York: Warner Books.

Fisher, B. A. (1978). *Perspectives on human communication.* New York: Macmillan.

von Foerster, H. (1974). *Cybernetics of cybernetics.* Urbana, IL: University of Illinois, Biomedical Computer Laboratory.

French, A. P., & Kennedy, P. J. (Eds.). (1985). *Niels Bohr: A centenary volume.* Cambridge, MA: Harvard University Press.

Heisenberg, W. (1958). *Physics and philosophy.* New York: Harper Torchbooks.

Hofstadter, D. R. (1985). *Metamagical themas: Quest for the essence of mind and pattern.* New York: Basic Books.

Jakobson, R. (1971). Two aspects of language and two types of asphasic disturbances. In R. Jakobson & M. Halle, *Fundamentals of language* (2nd ed., pp. 67–96). Paris: Mouton.

Kantor, D., & Lehr, W. (1975). *Inside the family.* San Francisco: Jossey-Bass.

Kline, M. (1980). *Mathematics: The loss of certainty.* New York: Oxford University Press.

Kraus, S., & Perloff, R. M. (Eds.). (1985). *Mass media and political thought: An information-processing approach.* Beverly Hills, CA: Sage.

Krippendorf, K. (1984). An epistemological foundation of communication. *Journal of Communication, 34,* 21–36.

Laing, R. D. (1967). *The politics of experience.* New York: Ballantine.

Laing, R. D., Phillipson, H., & Lee, A. R. (1966). *Interpersonal perception: A theory and a method for research.* New York: Harper & Row.

Lakoff, G., & Johnson, M. (1980). *Metaphors we live by.* Chicago: University of Chicago Press.

Luhmann, N. (1986). The autopoiesis of social systems. In F. Geyer & J. van der Zouwen (Eds.), *Sociocybernetic paradoxes: Observations, control and evolution of self-steering systems* (pp. 172–192). London: Sage.

Maruyama, M. (1975). The post-industrial logic. In A. A. Spekke (Ed.), *The next 25 years: Crisis and opportunity* (pp. 43–50). Washington, DC: The World Future Society.

Maturana, H. R. (1980). Introduction. In H. R. Maturana & F. J. Varela, *Autopoiesis and cognition* (pp. xi–xxx). Dordrecht, Holland: D. Reidel.

Mead, G. (1934). *Mind, self and society.* Chicago: University of Chicago Press.

Meyrowitz, J. (1985). *No sense of place: The impact of electronic media on social behavior.* New York: Oxford University Press.

Millar, F. E., & Bavelas, J. G. (1985, May). *The pragmatic/interactional perspective on conversation.* Paper presented at the meeting of the International Communication Association, Honolulu, HI.

Millar, F. E., & Rogers, L. E. (1976). A relational approach to interpersonal communication. In G. Miller (Ed.), *Explorations in interpersonal communication* (pp. 87–103). Beverly Hills, CA: Sage.

Millar, F. E., & Rogers, L. E. (1987). Relational dimensions of interpersonal dynamics. In M. E. Roloff & G. R. Miller (Eds.), *Interpersonal processes: New directions in communication research* (pp. 117–139) Newbury Park, CA: Sage.

Nimmo, D. R., & Sanders, K. R. (Eds.). (1981). *Handbook of political communication*. Beverly Hills, CA: Sage.

Parks, M. (1977). Relational communication: Theory and research. *Human Communication Research, 3,* 372–381.

Pribram, K. H. (1986). The cognitive revolution and mind/brain issues. *American Psychologist, 41,* 507–520.

Reddy, M. J. (1979). The conduit metaphor: A case of frame conflict in our language about language. In A. Ortony (Ed.), *Metaphor and thought* (pp. 284–324). Cambridge: Cambridge University Press.

Russell, B. (1938). *Power.* New York: Norton.

Scheff, T. J. (1967). Toward a sociological model of consensus. *American Sociological Review, 32,* 32–46.

Sillars, A. L. (1982). Attribution and communication: Are people "naive scientists" or just naive? In M. E. Roloff & C. R. Berger (Eds.), *Social cognition and communication* (pp. 73–106). Beverly Hills, CA: Sage.

Sluzki, C. E., & Ransom, D. C. (1976). *Double bind: The foundation of the communicational approach to the family.* New York: Grune & Stratton.

Watzlawick, P., Beavin, J., & Jackson, D. D. (1967). *Pragmatics of human communication.* New York: Norton.

Watzlawick, P., & Weakland, J. H. (Eds.). (1977). *The interactional view: Studies at the Mental Research Institute, Palo Alto, 1965–1974.* New York: Norton.

von Weizsacker, C. F. (1980). *The unity of nature* (F. J. Zucker, Trans.). New York: Farrar, Straus, & Giroux.

Wilber, K. (1977). *The spectrum of consciousness.* Wheaton, IL: A Quest Book.

Wilden, A. (1980). *System and structure: Essays in communication and exchange* (2nd ed.). London: Tavistock.

Wilder, C. (1979). The Palo Alto group: Difficulties and directions of the interactional view for human communication research. *Human Communication Research, 5,* 171–186.

Wilder-Mott, C. (1982). Rigor and imagination. In C. Wilder-Mott & J. H. Weakland (Eds.), *Rigor and imagination* (pp. 5–42). New York: Praeger.

II | STRATEGIES AND EFFECTS

5 Learning From Political News: Effects of Media Images and Information-Processing Strategies

Gerald M. Kosicki
The Ohio State University
Jack M. McLeod
University of Wisconsin—Madison

Readers and viewers of mass communication all have personal, "common-sense theories" about media and their products. These attributions regarding media refer to the knowledge and ideas that everyone has, based on direct experience with newspapers and television news. It does not matter very much, perhaps, whether these primitive theories are true or not. Rather, what is important from the standpoint of media research is that people act on them as if they are true. McQuail (1987) summed up this perspective handily:

> Any newspaper reader or television viewer has an implicit theory in the sense of a set of ideas about the medium in question, what it is, what it is good for, how it fits into daily life, how it should be "read," what its connotations are and how it may relate to other aspects of social life. Most people will carry an elaborate set of associations and ideas of this kind which enable them to act consistently and satisfactorily in relation to the media. (p. 5)

Assuming that people do hold such images, or schema, about the nature of media and their products, it is important to gain some insight into their specific content and structure. Once that is done, it becomes important to examine them in terms of their influence on media use and political learning, as well as other priority concepts and preoccupations of the field.

Of particular interest to us is the potential implications of these images for how people use the media and make sense of their messages. A further refinement we comment on here is how media images and information-processing strategies affect news comprehension and learning.

Our interest here goes yet a step further. We examine the topics of media

69

images, audience information-processing strategies, and news comprehension from the standpoint of metacognition—thinking about thinking. We locate our research in the cognitive realm, especially within the metacognition tradition, and discuss what insights that might provide into the overall sense-making process of audience responses to political communication.

It should be noted that for at least since the mid-1970s, cognitive perspectives have dominated the "new look" in mass communication effects research (cf. Becker, McCombs, & McLeod, 1975; Gunter, 1987). It is virtually an article of faith among contemporary mass media researchers that the audience is in some sense actively processing media products. Furthermore, it is widely recognized that the cognitive perspective provides an extraordinarily useful platform from which many interesting types of audience processes and effects can be examined.

THE METACOGNITIVE RESEARCH STRATEGY

In recent years, an important trend in political science and mass communication research has involved the explicit adoption of cognitive information-processing concepts, perspectives, and theories into field studies in substantively important areas of political science generally (Himmelweit, Humphreys, & Jaeger, 1985; Lau & Sears, 1986; Sears & Citrin, 1985). More specifically, this trend has been especially visible in political communication (Graber, 1988; Iyengar & Kinder, 1987; Kraus & Perloff, 1985). Such borrowing benefits both the borrowing and the lending fields. Among the potential benefits to the lending field are increased external validity and a richer substantive area. The borrowing field gains access to the powerful theoretical perspectives developed painstakingly in wave after wave of experimental manipulations.

The purpose of this chapter is to discuss media images and information-processing strategies as examples of *metacognition*. This perspective encompasses several key ideas highly relevant to the study of audience response to political communication. Certainly involved in metacognition is the idea of active self-monitoring of some aspect of our own mental processes. Implied in this monitoring is the notion of consequent self-regulation and orchestration of future strategies or processes.

The metacognitive perspective itself, although potentially quite helpful in addressing many psychological questions (Yussen, 1985) does have its limitations and drawbacks (cf. Bruner, 1957; Ericsson & Simon, 1980).

Yussen argued, however, that the study of metacognition and cognition generally has been unduly limited by several factors. The first limitation is the assumption of communality of information processes across individuals. That is, the experimental paradigm, which embraces so much of the information-processing domain, is well-suited to examining how information is processed across everyone. The assumption is widespread that such processes are consistent across individuals. Indeed, there could be substantial differences in how individuals accomplish information-processing tasks. The second problem is that because much of the work has been developmental, there has been a lack of attention to adult metacognition. Yussen suggested there is good reason to suppose that adult processes are quite different from childrens'. Third, Yussen also argued that there has been relatively too much research attention focused on what he called "puzzle-solving" research. In itself this is not a problem, but it can be argued that this focus on information puzzles distracts researchers from examining more ambiguous, and probably more common, tasks that adults deal with in everyday life. Among these other more ambiguous tasks is making sense out of public affairs information contained in the mass media. Fourth, we would argue that the puzzle-solving experiments most likely are characterized by examining cognitive processes at peak attention. In fact, much of political viewing and processing of media messages takes place with less than maximum attention. For many members of the audience, only partial attention can or will be paid to political news.

The specific goal of this chapter is to suggest some metacognitive information-processing strategies that people have for coping with the flow of the news and making sense of it, and to trace the origins of these strategies to the images that people hold of the news. Explicitly advocating metacognitive strategies would seem to benefit both fields in certain ways. Mass communication researchers gain access to the overall theoretical perspectives of cognitive science. The metacognitive researchers would be getting an interesting topic that can serve as a locus for many studies, as well as provide realistic contexts that would help satisfy some of the concerns previously offered. We also suggest what the cognitive perspective can add to the study of news comprehension, that is, going beyond mere memory for discrete facts toward an approach stressing the organization of thinking about politics and public affairs. The final point is to propose an overall conceptual model of this process linking social structural variables with media images and processing strategies, and these in turn to news comprehension. Before we turn to an examination of each of these three constructs, however, it is useful to review several points about the nature of the news itself and how it is produced.

THE NATURE OF POLITICAL NEWS

There are many points one can make about the nature of the news media and their products, but a selected few are especially relevant to our concerns here. As Carey (1986) has noted, the daily news itself is quite fragmentary, incomplete, and episodic. We have to make a conscious effort to keep up with developments as they occur. This process of keeping up with the news is particularly nettlesome because of the sheer volume and diversity of the news and news media (Graber, 1988). Even in the somewhat more narrow realm of political news, the volume is quite vast, more than anyone can ever use.

News has other noteworthy characteristics as well. News is quite brief, compressing a lot of unfamiliar information into a small amount of space or time. News often involves a truncated or highly stylized time frame, giving little sense of either the history or future consequences of the event or issue. News is also relentlessly "factual" (cf. Romano, 1986), implying a lack of abstraction and explicit generalizability. This fact may make it harder for the audience to make connections among events and note recurring patterns in the news.

Political news is also peculiar as a stimulus because it has social importance for virtually everyone. People, events, and policies discussed in the news have direct or indirect consequences for our lives, but people vary in the degree to which they recognize this relevance. Finally, the news does not come to us in a readily interpretable form. Journalists attempt to write for a mass audience, but this audience is amazingly diverse. The result is that the news contains something for everyone, but to find the specific part that is most appropriate for any given person takes considerable effort. Furthermore, even when the exact content of interest is located, the meaning is not always transparent. People might be expected to make rather different sense of the news, especially political news, depending on their party affiliation, ideology, level of political sophistication, and other cognitive and structural variables. Individual stories may not make much sense to the uninitiated reader or viewer who has not followed the developments of a particular story.

Carey's point about the news being fragmentary is not to suggest that the news is inherently incomprehensible, however. Rather, the news is quite comprehensible if viewed as a "curriculum." In other words, if viewed over time and across different media, the news can add up to a comprehensive picture of the world, at least for the idealized person who takes the initiative to so construct it.

Of course, in real life, there is no such perfect reader or viewer. Most of us are limited information processors, who use media to help us attain certain goals. We want to avoid being surprised by events, we want to be informed about politics, we want to understand something of our world. Whatever our specific goals or the ways we articulate them, we must be selective. The volume of news media messages is too great, and our time too limited, to use all of them. Thus, we come to adopt certain tactics for deciding which media to use and how to make sense of the ones we do use.

A final point about the nature of media is that they occupy a great deal of people's wakeful activities in one form or another. Media messages are thus important sources of mental activity for extraordinarily large numbers of people. For this reason, and because news represents such a distinctive content genre, generative of unique patterns of cognitive and attentional processes different from other types of mental activity, it is important to develop concepts appropriate to understanding people's use of news.

MOLAR INFORMATION-PROCESSING STRATEGIES

By *molar information-processing strategies* we generally mean a set of tactics individuals use to try to cope with the amount and kind of mass media information that they encounter in their everyday lives. Specifically, we use the term *molar* to refer to general trans-situational strategies a person might adopt in dealing with a specific type of content such as political news. This is in contrast to "molecular" processes reported at a specified moment with respect to a given message or to some feature within a message (Carter, Ruggels, Jackson, & Heffner, 1973; Forrest-Pressley & Waller, 1984). Such work often leads to discussion of a single strategy rather than studying a set of them. *Strategies* refers to the means a person reports using to cope with the amount of news and the problems of making sense of what is received. There are many such strategies and we devote much of this chapter to examining several of them in detail. First, however, it is helpful to outline our major assumptions:

1. People actively use media and over time find various strategies of coping with information very useful. These strategies are necessary because people are limited in their ability to process information and have limited time to devote to media.

2. These mental strategies are manifested in everyday habits or behaviors. People continue to use these strategies over time because they find them helpful. However, people may use differing amounts of them, in different patterns.

3. People are able to monitor their thought processes and strategies about thinking, as well as verbalize about them. We also assume these everyday habits and behaviors discussed in Assumption 2 can be recalled through self-report techniques. Problems of self-report data perhaps can be minimized by asking people to engage in exercises *recognizing their personal behavior patterns* rather than to discuss in detail their own mental processes.

4. These mental operations relate to interaction with *media* generally, and so cut across the use of both newspapers and television. Although there may be considerable cyclical fluctuations, patterns of information processing

strategies are sufficiently stable for a given media genre (e.g., political news) so as to merit their consideration as molar, recurrent strategies.

The strategies of using media to achieve personal goals that we discuss here have several distinguishing aspects. First, unlike many commonly used measures of media use, they do not primarily involve media time budgeting. Second, they have strong volitional elements such as focusing attention or employing increased mental effort. Third, they involve manipulating or doing something with information. These manipulations might involve a variety of tasks, including, but not limited to, attending, selecting, interpreting, pondering, discounting, and judging.

References to such strategies are common in both popular discourse and scholarly writing. That strategies are apparent to users is reflected in the following response to one of our survey interviewers after a question about skimming the newspaper: "Oh, that's not me, I'm a cover-to-cover reader." A CBS "Nightwatch" program on media images (January 17, 1986) offered another bit of anecdotal evidence that people not only have the capability of using information in sophisticated ways, but can, under some circumstances, discuss these strategies. A person was quoted as saying, "Sometimes there is some sensationalism, but that is what sells newspapers, and most of us have learned to read through that."

Fiske and Taylor (1984), in discussing a dimension of attention known as *salience*, noted that certain kinds of information recurrently occupy an individual's mind. This phenomenon is said to allow a person to ponder the material and reflect upon ways it may relate to other bits of information. Robert Lane (1962) discussed the obverse of this kind of reflection when he wrote of a tendency for people to "morselize" their experiences of the world, leading to a view of life as "itemized and fragmented":

> a union demand is a single incident, not part of a more general labor-management conflict; a purchase on the installment plan is a specific debt, not part of a budgetary pattern—either one's own or society's. (p. 353)

Graber (1988), based on detailed, clinical-style personal interviews with a small panel of respondents over nearly 1 year, has collected many similar comments, and interpreted them in a very detailed fashion. But her analysis of individual sense-making strategies focuses largely on the interpretation of information once it is *received* by the respondent from mass media. Our own interests here are somewhat more general in nature. Our goal is to develop concepts that are useful in understanding individuals' *confrontation* of the media and their messages, as well as the subsequent interpretation. This means more than performing a mental calculus on the information after it is made available, and goes to the heart of choice making regarding media strategies.

Considering the interaction of a single individual and the news media, several things become immediately apparent. First, there is too much information for most people to pay attention to it all, even assuming a great deal of interest in it. Second, messages may not come to many people in a "ready-to-eat" format. For at least some people, media messages need to be *interpreted*, as the individual mentioned above so concisely stated. Graber (1988) discussed this problem as one of "processing difficulties." Some problems with the information encountered by respondents that lead to processing difficulties included the perception of deception by the source of the information, a lack of background information by the respondent, or, relatedly, a feeling that the information was too complex.

A third quality of mediated information for many people may be that it holds their mental attention for a period *after exposure*. This mental effort directed at pondering the news and talking about it with others could be an important clue to understanding learning from media. People who find certain information highly salient or attention-holding should be, through increased mental effort and integration, more successful at integrating the new information into what they already know about the world. Graber (1988) reported that several of her respondents felt the information presented in news stories was too fragmented or incomplete and required mental effort to "put it all together" (p. 175).

These considerations lead us to propose three information-processing strategies for mass-mediated information. We have measured and studied these three concepts in each of three public surveys[1] (Kosicki, McLeod, & Amor, 1987, 1988; McLeod, Pan, & Rucinski, 1988a). We call them, in turn, *selective scanning, active processing, and reflective integration.*

Selective scanning is a reader or viewer's response to the volume of mediated information and the limited time and energy available for using media. Primarily the strategy involves tuning out items that are not of interest or use to the audience member.

Active processing reflects the audience member's attempt to make sense of the story, going beyond the exact information given to interpret the information according to his or her own needs. The strategy captures the person's need to "figure out" the story.

Reflective integration represents the postexposure salience of information such that it occupies the mind and is the subject of interpersonal discussion.

---

[1]See Kosicki et al. (1987) for more detail on these concepts and their use in subsequent analyses. Sample items, to which people are asked to respond on a 5-point Likert strongly agree to strongly disagree scale are: Selective scanning: When reading a magazine or newspaper, I flip through and only read stories when a photo or headline catches my eye. Active processing: When I'm using the news media, I always try to figure out what the real story is that they are not telling me. Reflective integration: Often when I've learned something in the news I'll recall it later and think about it.

The key, however, is the incorporation of new information into the person's existing cognitive framework for understanding the subject.

The strategies we propose are somewhat similar to those discussed by Levy and Windahl (1984) in their "communication sequence" ordered in the times before, during, and after exposure to media messages, and their notion of "audience orientations" as selective, involved, and using. Levy and Windahl's resulting typology is somewhat similar to ours in that the concepts are ordered in time. Our notion of selectivity, however, is more volitional and operates at the point of encounter with the information, and is not a matter of time budgeting or scheduling. To that extent, it seems our first and second factors, selective scanning and active processing, correspond to Levy's "duractivity" phase, whereas the reflective integration is the time after exposure. Also, Levy discussed postactivity use as merely a "coin of exchange" or "chit-chat" with friends, whereas we are thinking of reflective integration as the final step in sense-making, which can take place either through pondering or social interaction.

PUBLIC IMAGES OF THE MASS MEDIA

The cognitive-processing strategies we have discussed so far have their origins in social structural concerns, as well as the images of media and media products that audience members hold. These images have also been the subject of some previous empirical work (Amor, McLeod, & Kosicki, 1987; Kosicki & McLeod, 1989; McLeod, Kosicki, Amor, Allen, & Philips, 1986). In these papers several basic images of media were suggested, empirically measured with survey questions, and analyzed in relation to various measures of media use, political learning, and cultural and social structural factors.

There were five distinct dimensions of images developed in the course of this research. These dimensions, which are meant to be hypothetical, unmeasured, complex constructs, were developed with original questions after examining the existing literature on media credibility and related areas. The questions were extensively pretested, and have been replicated in 3 successive years of data collection.[2]

The dimensions are as follows:

News information quality is a positive summary evaluation of media being accurate, complete, thoughtful, and responsible.

Patterning of news, focuses on the "sense-making" function of news, that

---

[2]These studies were conducted at the Mass Communication Research Center at the School of Journalism and Mass Communication at the University of Wisconsin—Madison.

is, the ability of the news to add up to a comprehensive picture of the world over time. Put another way, it expresses faith in the ability of the news to reveal meaningful patterns out of the diversity of information presented.

Negative aspects of content is the third image factor. This is a summary of four often-heard criticisms of the news: it is dull, sensationalistic, dominated by bad news, and biased.

Dependency and control, the fourth image, represents a tendency to see media institutions as hegemonic. That is, they are too consonant and too powerful, and people rely on them too much.

Special interests is a view of media as representing special interests in their reports, themselves being special interests within society, or possibly both perspectives simultaneously.

Available evidence developed to date indicates that these media images arise from several sources in the social world: general structural variables, political orientations, and general cultural orientations to the world such as religious values, and general world views (Amor et al., 1987). World views is perhaps the most interesting and novel of these cultural antecedents we have identified. From cultural anthropology we adapted the definition of world view offered by Kearney (1984) that "basic assumptions and images that provide a more or less coherent, though not necessarily accurate, way of thinking about the world" (p. 41).

Building on this, Amor et al. (1987) noted that world view was meant to designate a specific characterization of the external world including institutions, that not only summarizes key attributes of the world but also encompasses the orientation of the subject toward them.[3] The dimensions of world view we examined included existential pessimism, an image of the world as a hard place unlikely to get better; quiet fatalism, representing passivity and detachment from the world's problems; belief in a knowable world, a positive view such that coordinated mental effort is rewarded in understanding; and confidence in science, the view that science and technology can improve the world, not make it worse. This set of variables makes significant contributions to the prediction of the media image factors, even after simultaneous multivariate controls on 18 variables.[4]

---

[3]As Amor, McLeod, and Kosicki (1987, p. 8) explained, the concept is meant to be distinct from the related sociological concept of "social values" (Kluckhohn & Strodtbeck, 1961) and the psychologically based "locus of control" (Fiske & Taylor, 1984).

[4]See Amor, McLeod, and Kosicki (1987) for details of this procedure and other antecedents of media images. In this and subsequent references to such data analysis procedures, we used hierarchical multiple regression.

MEDIA IMAGES
AND INFORMATION-PROCESSING STRATEGIES

The argument so far has been that audience members hold distinctive images of the mass media that arise out of structural locations and political and cultural values. Furthermore, people also have developed regular habits of mind that affect their use and interpretation of media that are, at least in part based on their images of media. These habits of mind, under the individual's volitional control, are known as *information-processing strategies*. Despite cyclical fluctuations, patterns of cognitive information-processing strategies are sufficiently stable for a given media genre, for example, political news, as to merit their consideration as molar, recurrent strategies. It is reasonable to talk about them generally, although people have the ability to control and switch them if they so desire.

Evidence developed so far suggests that these strategies are in part responses to differential images audience members hold of media and their products. For example, Kosicki et al. (1987) reported that even under simultaneous controls in for 29 structural, cultural, political, and media use variables, the largest single predictors of active processing were media images. Specifically, the active processing strategy was most likely to be employed among those who found news quality of relatively poor quality, had high negative affect for media content, as well as strong feelings of dependency about media. Those high on active processing were also likely to feel that the media were the mouthpieces of special interests in society or were themselves special interests. Presumably, active processing is a strategy most useful for defending oneself against manipulation by powerful elites who work with or through media.

Similarly, it is useful to note that reflective integration, pondering and thinking about the news and talking about it with friends, was also strongly predicted by media images. Here, however, the profile is somewhat different. Reflective integration was positively related to perceptions of news quality, as well as the tendency to see news as patterned and adding up to a comprehensive view of the world over time. Reflective integration was also negatively related to negative affect for content and dependency and control. People who feel negatively about such content would thus be unlikely to want to waste much of their time pondering it deeply.

Selective scanning, the final processing strategy, which represents a kind of coping mechanism for the volume of news and information available to audience members, had yet another distinctive pattern of relations to the images. Selective scanners were likely to see the news as being a quality product, but this is mixed with negative affect for content and feelings of dependency and control.

In addition, new results of a more recent investigation not yet published indicate that the active processing strategy is consistently used by certain people across content categories such as news and advertising (McLeod et al., 1988a). That is, certain audience members consistently apply this strategy to very different types of media content. Reflective integration, on the other hand, shows no such consistency, reflecting perhaps a view that certain types of content, namely advertisements, are simply not worth reflecting about. The selective scanning results are mixed and we expect to find that what kind of content one is skimming, and for what purpose, is an important consideration. Scanning behavior, however, seems so far to be more a way to avoid information that is not of interest than a strategy for searching for more suitable information.

These results are somewhat tentative, but they do bolster our contention that these strategies, arising out of people's self–reports about their own mental processes, are systematically related in sensible, but nonobvious ways to important independent variables. Chief among these variables are people's attributions about the media and their uses.

LEARNING FROM THE MASS MEDIA

The final step in the model we have been developing is learning from media, or news comprehension. The crucial point here is a deceptively simple one. The most important things that individuals learn from media presentations are probably not lists of "facts" or discrete bits of information such as candidate names or terms of office for various politicians. To be sure, such questions have given good service over the years in many studies primarily interested in demonstrating some effect of the independent variables such as media use or attention. But when the goal is to examine how subtle media images or information-processing strategies influence learning, a more diversified approach to the dependent variables is required.

Generally, our approach—reported in McLeod, Kosicki, Pan, and Allen (1987) and McLeod, Pan, and Rucinski (1988b)—incorporates a method of open-ended structured probes to encourage respondents to talk about a particular public issue. The issue we examined in the Fall of 1986 happened to be the deliberations surrounding the passage of the U.S. Tax Reform Act, a sweeping overhaul of the American income tax system. This issue was in the news at the time we were doing our fieldwork. However, we believe our method of probing respondents and coding the responses is sufficiently flexible to allow it to be used in a variety of contexts and issues.

Conceptually, the open-ended responses were coded to reflect two sets of concepts. The first involved the complexity with which individuals thought about the issue and employed multiple perspectives, or frames, in thinking about it. Frames were things such as a thinking style incorporating multiple time referents, that is, talking about the history of an issue, the present state of affairs, and implications for the future or some combination of these. Another frame was that of self-interest versus sociotropic economic concerns. People were classified as employing a self-interest frame if they discussed the issue largely in terms of the implications for their own economic condition. Sociotropic concerns were those involving the entire U.S. economy or other widely shared social benefits. Conventional newsroom wisdom seemed to suggest that the audience was primarily interested in the bottom line on tax reform, that is, how will it affect how much they have to pay. But our open-ended data suggested, for example, that at least one third of the audience was concerned about the overall economic benefits of the plan.

McLeod et al. (1988b) studied audience response to the U.S. involvement in Nicaragua in a similar manner to the tax reform issue. They identified three major frames: multiple time perspectives, ideology, and self-determination. The frames are related to more traditional knowledge holding, and especially to the desire to seek more information about the issue.

Our initial conclusion is that the frames serve as a way of organizing what one knows about public issues such that one tends to become more confident in one's ability to handle and seek new information. Having well-developed frames makes an event "knowable" to a person and fosters an interest in information seeking about that issue. Furthermore, it seems clear, at least to us, that the effects of mass media on what people learn about politics and public affairs goes well beyond memory for discrete facts. News "fact quizzes" commonly employed in political communication studies are inadequate representations of the range of possible outcomes. Furthermore, the ways the audience structures and thinks about political issues may have important implications for political action. We have not said much until now about the translation of political knowledge into conjoint political action. However, such a process would seem to require the synthesis or reorganization of facts in distinctive ways. That is, simple remembering of names and candidates may be necessary to begin this process, but is certainly not sufficient.

CONCLUSION

We have tried in this chapter to outline a set of constructs developed from an explicitly metacognitive framework in which we asked people to report on their strategies for confronting the mass media. One goal throughout has been to suggest ways metacognition can inform and shape contemporary research in political communication. One way is to foster the development of cognitively ambitious concepts for the use of information that go beyond simple measures of amount of media exposure. People do more with media and their products than merely soak them up like so many rays of sunshine. Political communication researchers would do well to incorporate such information-processing strategies into their future work.

Another strand of our research is directed toward organizing the various attributions people make regarding media. These primitive theories that people employ in daily life about media were suggested by the very fragmented and incomplete literature on media credibility. We have demonstrated empirically over several years of data collection and analysis that people's perceptions of media can be meaningfully organized along a relatively parsimonious set of constructs. Furthermore, these constructs are related in meaningful ways to processing strategies. Finally, we have generated evidence consistent with the interpretation that processing strategies are significant outcomes of media images, but also have links to politically important criterion variables such as interest, learning, and participation.

Clearly there is more work to be done. The media attributions or images need to be explicated more fully. Processing strategies should be refined and improved, and their antecedents and consequences subjected to additional tests. Perhaps the most work remains in the areas of structuring public issues. Indeed, the final payoff of our work is the implications of these images and strategies for what people learn about politics, and how they organize what they know so it can be put to use. It is one thing for cognitive psychologists to suggest that individuals use schema, frames, or categories in organizing information in memory. It is quite another to attempt to "fill up" the schema with real information tied to important political concerns.

More importantly, the overall framework proposed here shifts discussion about political communication from simple notions of "media use" affecting knowledge of idiosyncratic "facts." Instead, we need to focus on complex relationships among the ways people use, explain, evaluate, and make sense of the news, and their understanding and organization of the larger world it reports.

ACKNOWLEDGMENTS

The authors acknowledge the contributions of their various co-authors and colleagues who have been closely involved in the planning and execution of the various studies discussed here, especially David Amor and Zhongdang Pan, both of the University of Wisconsin—Madison. Eric Fredin of The Ohio State University has been insightful, supportive, and critical. We also appreciate the encouragement of Sidney Kraus of Cleveland State University.

REFERENCES

Amor, D. L., McLeod, J. M., & Kosicki, G. M. (1987, May). *Images of the media, orientations to the world: Where do public images of the mass media come from?* Paper presented to the Mass Communication Division, International Communication Association, Montreal.

Becker, L. B., McCombs, M. E., & McLeod, J. M. (1975). The development of political cognitions. In S. H. Chaffee (Ed.), *Political communication* (pp. 21–63). Beverly Hills, CA: Sage.

Bruner, J. S. (1957). Going beyond the information given. In J. S. Bruner (Ed.), *Contemporary approaches to cognition: A symposium held at the University of Colorado* (pp. 41–74). Cambridge, MA: Harvard University Press.

Carey, J. (1986). The dark continent of American journalism. In R. K. Manoff & M. Schudson (Eds.), *Reading the news* (pp. 146–196). New York: Pantheon.

Carter, R. F., Ruggels, W. L., Jackson, K. M., & Heffner, M. B. (1973). Application of signaled stopping technique to communication research. In P. Clarke (ed.), *New models for mass communication research* (pp. 15–43). Beverly Hills, CA: Sage.

Ericsson, K. A., & Simon, H. A. (1980). Verbal reports as data. *Psychological Review, 87,* 215–251.

Fiske, S., & Taylor, S. (1984). *Social cognition.* New York: Random House.

Forrest-Pressley, D. L., & Waller, T. G. (1984). *Cognition, metacognition and reading.* New York: Springer-Verlag.

Graber, D. A. (1988). *Processing the news: How people tame the information tide* (2nd ed.). New York: Longman.

Gunter, B. (1988). *Poor reception: Misunderstanding and forgetting broadcast news.* Hillsdale, NJ: Lawrence Erlbaum Associates.

Himmelweit, H. T., Humphreys, P., & Jaeger, M. (1985). *How voters decide: A longitudinal study of political attitudes and voting extending over fifteen years* (rev. ed.). Milton Keynes and Philadelphia: Open University Press.

Iyengar, S., & Kinder, D. R. (1987). *News that matters: Television and American opinion.* Chicago: University of Chicago Press.

Kearney, M. (1984). *World view.* Novato, CA: Chandler & Sharp.

Kluckhohn, F., & Strodtbeck, F. (1961). *Variations in value orientations.* Evanston, IL: Row, Peterson.

Kosicki, G. M., & McLeod, J. M. (1989, April). *Media information processing strategies and media images: Effects on learning, interest, and participation.* Paper presented to the Midwest Political Science Association, Chicago, IL.

Kosicki, G. M., McLeod, J. M., & Amor, D. L. (1987, May). *Processing the news: Some individual strategies for selecting, sense-making and integrating.* Paper presented at the meeting of the Political Communication Division, International Communication Association, Montreal.

Kosicki, G. M., McLeod, J. M., & Amor, D. L. (1988, April). *Processing strategies for mass media information: Selecting, integrating and making sense of political news.* Paper presented at the meeting of the Midwest Political Science Association, Chicago, IL.

Kraus, S., & Perloff, R. (Eds.). (1985). *Mass media and political thought: An information processing approach.* Beverly Hills, CA: Sage.

Lane, R. (1962). *Political ideology.* New York: The Free Press.

Lau, R. R., & Sears, D. O. (1986). *Political cognition.* Hillsdale, NJ: Lawrence Erlbaum Associates.

Levy, M. R., & Windahl, S. (1984). Audience activity and gratifications: A conceptual clarification and exploration. *Communication Research, 11,* 51–78.

McLeod, J. M., Kosicki, G. M., Amor, D. L., Allen, S. G., & Philps, D. M. (1986, August). *Public images of mass media news: What are they and does it matter?* Paper presented at the meeting of the Communication Theory and Methodology Division, Association for Education in Journalism and Mass Communication, Norman, OK.

McLeod, J. M., Kosicki, G. M., Pan, Z., & Allen, S. G. (1987, August). *Audience perspectives on the news: Assessing their complexity and conceptual frames.* Paper presented to the Communication Theory and Methodology Division, Association for Education in Journalism and Mass Communication, San Antonio, TX.

McLeod, J. M., Pan, Z., & Rucinski, D. M. (1988a, July). *Processing news and advertising: Same strategies and same effects?* Paper presented to the Communication Theory and Methodology Division of the Association for Education in Journalism and Mass Communication, Portland, OR.

McLeod, J. M., Pan, Z., & Rucinski, D. M. (1988b). *Framing a complex issue: Beyond remembering facts.* Unpublished manuscript, University of Wisconsin—Madison, Mass Communications Research Center, Madison, WI.

McQuail, D. (1987). *Mass communication theory* (2nd ed.). London and Newbury Park, CA: Sage.

Romano, C. (1986). The grisly truth about bare facts. In R. K. Manoff & M. Schudson (Eds.), *Reading the news* (pp. 38–78). New York: Pantheon.

Sears, D. O., & Citrin, J. (1985). *Tax revolt: Something for nothing in California* (enlarged ed.). Cambridge, MA: Harvard University Press.

Yussen, S. R. (1985). The role of metacognition in contemporary theories of cognitive development. In D. L. Forrest-Pressley, G. E. MacKinnon, & T. G. Waller (Eds.), *Metacognition, cognition and human performance* (Vol. 1, pp. 253–283). Orlando, FL: Academic Press.

6 | Mass Media Effects on Political Cognition: How Readers' Images of Journalists Shape Newspaper Impact

Klaus Schoenbach
Academy for Music and Theater, Hannover, West Germany
Stanley J. Baran
San Jose State University

Few studies have attempted to describe the images, the stereotypes, journalists hold of their audiences (e.g., Flegel & Chaffee, 1971; Koecher, 1986; Pool & Shulman, 1959). Even fewer have shed light on what those audiences think of the journalists who report the news for them (e.g., Atwood, 1970). The small degree of interest in this area is certainly due at least in part to the assumption that it may be particularly difficult for those involved in a mediated communication process to construct clear images of one another: Journalists usually know only tiny portions of their audiences through letters to the editor or phone calls to their media organizations. Conversely, only on television, for example, do recipients at least see a small number of journalists. Print practitioners, however, are rarely ever directly known to their audiences.

But still, clear-cut images of different groups, even of relatively impersonal institutions, are often held by people who have little actual contact with even one of their members. Ethnic groups, for example, often evoke very distinctive stereotypes in some individuals, even though they may never have actually interacted with members of those groups. Institutions and organizations like the Bush Administration, the Catholic Church, and Procter and Gamble are pictured quite clearly in many people's minds. This, too, has been found to be the case where media institutions like "the press" or specific outlets like individual television stations are concerned (see the literature review in McLeod, Kosicki, Amor, Allen, & Philips, 1986).

To be sure, these impressions may be inaccurate in terms of what those affected or "media experts" may think. As such, many of the components of these images may be called *prejudices*. But as is often the case with such prejudices, their owners are not aware of the inaccuracies and behave as if their images are correct. We know, for instance, that journalists' notions of their audiences lead to modifications of media content (Bauer, 1958; Martin, O'Keefe, & Neyman, 1972; Pool & Shulman, 1959; Schramm & Danielson, 1958; Zimmerman & Bauer, 1956). It should be obvious, then, that this sort of journalist behavior, based on stereotypes of audiences, should and would have consequences in terms of the impact of their media messages. It can be assumed that modified media messages—meaning a modified stimulus potential—shape effects on audiences.

Logically, too, what the audience thinks of the producers of the content it consumes should impact the effectiveness of those messages. It could be assumed, for instance, that readers of a newspaper who view its writers as dishonest or selfish may not be as impressed by what they read as would others who see those same journalists as serious people, working hard to provide up-to-date and useful information. Some hints of this notion exist in the persuasion literature (e.g., see Hovland & Weiss, 1951; Hovland, Janis, & Kelley, 1953).

In this chapter, we examine how the influence of media content is shaped by images of its producers that are held by its consumers. This is done in a nonexperimental, everyday, and fairly pragmatic situation: reading the local section of the local newspaper and its impact. More specifically, how do newspaper readers' stereotypes of local reporters intervene in the process of newspaper use effects on political cognitions on the local level?

DATA COLLECTION

The data in this study were collected in a panel survey of newspaper readers in the city of Dortmund, West Germany. The survey was part of a multimethod study including a second, parallel panel of all the 48 journalists working for the local sections of the three Dortmund papers. A third component of the study consists of a large-scale content analysis (about 17,000 articles) of those sections (see also Schoenbach & Weischenberg, 1984). This enterprise was funded by the German National Science Foundation (*Deutsche Forschungsgemeinschaft*) within a program the Foundation initiated in 1983 under the title "Effects of Mass Communication."

Dortmund is a large city (about 620,000 inhabitants) located in the industrial region of the Ruhr Valley in the northwestern part of Germany. It was selected for study because a municipal election was held in Dortmund in the Fall of 1984 around which the surveys were administered. It was assumed that the images readers and local reporters have of each other would be activated by the election campaign and the election itself. Moreover, as there were neither local radio nor television stations in Dortmund, the possible sources of specific information about the election were narrowed considerably. It could be expected then, for most Dortmund citizens, that changes concerning knowledge and attitudes of the local political scene could be attributed largely, if not exclusively, to the local newspapers, campaign literature, and to personal conversations.

This chapter presents highly selective results of the reader survey section of our study (additional analyses and results can be found in Schoenbach & Weischenberg, 1987). In this survey, four personal interviews of 30 to 40 minutes each were conducted with a sample of readers. Sampling originated with three equally sized subsamples, each composed of 730 randomly selected households subscribing to one of the three Dortmund newspapers. In each of the 2,001 households with correct addresses, respondents were selected randomly among those household members who were over 18 years old, and read the household's newspaper at least occasionally.

The first wave of interviews commenced August 1, 1984, and ended on August 22, 1984, shortly before the local election campaign began. This panel contained 1,329 successfully interviewed respondents, 66% of the originally drawn sample. The second wave was fielded on August 28 and completed on September 10, in the middle of the election campaign. Remaining in the sample were 927 respondents. The third wave started 11 days before election day (September 30) and was in the field until September 29. Interviewed during that period of time were 797 people. The fourth wave, finally, was conceived of as a postelection survey. It was conducted between October 28 and November 7. Still, 717 respondents were in the sample.

THE MODEL OF ANALYSIS

This study assumes effects of local newspaper use on knowledge about and images of local politics. As such, it is further presumed that the size of those effects is determined by how extensively and intensively respondents read their newspaper, by their motives for reading, and by various sociodemographic characteristics as is traditionally suggested by the stimulus–response and uses-and-gratifications models of media effects. The possible alternative sources of political cognitions, personal conversations, and campaign literature are also taken into account. We assume even further, however, that the audience's image of the producers of media messages plays just as important a role in the effects process. Of particular interest, then, is whether and how different stereotypes of local journalists shape the effects of newspaper use, even after types of use, motives, and sociodemographic factors are considered.

MEASUREMENT

Overall, we incorporated six categorical variables with which to examine the responses in the study. These were effects, newspaper use, campaign literature as a source of political cognitions, motives for reading the newspaper, socio-demographic, and images of journalists.

Effects Variables

A number of political cognition variables were examined. For the purpose of this investigation, however, three specific cognitions of different levels of complexity were selected for analysis.

Date of the Election. The simplest was the date of the election, known by only one-fifth (21%) of the respondents at the outset of the campaign. At the end of it, as many as 80% could name the date correctly. The variable used in the analysis was a recoded version of responses to an open-ended question. A 2 meant the exact date (September 30, 1984); 1 was a date within either a week before or after election day; and 0 signified all other answers.

Party Knowledge. Two small parties fought for entry into the city council, the ecological party of the "Greens" and a free-enterprise-oriented party, the Free Democrats. Respondents who knew that both parties were not represented in the council, got a score of 2, one right answer counted 1, none, 0. This variable, presumably a bit more difficult to learn than the date of the election, was named party knowledge.

Perceived Election Interest. In addition to these two factual knowledge indicators, a third, somewhat different measure of political cognitions, perceived election interest, was used. Respondents were asked:

> And what do you think, how interested in the local election are most of the people here in Dortmund? Would you say they are very interested, fairly interested, little interested, or not interested at all?

Newspaper Use Variables

Extensiveness of Newspaper Use. This variable was measured by a combined index of both the weekly frequency of reading the newspaper and the average daily duration of that reading.

Intensity.   In addition to this "nonspecific basic extensiveness" of using the newspaper, also included was the more specific measure, intensity of reading. By means of a card with eight headlines from the previous 2 weeks, respondents in each panel wave were asked how intensively they had read each story. Here the index was formed by summing the levels of intensity for each article.

Perception of Election Coverage.   After the election, panel members were asked even more specifically how often they had seen anything about the election in their newspaper, "often," "occasionally," or "never." This variable was labeled perception of election coverage.

Personal Conversations As a Source of Political Cognitions

In each of the panel waves, respondents were handed a card with 19 topics of conversation. Interviewers then asked the question:

On this card, you'll find some topics one can talk about with other people. Please, remember the last days: About which of those topics did you talk with other people?

One of the 19 topics was *"politics in Dortmund."* Respondents who answered affirmatively were given a score of 1, others, a 0.

Campaign Literature As a Source of Political Cognitions

After the election, respondents were presented a list of different sources of campaign information. In addition to the already mentioned local newspaper, there were three alternative sources of such information: partisan leaflets and brochures, ads in newspapers and magazines, and billboards. Again, as was the case with the perception of election coverage in the newspapers, use was measured on a 3-point scale of "often," "occasionally," and "never."

Motives for Reading the Newspaper

General Interest in Local Coverage.   A relatively unspecific motive for reading the newspaper was the general interest in local coverage. For this purpose, respondents were asked to indicate their interest in the local section of their newspaper on a 6-point scale.

Interest in Political Coverage.   A second, more specific motive, was called interest in local political coverage. It was measured by the additive index of the personal importance of two functions of reading the local newspaper. These were "To be informed about the decisions of the Dortmund city council" and "To know what the plans of the political parties in Dortmund are."

Responses were coded as 2 for "very important," 1 for "important," and 0 for "not so important."

Vote Guidance. The third motive to attentively read the local coverage is referred to as vote guidance (see, e.g. Blumler & McQuail, 1968). It is the readers' need for orientation in terms of their voting decision. This motive was measured by using the personal importance of reading the newspaper in order "to be able to decide properly in elections" on a 6-point scale.

Sociodemographic Variables

Age, education, and general political interest are the control variables in the following analysis. Age was measured in years, condensed into four categories that were used as dummy variables. Education was represented by a 5-point scale describing the highest level reached in one's formal education. It, too, was collapsed into three categories that were introduced into the analysis as dummy variables. Political interest was assessed by the simple question, "Speaking quite generally, are you interested in politics?" Respondents could answer "yes," "not particularly," and "no."

Images of Journalists

A semantic differential was undertaken to assess reader images of journalists. The question for this purpose read,

> Would you please read this card? You will see some contradictory attributes on it. When you think of the journalists writing about Dortmund in your newspaper, which of these attributes do you think are appropriate? Please check one of the boxes between each pair of attributes according to how appropriate you find one of the two characteristics. So, if you think, for instance, that the journalists reporting about Dortmund in your newspaper are generally more critical, then check a box more to the left, that is, closer to that word. If you don't think so, go to the right.

The interviewer then handed a card to the respondent presenting 18 pairs of attributes and 6 boxes between each pair.

Analysis of this semantic differential demonstrated that the stereotypes readers assign to their journalists are generally unidimensional. A factor analysis showed only one significant factor emerging, explaining 77% of the variance. Many attributes can be combined to produce a one-dimensional scale, the poles of which were simply "positive image" and "negative image." That is, summing the semantic differential scores of 13 of the 18 characteristics produces a scale with a surprisingly high scale reliability ($\alpha = .88$). This scale included the scores of "critical," "interested in politics," "open-minded," "versed in the ways of the world," "accurate," "educated," "self-confident," "honest," "industrious," "approachable," "intelligent," "influential," and "responsible." It ranged from 13 (13×1, i.e., the strongest disagreement with the above-mentioned items) to 78 (13×6, i.e., the strongest agreement with the items).

Even when respondents were divided into three groups according to the newspaper they read, the scores they assigned to the local reporters virtually did not differ; and, although they changed somewhat during the course of the panel survey, even these changes were uniform among readers of the three papers. It is as if there was one prevailing image of the local reporter in Dortmund.

PROCEDURE OF THE ANALYSIS

The following section presents results derived from multiple regressions. In these analyses, the stages of the effects variables at the end of either of two periods were the dependent variables: The first period was the one between the first two panel waves—before the campaign started and at the beginning of the "hot phase." The second encompassed this "hot phase" (from the campaign's beginning to its end).

Newspaper use variables, personal conversation, campaign literature, motives for reading the paper, and sociodemographic characteristics were simultaneously entered as independent variables, controlling for each other. Whenever possible, included was not only the stage of those variables at the beginning of either survey period, but also their individual change during that period. This was the case for those variables that were measured in each panel wave. These were intensity of reading the newspaper, personal conversations, and all three motives for reading the newspaper, with a slight exception: Interest in local coverage was measured in the first and third waves, but not in the second. In addition, to control for any possible ceiling effect (a limit on cognitive change resulting from the initial levels of the effects variables), the basic stage of the dependent variable was entered into the analysis.

All regression analyses were conducted separately for three different groups of respondents: those holding positive, neutral, and negative images of the Dortmund journalists at the beginning of either of the two survey periods. For this purpose, the evaluation scale described earlier was used. The scale was divided into three sections so that each contained roughly equal numbers of respondents. Of interest, obviously, is whether positive, neutral, or negative images of journalists strengthened or weakened the relationships between newspaper use and motives for reading on the one hand, and cognitions about Dortmund politics on the other.

For the three dependent variables used, the sample was not further divided according to the specific newspaper read. An exploratory analysis had shown that in these three instances there were no significant differences in effects attributable to the different newspapers.

RESULTS

The following tables demonstrate that reader-held images of their local journalists did indeed influence the impact of newspaper reading. Different patterns of how newspaper use and motives for reading influence factual knowledge and the perception of other people's interest in the election clearly emerged. Surprisingly, however, not only a positive opinion of those who write the local reports enhances newspaper effects on factual knowledge; so too do negative opinions. Those respondents holding an either positive or negative image learned more from simply reading the newspaper. In this case, their motivation to read did not have to be as strong or as specific as for those with a middle-of-the-road attitude toward the local journalists. This pattern shows, for instance, in Table 6.1. In the first survey period, we find that for people with an either positive or negative image of journalists, extensive reading of the paper suffices to learn about election day. Any particular interest in either local, local political, or election content did not have to be added to increase that knowledge. In the neutral image group, however, vote guidance as an incentive to read the newspaper—the strongest motive we measured—was necessary to stimulate any newspaper impact. That was true for the second survey period as well. The role of people's recall of having encountered campaign reports in their newspaper proved interesting here. The perception of election coverage variable showed a negative relationship to increase in factual knowledge.

In Table 6.2, a similar pattern for the knowledge of whether "Greens" and Free Democrats are represented in the City Council emerged. One exception is striking, though. In the second survey period, the one encompassing the "hot phase" of the campaign, one of the two groups with non-neutral opinions of journalists also needed their newspapers even for vote guidance in order to learn from them. But still, in the neutral group, this motive definitely shows a stronger relationship to increased knowledge. Oddly, general interest in local political coverage was negatively related to knowledge (Table 6.2).

As to our third variable, the perception of how interested other people were in the election, a modification of the previous findings could be found: Up to this point, positive and negative images of the Dortmund journalists had helped the newspaper increase knowledge even for people who were not specifically interested in getting that information. Somewhat analogous were the results for our perceived election interest variable in the first period surveyed (beginning of August to end of August/beginning of September,

TABLE 6.1
Date of the Election.
Impact of Newspaper Use and Motives for Reading. Results of
Multiple Regressions (significant betas only[a]) by Image of Journalists.

	Readers' Opinions		
	Negative	Neutral	Positive
Beginning of August– **End of August/** **Beginning of September**			
Net Change of Dependent Vairable	.5 − 1.4	.4 − 1.4	.4 − 1.5
n	241	238	228
	Extensiveness of Newspaper Use .23** Perception of Election Coverage −.16*	Increase in Vote Guidance .24*	Extensiveness of Newspaper Use .25**
End of August/ **Beginning of** **September–End of** **September**			
Net Change of Dependent Variable	1.4 − 1.8	1.3 − 1.8	1.4 − 1.9
n	223	244	216
		Vote Guidance .23* Increase in Vote Guidance .19* Perception of Election Coverage −.24**	

[a]Control variables not shown *$p<.05$; **$p<.01$

1984): in both the positive and negative image groups either no specific motivation or a less specific one than demonstrated by the neutral group showed significant relationships to the belief that others were more interested in the election in early September than they had been the previous August. For the group with a positive attitude toward the Dortmund journalists, interest in coverage of local politics in the newspaper was enough. Again, in the neutral group "vote guidance" made a difference.

This picture changed in the second survey period, however. Still, interest

TABLE 6.2
Party Knowledge.
Impact of Newspaper Use and Motives for Reading. Results of
Multiple Regressions (significant betas only[a]) by Image of Journalists.

	Readers' Opinions		
	Negative	Neutral	Positive
Beginning of August-End of August/Beginning of September			
Net Change of Dependent Variable	1.5 − 1.6	1.5 − 1.6	1.5 − 1.7
n	243	240	230
	Intensity of Reading .26*	Vote Guidance .22*	Increase in Intensity of Reading .23*
End of August/Beginning of September-End of September			
Net Change of Dependent Variable	1.6 − 1.6	1.6 − 1.6	1.7 − 1.7
n	227	247	218
		Vote Guidance .46** Increase in Vote Guidance .24*	Vote Guidance .24* Interest in Local Political Coverage −.29**

[a]Control variables not shown; *p<.05; **p<.01.

in local political coverage augmented the impression that others were becoming interested in the campaign among those with polar opinions of the journalists. In the neutral group, on the other hand, the impact of the vote guidance motive was reversed. There, it led to the perception that other people were increasingly *less* interested. Somewhat similar is the function of that motive for people with a negative image of Dortmund journalists. This belief was also held by neutral group members who read the newspaper extensively but without our specific motives. Also, those with a positive image believed less in others' interest in the election, the more they saw campaign reports in their newspaper (Table 6.3).

These last results reveal how complex the network of effects may be and

TABLE 6.3
Perceived Election Interest.
Impact of Newspaper Use and Motives for Reading. Results of
Multiple Regressions (significant betas only[a]) by Image of Journalists.

	Readers' Opinions		
	Negative	*Neutral*	*Positive*
Beginning of August–End of August/ Beginning of September			
Net Change of Dependent Variable	2.6 − 2.6	2.6 − 2.6	2.6 − 2.6
n	241	239	229
		Increase in Vote Guidance .23*	Interest in Local Political Coverage .39** Increase in Interest in Local Political Coverage .39**
End of August/ Beginning of September-End of September			
Net Change of Dependent Variable	2.6 − 2.6	2.6 − 2.7	2.6 − 2.6
n	207	229	198
	Vote Guidance −.41** Increase in Vote Guidance −.21* Interest in Local Political Coverage .26** Increase in Interest in Local Political Coverage .21**	Increase in Vote Guidance −.28** Extensiveness of Newspaper Use .16*	Interest in Local Political Coverage .30** Increase in Interest in Local Political Coverage .29** Perception of Election Coverage −.17**

[a]Control variables not shown; *$p<.05$; **$p<.01$.

how many different factors are obviously part of it. For instance, the neutral group needed a very specific motive to be influenced by the newspapers. But this motive did not work in the same direction all the time: During the hot phase of the election campaign, for instance, it turned respondents' perceptions of other people's campaign interest around. Obviously, it must be assumed that an additional influence factor may be responsible for this switch. It could be, for instance, a raised, nonspecific attention or activation level of virtually everyone after the election campaign had actually started. If a need for orientation as strong as vote guidance was added to this general attention, people finally noticed that the coverage of that election in the Dortmund newspapers was probably not exciting enough and that their fellow citizens' interest may not have been that great after all. Indeed, the content analysis of the larger study showed that only up to 1% of all local reports in all three papers in any given week dealt with the election as their central topic. Less specific motives for reading the newspaper, however, did not make people realize the scarcity of the election coverage and thus still somewhat furthered the effects of those weak stimuli.

DISCUSSION

In the preceding analysis, newspaper use variables and motives for reading as prerequisites of newspaper impact on political cognitions were examined simultaneously. In addition, we considered the image readers hold of the producers of the messages they read. More specifically, we tried to find answers to the question of how images of local journalists shape the impact of newspaper use on their readers. First of all, it can be said that, when it comes to newspaper use effects, journalists' stereotypes do make a difference: Whether readers had a positive, neutral, or negative image of their local reporters proved to be an important contingent condition.

Our evidence about how this condition works, however, is somewhat puzzling. In our study, it is clearly not true that the more positive the image of journalists the stronger the impact of their messages. Both negative and positive images of journalists enhance reading effects. McLeod, Kosicki, Amor, Alan, and Philips (1986) found surprisingly similar effects in their study of the influence of *media* images on knowledge gain.

These results suggest an involvement model of the effects process: Changes in cognitions caused by newspaper reading are furthered by any strong opinion about the journalists, may it be positive or negative.

But this statement is obviously too general: Content, the quality and quantity of newspaper coverage, naturally plays a role, too. For example, in the case of the two factual knowledge indicators, the impact of the somewhat meager coverage of the election was boosted by extensive and intensive reading as well as by specific motives to follow the papers' reports; but, it was not uniformly in the case of perceived interest in the local election. Here there was even evidence for reverse effects: Specific motives led readers to realize how little coverage there was, turning them away from the idea that others were becoming more and more interested in the campaign. This effect, again, was enhanced by the holding of polar images of the journalists.

This is a fairly tentative explanation for our results. What we definitely can say, however, is that in addition to traditional contingent conditions, the evaluation of those in charge of producing media messages is an important mediating factor in the media effects process.

REFERENCES

Atwood, L. E. (1970). How newsmen and readers perceive each other's story preferences. *Journalism Quarterly, 47,* 296–202.

Bauer, R. A. (1958). The communicator and the audience. *Journal of Conflict Resolution, 2,* 67–77.

Blumler, J. G., & McQuail, D. (1968). *Television in politics.* London: Faber & Faber.

Flegel, R. C., & Chaffee, S. H. (1971). Influences of editors, readers, and personal opinions on reporters. *Journalism Quarterly, 48,* 645–651.

Hovland, C. I., Janis, I. L., & Kelley, H. H. (1953). *Communication and persuasion.* New Haven, CT: Yale University Press.

Hovland, C. I., & Weiss, W. (1951). The influence of source credibility on communication effectiveness. *Public Opinion Quarterly, 15,* 635–650.

Koecher, R. (1986). Bloodhounds or missionaries: Role definitions of German and British journalists. *European Journal of Communication, 1,* 43–64.

Martis, R. K., O'Keefe, G. J., & Nayman, O. B. (1972). Opinion agreement and accuracy between editors and their readers. *Journalism Quarterly, 49,* 460–468.

McLeod, J. M., Kosicki, G. M., Amor, D. L., Allen, J. G., & Philips, D. M. (1986). *Public images of mass media news: What are they and does it matter?* Paper presented at the annual convention of the Association for Education in Journalism and Mass Communication, Norman, OK.

Pool, I. de S., & Shulman, I. (1959). Newsmen's fantasies: Audiences and newswriting. *Public Opinion Quarterly, 23,* 145–158.

Schoenbach, K., & Weischenberg, S. (1984). Inter-und Intra-Transaktionen im Medienwirkungsprozess [Inter- and intra-transactions in the media effects process]. *Publizistik, 29,* 88–89.

Schoenbach, K., & Weischenberg, S. (1987). *Inter-und Intra-Transaktionen im Medienwirkungsprozess* [Inter- and intra-transactions in the media effects process]. Hannover, West Germany: Hochschule fuer Musik und Theater.

Schramm, W., & Danielson, W. (1958). Anticipated audiences as determinants of recall. *Journal of Abnormal and Social Psychology, 56,* 282–283.

Zimmerman, C., & Bauer, R. A. (1956). The effects of an audience upon what is remembered. *Public Opinion Quarterly, 20,* 238–248.

7 | News for the Other Person: Editors' Processing of Readers' Interest

Tsan-Kuo Chang
Sidney Kraus
Cleveland State University

News as presented in the mass media is for the ultimate consumption of the audience. To paraphrase an old cliché, if an event is reported in the mass media but no one cares to read, listen, or watch, does it become news? This question is critical in our understanding of the news as a social phenomenon and a pervasive political force. It is primarily the notion of audience interest that, for different reasons, has attracted the attention of both mass communication scholars and professional journalists.

For decades, news writing and reporting textbooks have recognized the importance of audience interest as a significant element influencing what is newsworthy. A survey of recent textbooks about the definition of news, for example, reveals that audience interest appears to be the underlying factor that accounts for most, if not all, of the news ingredients: timeliness, proximity, conflict, prominence or eminence, impact or consequence, human interest, sensationalism, and novelty, oddity or the unusual (e.g., Brooks, Kennedy, Moen, & Ranly, 1988; Hough, 1988; Itule & Anderson, 1987; Mencher, 1987). Each of these ingredients is more or less defined according to whether the news could be related to the taste of readers and viewers. Because of the concern over audience interest, many editors are likely to give the readers, as Hough (1988) stated, "what they ask for, whether it is local news or features or high school football" (p. 2).

How do the editors decide what to give to their readers? To cater to the news appetite of their readers and viewers, editors of course will need to develop means to assess audience interest. Editors can determine readers' preferences through readership surveys, letters to the editor, and circulation figures. More often than not, however, editors tend to rely on their instincts

99

and "have to second guess" what the "readers really want to know" (Mock, cited in Itule & Anderson, 1987, p. 46). There seems to be common agreement that editors just have a sense for readers' interest in the news.

Such a sense of audience interest undoubtedly involves editors' perceptions of what the news should be that would capture the attention of their readers and viewers on a regular basis. Perceptions are something people believe to be true, and often people act on those perceptions (Petty & Cacioppo, 1981). As part of individual paradigm, one's perceptions of the relationship with other people largely define and shape his or her communicative behavior. This was suggested by Lippmann (1922) in his classic discussion of pseudo-environment. For the editors, the perceptions of the news become for the most part their journalistic paradigms in which how they see their relationship with the readers is a key building block. In the views of Rothman and Lichter (1984), "the paradigms journalists (like all of us) unconsciously accept as guides affect the manner in which they see the world and describe it" (p. 40).

In the process of news collection, reproduction, dissemination, and consumption, the relationship between editors and their audiences is similar to that of suppliers and consumers. If editors tend to give the readers and viewers the news they want or ask for and if editors usually depend on their news instincts, then, there should be little doubt that editors' perceptions of audience interest are likely to play a critical part in their news decision making. As filtered through the interpretations made by editors, however, the effect of readers' interest on news content is more indirect than direct (McQuail, 1987). Apparently, readers per se do not actually dictate the types of news that should appear in the mass media. It is the end result of journalistic judgement by editors who try to find the best goodness of fit between the news and their readers' interest.

More importantly, how editors perceive their readers' interest in the various types of news may influence the ways editors process the number of stories they receive daily. Knowing the dynamics of the perception process could help editors better organize and classify information going through the newsroom, reduce the volume of information flow in the news channel, and avoid uncertainty in news selection. In other words, a mere perception of what the readers ask for serves some useful purposes for the editors in their daily management of the news flow. If the perceptions are accurate, editors would be able to minimize the "number of errors" in deciding which stories should get covered and which should not in order to give something that is interesting to their readers.

How editors process news could be considered essentially as a matter of classification of various news types. Research on editors' cataloging news has been well documented. Since the classic study of "Mr. Gates" (White, 1950), numerous studies have examined, either empirically or impressionistically, how editors define news (for a recent review, see Gaudino, 1988). A general conclusion suggests that editors do not rely on formal, external rules or guidelines to limit the daily flow of information they process. Instead, their selection of news appears to be based on a set of subjective and selective perceptions of how the news would be related to their readers. Knowing readers' news interest, whether real or imagined, of course allows editors to classify news stories accordingly. As Stempel (1967) argued, it offers editors a way to gain from grouping news stories.

According to Burgoon, Burgoon, and Atkin (1982), interest and importance are the main criteria journalists use in their news decision making. The interesting news is what the readers and viewers "want to know"; the important news is what editors think their audience "need to know." Both criteria are not necessarily independent of each other because the "want to know" news and the "need to know" news are largely determined by editors' perceptions of the readers. The goodness of fit between editors' perceptions of their readers' interests will have a great deal to do with the presentation and interpretation of the news as well as the success of the news organization.

Although it is generally agreed or assumed that editors have developed a sense for audience interest, there is little empirical evidence documenting how editors perceive their readers' interest and what effects such perceptions would have on news decision making. A search of survey studies published in *Journalism Quarterly* from 1950 through 1987 yielded a number of studies that examined perceptions as an important factor in the flow of news and information within and without the news organizations.

EDITORS' PERCEPTIONS AND READERS' INTEREST

In an earlier study of wire editors, Gieber (1956) found that most editors had little perception of readers' interest and their perceptions were not affected by social contacts. According to Gieber, readers as the ultimate consumers of the news were "not perceived clearly by most of the wire editors; some were not concerned whether or not the output of the wire desk was read by their audience" (p. 431).

Later, Atwood (1970) suggested that among newsmen, editors were least able to predict readers' interest and might judge news stories differently than did their readers. Using a Q-sort analysis, Atwood found that newspaper staffers "who were poorest in predicting audience preferences held desk jobs" (p. 302). In a related study of student press, Bornholdt (1966) concluded that journalists might have an inaccurate perception of audience interest. Recent studies by Burgoon et al. (1982) and Wulfemeyer (1984) also offered observations indicating that many journalists had a false image of audience interest or did not know their audience as well as they might.

Similar conclusions concerning how editors viewed public relations practitioners have been documented by other researchers. Kopenhaver, Martinson, and Ryan (1984) reported evidence suggesting that journalists "do not perceive practitioners stated positions about the news elements well at all, and they perceive a large gap (which apparently does not exist) between their views and practitioners' views" (p. 865). They also said that whether the gap exists or not, "the editors' presumption that a gap exists can have an important impact on the communication process" (p. 865).

Other studies reported how perceptions of audience interest affected news decision making by journalists. Flegel and Chaffee (1971) indicated that reporters tended to cover news according to their own opinions and the perceptions of readers' views were less influential in their reporting. They studied two daily newspapers in Madison, Wisconsin, and found that for both news and feature stories, the order of influence described by the reporters was the same: "they feel that their own opinions guide their reporting more than do those of their editors; readers' opinions are even less important" (p. 649).

In a related study, however, Martin, O'Keefe, and Nayman (1972) disagreed. They provided evidence suggesting that editors perceived readers' interest fairly well and the perceptions influenced their news decision making. Based on the coorientation model, their study of opinion agreement and accuracy between editors and their readers found that "there appears to be a discernible association between Wisconsin editors' perception of their readers' beliefs and the direction of the stories that appeared in their newspapers" (p. 464).

THIRD-PERSON EFFECT HYPOTHESIS

The assertion that editors' perceptions of readers' interest may have an effect on the process of news selection, reproduction, and dissemination is analogous to what Davison (1983) called the "third-person effect" in communication. As Davison stated, any effect that the communication achieves may be "due not to the reaction of the ostensible audience but rather to the behavior of those who anticipate, or think they perceive, some reaction on the part of others" (p. 3).

According to the third-person effect hypothesis, then, editors' news decisions need not be based on direct feedback from the readers. In fact, responses from the readers may not even be necessary for the editors to decide what they want or ask for. In his study of how journalists decided news, Gans (1979) indicated that when making story-selection judgments "journalists explicitly think about and act on their audience-images." In the process, "the imagined audience becomes a veto group" (p. 241).

As is usually the case, when the news sources (first person) provide raw information input through stories written by reporters, editors (second person) may anticipate or guess how their readers (third person) will react to the news in order to grab their interest. The perceptions or misperceptions of such reaction in turn would no doubt affect editors' subsequent news selection in response to the news and information in question. For example, some news and information may be ignored and presentations and interpretations of the selected items may be likely to include incomplete, unclear, or inaccurate information in the stories because of perceptions.

Although not directly related to news processing and decision making, recent studies on the third-person effect have provided evidence supporting the notion that perceptions of others involved in communication are an important factor in determining the nature of public debate (e.g., Mutz, 1987). There is little doubt that audiences are the most important component in the flow of mass communication. Indeed, without the audiences there would be no mass communication. In the process of mass communication, therefore, the implications of audience involvement for information dissemination are significant. As a source of influence on editors' performance as gatekeepers in the flow of information (Flegel & Chaffee, 1971), perceptions of readers' interest can be expected to have a considerable impact on the nature of mass production of news and the effectiveness of communication. What the perceptions are deserves more attention and systematic analysis.

The purpose of this chapter is to determine how newspaper editors across the country perceive their readers' interest in the news and whether the perceptions relate to perceived coverage of various news categories. Specifically, the following research questions were addressed: What did newspaper editors think of their readers' interest in the news? How closely did editors' perceptions of readers' interest agree with their own news interest? What factors affected editors' perceptions of readers news interest? Was perceived news coverage related more to editors' own news interest or more to their perceptions of readers interest?

METHOD

In a mail survey, based on probability proportionate to size, a national sample of 550 daily newspapers was randomly selected from the *1987 Editor & Publisher International Yearbook*. The sampling method was used to ensure that newspapers with larger circulation would be included in the sample because the majority of papers (85%) in the United States have a circulation of less than 50,000. The assumption is that larger newspapers tend to cover both domestic and foreign news more extensively, are able to reach a wide range of readership, and thus have a stronger impact on public policy. Of the 550 newspapers, 9 shared the same editorial staff with other larger papers in the sample and 1 was later merged with another paper. These 10 papers were therefore eliminated from the sample. The final sample of 540 newspapers represented 33% of the 1,657 papers listed in the 1987 yearbook.

A six-page questionnaire, composed mostly of multiple-choice questions, was first mailed to the top editor (in most cases, either editor or managing editor) of each newspaper in mid-December 1987. None of the questionnaires was returned by the post office as undelivered. In mid-January 1988, approximately 4 weeks after the initial mailing, a second packet was sent to those newspaper editors who had not responded to the first mailing. In late February 1988, nonrespondents were again reminded and encouraged to return the questionnaire by an early March deadline. And finally, 1 week after the deadline, a postcard was sent to all the remaining nonrespondents, asking why they had not returned the questionnaire.

The initial mailing drew 121 responses (22.4% of the total sample) and the second mailing produced another 114 responses of which 109 (20.2%) completed the questionnaire, 4 refused to participate, and 1 was merged with another newspaper. The third mailing generated 48 usable questionnaires (8.9%), 3 refusals, and 1 ineligible. The three mailings yielded 278 respondents, a response rate of 51.7%. Responses to the postcard inquiries were not included in the present analysis.

In the questionnaire, the editors were asked, among other things, to rate their readers' interest in each of the following news categories: government, business/finance, politics, sports, U.S. foreign affairs, crime/violence, military/defense, foreign news, human interest, law/justice, fashion/food/living, and arts/entertainment. Editors indicated their readers' interests in each of the news categories on a 5-point scale, with 1 representing "not at all interested" and 5 representing "very interested." On a similar 5-point scale, editors were also asked how interested they were personally in the same 12 news categories.

Such ratings of readers' interest and editors' own interest in the same news categories measured congruency, or the extent to which newspapers editors' interest agreed with what they thought would interest their readers. In the coorientation model, congruency is the extent to which one's attitudes are similar to his or her perceptions of another person's attitudes.

To measure coverage of the 12 news categories, editors were asked to rate their newspaper's overall coverage of those categories on a 5-point scale, with 1 representing "not at all adequate" and 5 representing "very adequate." Although not a precise measure of the actual amount of coverage of various news (which would require an extensive content analysis), the perceived adequacy of coverage by the editors may serve as indicators of how the 12 news categories were covered in the editors' newspapers. Presumably, newspaper editors would have a good reading of how much space is given to the different types of news. Other measures used in the study included newspaper circulation, region, editor's political leanings, party affiliation, education, presence of competing newspapers, and editor's years of working experience. These internal and external factors were used as control variables in the subsequent analysis.

RESULTS

Questionnaires were returned by newspaper editors from all parts of the country. Compared to the total sample, there appears to be no geographic bias caused by the nonrespondents. Furthermore, comparisons between respondents and nonrespondents on a number of internal and external variables (e.g., circulation, city population, market, and organizational characteristics) show no significant differences. Although such similarities do not necessarily suggest that nonrespondents would have perceptions of readers interest similar to that of respondents, they should increase confidence in the broader generalization of the results regarding how newspaper editors perceived their readers' interest in the news.

As reported in Table 7.1, newspaper editors nationwide perceived their readers' interest in the various news categories to be different from their own interest. Such differences were not only in kind, but also in degree. Of the 12 different types of news, not a single category showed any congruency between editors' interest and the perceived readers' interest in the news. The

TABLE 7.1
Mean Differences Between Editors' Interest and Perceived Readers' Interest in the News

New Categories	Perceived Readers' Interest	Editors' Interest	Mean Difference	T	P
Government	3.3986	4.1486	−.7500	−12.22	.000
Business	3.5181	3.7790	−.2609	−4.07	.000
Sports	4.3026	3.5424	.7601	8.79	.000
Foreign affairs	2.8352	3.9341	−1.0989	−17.70	.000
Crime	3.7766	3.1575	.6190	10.18	.000
Military/defense	3.0256	3.6300	−.6044	−9.46	.000
Foreign news	2.6109	3.7709	−1.1600	−19.06	.000
Human interest	4.1091	3.7964	.3127	5.27	.000
Law/justice	3.0554	3.6310	−.5756	−9.40	.000
Fashion/food	3.6496	2.5766	1.0730	15.08	.000
Arts/entertainment	3.7782	3.2909	.4873	6.23	.000
Politics	3.3212	4.0912	−.7701	−11.69	.000

Note: A "1" on the original scale represented "not at all interested," while a "5" represented "very interested." Therefore, the larger the means in the table, the greater the interest in the news.

discrepancies were even more striking when the nature of the news was considered.

On the whole, editors considered themselves to be more interested in the following news categories than were their readers: government, politics, business, foreign affairs, military/defense, foreign news, and law/justice. On the other hand, they perceived their readers to be quite interested than they were in sports, crime, human interest, fashion/food/living, and arts/ entertainment. Consistent with previous studies (e.g., Burgoon et al., 1982; Schiltz, Sigelman, & Neal, 1973), editors showed a substantially high interest in foreign affairs news and foreign news and perceived their readers to have relatively low interest in the same news categories. The only news category that readers' interest was perceived to be substantially higher than editors' own interest was fashion/food/living. As is evident, the differences between editors' own interest and the perceived readers' interest seem to follow a conventional classification of news: hard news versus soft news. Editors rated their own interest to be high in hard news and perceived their readers to be mostly interested in soft news.

The incongruency between editors' own interest and the perceived readers' interest can be best seen in the overall rankings of the 12 categories in Table 7.2. The rank order correlation (Spearman rho = −.3846, n.s.) showed a moderate negative, but insignificant, relationship between editors' own inter-

TABLE 7.2
Rank Comparison Between Editors' Interest and Perceived Readers'
Interest in the News

News Categories	Editors' Interest	Rank	Perceived Readers' Interest	Rank
Government	4.1486	1	3.3986	7
Politics	4.0912	2	3.3212	8
Foreign affairs	3.9341	3	2.8352	11
Human interest	3.7964	4	4.1091	2
Business	3.7790	5	3.5181	6
Foreign news	3.7709	6	2.6109	12
Law/justice	3.6310	7	3.0554	9
Military/defense	3.6300	8	3.0256	10
Sports	3.5424	9	4.3026	1
Arts/entertainment	3.2909	10	3.7782	3
Crime	3.1575	11	3.7766	4
Fashion/food	2.5766	12	3.6496	5

Spearman rho: −.3846 (n.s)

Note: A "1" on the original scale represented "not at all interested," while a "5" represented "very interested." Therefore, the larger the means in the table, the greater the interest in the news.

est and perceived readers' interest in the news. In other words, there was disagreement between editors' own interest and what they thought would be interesting to their readers. Although not statistically significant, editors seemed to view their readers' news interest to be opposite to their own interest. For example, of the 12 news categories, government, politics, and foreign affairs were rated the top 3 by editors' own interest, but were rated to be fairly low with regard to their readers' interest. On the other hand, editors indicated that they had less interest in news about arts/entertainment, crime, and fashion/food/living, but considered their readers to be quite interested in such news. These results suggest that editors perceived their readers to have different news interest than their own and are in line with previous studies (e.g., Atwood, 1970; Kopenhaver et al., 1984).

What was the coverage of the 12 news categories in the newspapers? Editors were asked to rate their newspaper's overall coverage of the news in terms of adequacy. The results are reported in Table 7.3. Sports was considered by editors to have quite adequate coverage in their newspapers, followed by news about government, politics, and crime. The news categories that were perceived to have less adequate coverage were military/defense, foreign affairs, and foreign news. In the middle was news about human interest, arts/entertainment, fashion/food/living, law/justice, and business.

TABLE 7.3
Rank Comparison among Adequacy of Coverage, Editors' Interest and
Perceived Readers' Interest in the News

News Categories	Adequacy of Coverage*	Rank	Editors' Interest Rank	Perceived Readers' Interest Rank
Sports	4.066	1	9	1
Government	3.863	2	1	7
Politics	3.669	3	2	8
Crime	3.585	4	11	4
Human interest	3.473	5	4	2
Arts/entertainment	3.453	6	10	3
Fashion/food	3.435	7	12	5
Law/justice	3.133	8	7	9
Business	3.126	9	5	6
Military/defense	3.022	10	8	10
Foreign affairs	2.841	11	3	11
Foreign news	2.716	12	6	12

Spearman rho between coverage rank and editors' interest rank: .028

Spearman rho between coverage rank and readers interest rank: .713

*Note: A "1" on the original scale represented "not at all adequate," while a "5" represented "very adequate." Therefore, the larger the means in the table, the more adequate the coverage of the news.

If the perceived amount of coverage could be taken as an indication of how newspapers across the country actually covered various news categories, it would seem that sports and political news enjoyed relatively large space, whereas news that dealt with international relations and military affairs received less attention. Although not based on content analysis, the perceived paucity of coverage of international news in the newspapers appears to be consistent with existing studies that showed a minimal amount of space and time devoted to foreign news in the U.S. mass media (e.g., Hart, 1963; Kaplan, 1979; Larson, 1979; McAnany, Larson, & Storey, 1982; Peterson, 1980).

How did perceived news coverage relate to editors' own news interest and their perceptions of readers interest in the news? The Spearman rank order correlation (rho = .028) reported in Table 7.3 indicates that there appears to be no relationship between editors' interest in the news and the ratings of their newspapers' overall coverage of the news. For example, editors rated sports as the top news category to have quite adequate coverage in their newspapers. They did not, however, show much interest in sports as compared to other news stories. In fact, of all the news categories, sports was rated fairly low by editors' interest.

The rank-order correlation between perceived amount of news coverage and editors' perceptions of readers' interest in the news suggests a high, positive relationship (rho = .713, $p < .05$). It appears that perceived readers' news interest is related to the overall amount of coverage rated by the editors. In other words, when readers' interest in the news was perceived to be high, editors were likely to report that coverage of the news was fairly adequate. This finding implies that editors gave what their readers asked for. This is especially true with regard to news that dealt with international relations and military affairs. When these news categories were removed from the rankings, the substantial rank-order correlation dropped and became insignificant.

The implication that readers got what they wanted in the news can be best shown in Fig. 7.1. As discussed earlier, a clear distinction exists between editors' own news interest and their perceptions of readers' interest. What is more interesting is the pattern shown in the figure. When readers were perceived to be more interested in the news, coverage of the news tended to be rated fairly adequate, as compared to coverage of the news in which editors showed a higher interest than their readers. It is evident that the five news categories associated with high readers' interest (sports, crime, fashion/food/living, human interest, and arts/entertainment) were all considered to have more coverage in the newspapers than were most of the remaining categories in which editors were more interested.

With only very slight variation, the pattern holds even after controlling for variables like geographic region, circulation, editors' working experience, editors' education, presence of competitive newspapers, editors' political ide-

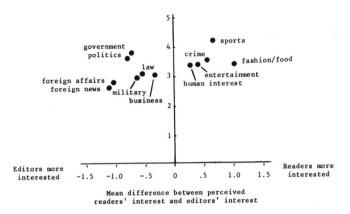

FIG. 7.1. Relationship among adequacy of coverage, editors' interest and perceived readers' interest in the news. Mean difference was calculated as follows: perceived readers' interest–editors' interest. Therefore, negative mean difference indicates that editors were more interested in the news than were their readers. Positive mean difference indicates that readers were perceived to be more interested in the news.

ology, and their political party affiliation. In other words, regardless of internal and external differences, newspapers editors across the country appear to perceive readers' interest in the news in a similar manner. It makes no difference whether the newspapers had a circulation of less than 50,000 or more than 500,000. And it does not matter whether editors had working experience of less than 10 years or more than 30 years. The perceptions of readers' interest are mostly the same and the perceived amount of coverage remains largely unchanged.

DISCUSSION

The agreement of editors on readers' interest in the news and the perceived news coverage suggests standardization of news content among newspapers in the United States. Such standardization not only helps to reduce uncertainty in news selection, but also serves some practical purposes for the editors. As Lippmann (1922) argued long ago, "Without standardization . . . the editor would soon die of excitement . . . The thing could not be managed at all without systematization, for in a standardized product there is economy of time and effort, as well as a partial guarantee against failure" (p. 222).

We may have uncovered another clue to understanding what has been

called the agenda-setting function of the media—"[The] impact of mass media—ability to effect cognitive change among individuals" (McCombs &
Shaw, 1972, p. 1). Research on agenda-setting may be classified into two
basic divisions—issues related to systemic and to individual agendas. Kraus
and Davis (1976) pointed out that,

> The *systemic agenda* refers to a general set of political controversies that fall within
> the range of legitimate concerns meriting the attention of the public. *Institutional
> agenda* denotes a set of concrete items scheduled for active and serious consideration
> by a particular institutional decision-making body. (p. 220)

Considering this study, newspaper editors may be defined as an "institutional decision-making body" that may be setting the agenda for its readers.
A recent study has provided strong evidence regarding the agenda-setting
function of the news media. In their experiment on television news, Iyengar
and Kinder (1987) concluded that "Americans' views of their society and
nation are powerfully shaped by the stories that appear on the evening news"
(p. 112).

It would be difficult to demonstrate that editors engage in "conspiratorial
activities" about news items, or that they consult each other to form an
agreed upon approach to the selection and editing of news items. Still,
the findings herein suggest that an "agreement" can be found in the *process*
by which editors determine the *news value* of different kinds of information.
That "agreement" is the editors' predictions about readers' interest in news.

Lippmann's opinion about standardization notwithstanding, one could
argue that such unanimity among gatekeepers in a free society may have
negative effects on democratic institutions. Indeed, editors' concordance of
what interests readers may be the "hidden" practice partly responsible for the
current rash of press criticism. If the negative effects on democratic institutions
is more ponderous than the benefits of standardization, it may be difficult to
alter the relationship between the editors and readers since this systemic
influence is probably *learned* in the process of being socialized into the role of
editor.

REFERENCES

Atwood, L. (1970). How newsmen and readers perceive each others' story preferences. *Journalism
    Quarterly, 47*, 296–302.
Bornholdt, J. N., Jr. (1966). Should the student press be more serious? *Journalism Quarterly, 43*,
    560–562.

Brooks, B. S., Kennedy, G., Moen, D. R., & Ranley, D. (1988). *News reporting and writing* (3rd ed.). New York: St. Martin's Press.

Burgoon, J. K., Burgoon, M., & Atkin, C. K. (1982). *The working world of the journalist.* New York: Newspaper Advertising Bureau, Inc.

Davison, W. P. (1983). The third-person effect in communication. *Public Opinion Quarterly, 47,* 1–15.

Flegel, R. C., & Chaffee, S. H. (1971). Influences of editors, readers, and personal opinions on reporters. *Journalism Quarterly, 48,* 645–651.

Gans, H. J. (1979). *Deciding what's news.* New York: Pantheon.

Gaudino, J. L. (1988, July). *A predictive framework for determining how journalists determine news.* Paper presented at the annual conference of the Association for Education in Journalism and Mass Communication, Portland, OR.

Gieber, W. (1956). Across the desk: A study of 16 telegraph editors. *Journalism Quarterly, 33,* 423–432.

Hart, J. A. (1963). The flow of news between the United States and Canada. *Journalism Quarterly, 40,* 70–74.

Hough, G. A. (1988). *News writing* (4th ed.). Boston: Houghton Mifflin.

Itule, B. D., & Anderson, D. A. (1987). *News writing and reporting for today's media.* New York: Random House.

Iyengar, S., & Kinder, D. R. (1987). *News that matters.* Chicago, IL: The University of Chicago Press.

Kaplan, F. L. (1979). The plight of foreign news in the U.S. mass media: An assessment. *Gazette, 25,* 233–243.

Kopenhaver, L. L., Martinson, D. L., & Ryan, M. (1984). How public relations practitioners and editors in Florida view each other. *Journalism Quarterly, 61,* 860–865, 884.

Kraus, S., & Davis, D. (1976). *The effects of mass communication on political behavior.* University Park, PA: Pennsylvania University Press.

Larson, J. F. (1979). International affairs coverage in U.S. network television. *Journal of Communication, 29,* 136–147.

Lippmann, W. (1922). *Public opinion.* New York: Harcourt, Brace.

Martin, R. K., O'Keefe, G. J., & Nayman, O. B. (1972). Opinion agreement and accuracy between editors and their readers. *Journalism Quarterly, 49,* 460–468.

McAnany, E., Larson, J. F., & Storey, J. D. (1982, May). *News of Latin America on network television, 1972–1982: Too little too late?"* Paper presented at the annual conference of the International Communication Association, Boston, MA.

McCombs, M. E., & Shaw, D. L. (1972). The agenda–setting function of the mass media. *Public Opinion Quarterly, 36,* 176–87.

McQuail, D. (1987). *Mass communication theory: An introduction* (2nd ed.). Beverly Hills, CA: Sage.

Mencher, M. (1987). *New reporting and writing* (4th ed.). Dubuque, IA: Wm. C. Brown.

Mutz, D. C. (1987, May). *Perceptions of others in the public opinion process: The third person effect and the spiral of silence.* Paper presented at the 37th annual conference of the International Communication Association, Montreal, Canada.

Peterson, S. (1980). A case study of third world news coverage by western news agencies. *Studies in Comparative International Development, 15,* 62–98.

Petty, R. E., & Cacioppo, J. T. (1981). *Attitudes and persuasion: Classic and contemporary approaches.* Dubuque, IA: Wm. C. Brown.

Rothman, S., & Lichter, S. R. (1984). Personality, ideology and world view: A comparison of media and business elites. *British Journal of Political Science, 50,* 29–49.

Schlitz, T., Sigelman, L., & Neal, R. (1973). Perspective of managing editors on coverage of foreign policy news. *Journalism Quarterly, 50,* 716–721.

Stempel, G. H., III. (1967). A factor analytic study of reader interest in news. *Journalism Quarterly, 44,* 326–330.

White, D. M. (1950). The "gatekeeper": A case study in the selection of news. *Journalism Quarterly, 27,* 383–390.

Wulfemeyer, K. T. (1984). Perceptions of viewer interests by local TV journalists. *Journalism Quarterly, 61,* 432–435.

8 | Pat Robertson's Fall From Grace: Viewer Processing of PTL Scandal Information

Robert Abelman
Cleveland State University

Pollster George Gallup declared 1976 the "Year of the Evangelical." This was in response to Jimmy Carter's public profession that he was a "born again" Christian, and the fact that his electoral margin of victory may well have been provided by evangelical Christians. Interestingly, however, most analysts either missed or underplayed the importance of this group as a potentially powerful voting bloc in future elections. According to Hadden and Swann (1981), "there was a tendency to see Carter's candidacy and victory as an aberration. He ran primarily against Washington in the fallout of Watergate. . . . Thus, there was no real need to assess seriously the significance of the 'evangelical vote' " (p. 126).

Clearly, this is no longer the case. The emergence of the "New Christian Right," headed by Jerry Falwell's political arm the Moral Majority, has served to minimize the division between church and state in the past decade and, subsequently, has received its share of national exposure. On September 15, 1980, for instance, Falwell and his organization were the cover story in *Newsweek* (Mayer, 1980) and "Preachers and Politics" was the lead feature story in *U.S. News and World Report* (Mann & Peterson, 1980). That the religious community was "amassing a base of potential [political] power that dwarfed every other competing interest in American society" (Rifkin & Howard, 1979, p. 30), with the evangelical movement becoming the most active of all religious groups (Bromley & Schupe, 1984; Carey, 1985; Pierand, 1985), was made most apparent in the 1984 election. Evangelicals made up roughly 20% of Ronald Reagan's vote in 1984 (Wills, 1988), obtained largely through his close affiliation with the Moral Majority and religious broadcasters. Reagan's statement that "religion and politics are necessarily related" (Johnson

113

& Tamney, 1985, p. 124), made during the 1984 convention, and his regular participation in national religious broadcaster conferences, typifies the efforts of Republican conservatives to enlist the aid of evangelicals and their followers. According to Horsfield (1984):

> For some fearful observers, the growth of evangelical broadcasting represented a massive takeover by the political and moral right and a plot to establish a religious republic with the evangelical and fundamentalist broadcasters as the major spokespersons. More moderately, some journalists observed that the television preachers, by unifying and motivating otherwise inactive voters, could hold the key to [elections]. (p. xiii)

The 1988 media election coverage focused on evangelicals almost entirely within the context of televangelist Pat Robertson's presidential campaign . . . with due justification. Hal Quinley of the polling firm Yankelovich, Clancy, and Shulman said that "there is a core group of about 20% of those eligible to vote that is highly receptive to Robertson's evangelical message and can be mobilized" (cited in Wills, 1988, p. 28). Indeed, it has been suggested that Robertson's success as a candidate for the 1988 presidential election was largely contingent on the mobilization of this core group (Detwiler, 1988; Frankl, 1987; Mashsek, 1986). Furthermore, because "all evangelicals are not Republicans, all evangelicals are not in support of Robertson, and not everyone supporting Robertson is an evangelical" (Castelli, 1988, p. 8), Robertson's success was also dependent on the "halo effect" the evangelical vote would have on other Christians.

Several social critics (e.g., Alter, 1988; Fore, 1987) believed that Robertson was guaranteed the evangelical vote because of his high-profile position as religious television's entrepreneur. He pioneered the first religious TV station, the first religious network, and the first Christian programming to borrow the talk show/news program format from commercial television. According to a 1987 A. C. Nielsen report, episodes of Robertson's "The 700 Club" were tuned into 16.3 million homes per month and reached 27 million viewers, making it the top-rated daily program (followed by the 5.8 million households reached by Jim Bakker's "The PTL Club"), and nearly doubling the audience of the top-rated weekly program, "The Jimmy Swaggart Ministry" (9.3 million households). Robertson's Christian Broadcasting Network (CBN) reached 30 million cable subscribers, making it not only the largest Christian cable operation at the time but the fifth largest of any kind (Ostling, 1986). In addition to extensive exposure, Robertson's "The 700 Club" was among the most political of all religious broadcasts and narrowcasts (Abelman & Neuendorf, 1985). It became increasingly political, and less religious, as his entrance into the political arena became more apparent (Abelman & Pettey, 1988; Alter, 1988).

Although Robertson's exposure as a televangelist has made him a recognizable personality, and his politically peppered telecasts confirmed his political ambitions and positions, Robertson nonetheless failed to generate the evangelical vote. He subsequently dropped from the race for the Republican nomination. Castelli (1988) suggested that Robertson's failure to dominate among evangelicals stems from the fact that his base represented only a small segment of the evangelical population—charismatics[1]—and that he could not attract votes beyond this base. However, a recent *Time* survey (Shapiro, 1988) found that 57% of the country agreed with the statement that "we are a religious nation and religious values should serve as a guide to what our political leaders do in office." The survey concluded that this serves to broaden rather than limit Robertson's appeal. As Wills (1988) pointed out, the country's "yearning for moral reassurance is not likely to find satisfaction in the regular Republican candidates this year—certainly not in the unburning Bush or the mournful Dole" (p. 27).

Hadden and Shupe (1988) forecasted Robertson's failure by noting that voters with low income and education, like many of Robertson's supporters and "The 700 Club" viewers, are traditionally less active and influential in party politics. However, Iowa caucus returns showed that half of Robertson's people did not go to college (for Bush that total was 29%) and 41% of them made $30,000 or less a year (compared with 26% of Bush's total) (Wills, 1988, p. 28). Similarly, Hoover's (1985, 1989) extensive analysis of the "The 700 Club" audience suggested that it is basically comprised of politically aware members of the New Right, who see involvement in the program as being synonymous with their involvement in the political process.

Stacks (1988) attributed Robertson's failure to his "loose-lipped irresponsibility" that "did little for his hopes" (p. 12). He was, of course, referring to Robertson's declaration that God had provided him with knowledge of the whereabouts of U.S. hostages in Lebanon and that "Christians. . . and Jewish people. . . are the only ones that are qualified to have the reign" (Alter, 1988, p. 18). It should be noted, however, that supporters of Robertson are quite familiar and comfortable with his commitment to divine intervention and the insight it has apparently provided him. Recall that Robertson claimed to have diverted the course of Hurricane Gloria through prayer and regularly engaged in healing sessions on his television program. Indeed, early references to his pending declaration of candidacy (Robertson, 1986a) were placed within the framework of divine illumination:

I wouldn't consider it [the presidency] unless it was absolutely certain that, number one, I had heard from God, and absolutely certain that His people nationwide by the hundreds, thousands, and even millions heard the same thing.

---

[1]Charismatic Christians accept the literal interpretation of the Bible and practice an emotional style of worship, which includes speaking in tongues, faith healing, and "words of wisdom"—direct messages from God.

Although there are no doubt many factors that contributed to Robertson's inability to activate the evangelical vote for the 1988 election, it is quite possible that one of the most prominent was the recent demise of two of his religious broadcasting brethren. As we learned through the popular press (see Hackett, 1987; Martz, 1987; Ostling, 1987a, 1987b, 1987c; Press, 1987; Watson, 1987a, 1987b) Jim Bakker, founder and head of the Praise the Lord (PTL) television network, misappropriated ministry funds and engaged in hetero- and [alleged] homosexual affairs. Jimmy Swaggart confessed to sins of the flesh and, in an effort to ignore long-term punishment, denounced his affiliation with the Assemblies of God (see Kalette, 1988; Ostling, 1988b, 1988c). According to leaders in the evangelical community (ABC news, 1987a, 1987b, 1987c; Newhouse news, 1987; Ostling, 1988a), these activities have tarnished the image of the nation's most high-profile televangelists and their ministries. A recent Gallup poll of 1,026 Americans found that only "some" or "very little" of evangelical programming was said to be trustworthy. The survey concluded that "there have been extravagances and questionable tactics, and surely this has soured people's attitudes toward giving [contributions] and toward Christianity" (Ostling, 1987c, p. 70).

Evidence to this effect can be found in the televangelists' declaration of diminished offerings from the televiewing audience.[2] Jimmy Swaggart himself reported a $1.5–1.8 million decline per month; Robert Schuller, whose "Hour of Power" is carried by 172 TV stations, showed a 3% dip in donations in 1987. Jerry Falwell's income for the months immediately following the PTL scandal was $6 million less than projections. In one 7-month period, CBN revenues fell 32.5% compared with the same time in 1986 (Ostling, 1988a). "The 700 Club" in particular announced that donations were down 33% since the scandal (Ostling, 1987a) and, as a result, laid off 500 employees in June 1987.

This suggests the possibility that many viewers of "The 700 Club," a large, conservative, and traditionally supportive constituency, have abandoned Robertson in the wake of scandal within the televangelical community. Despite his repeated claims that he is "not a televangelist" (e.g., Alter, 1988; Martz, 1988), it is likely that Robertson's audience has not distinguished between the candidate and the television preacher. This chapter explores the impact of the PTL scandal on viewers' perceptions of televangelists in an effort to best explain the demise of Robertson's presidential candidacy.

---

[2]These figures are, of course, suspect due to the tax exempt status of televangelists which encourages financial unaccountability. Only a handful of the most popular televangelists are volunteer members of the Evangelical Council for Financial Accountability, Washington, DC.

THE VIEWERS OF THE "THE 700 CLUB"

Historically, analyses of the religious televiewing audience have concluded that it can be characterized succinctly as demographically downscale, older, and more religious than the average American (Dennis, 1962; Gaddy, 1984; Gerbner, Gross, Hoover, Morgan, & Signorielli, 1984; Parker, Barry, & Smyth, 1955). However, recent uses-and-gratifications research by Abelman (1988a) interrelated viewing patterns, viewing motivations, and demographic characteristics of high consumers of "The 700 Club," and found three distinctive types of television viewers.

The first type of viewer, representing approximately 52% of "The 700 Club" audience, engages in the *instrumental* use of religious television—that is, the viewing of informational programming and the viewing of entertainment programming for its informational content. This type of viewer is younger and better educated than the research previously cited has suggested. Although rating fairly high on religiosity—the importance of religion in one's life—religious conviction or expression is not a primary motivation for viewing "The 700 Club." General viewing preferences include religious programs that have adopted commercial television's informational programming formats (e.g., news, talk shows, game shows) and informational programming indigenous to religious broadcasting (e.g., Bible studies, sermons).

The second type of viewer extracted from this investigation, *ritualized* users of religious television, habitually use television and engage in extremely high levels of consumption. These viewers are highly religious, actively involved in church activities, watch television largely out of faith and religious conviction, and show a strong preference for and affinity toward evangelical programming in general and televised church services in particular. Of "The 700 Club" audience, 38% is best classified as ritualized viewers and fit within the traditional description of religious television viewers—older, poorer, and less educated than the average American.

The third type of viewer, the *reactionary* consumer, watches religious television as a result of a general dissatisfaction with secular television programming. Although the least religious and least active in church activities of the three types of viewers, the reactionary viewer (10% of the audience) seeks the spiritual guidance and moral support not typically found in programming on the commercial networks. Motivated also by a strong sense of curiosity, this type of viewer purposefully selects "The 700 Club" as an interesting viewing alternative.

These findings and other uses-and-gratifications-based examinations of the viewers of religious fare (e.g., Abelman, 1987, 1988c, 1989; Buddenbaum, 1981), secular genre (e.g., Carveth & Alexander, 1985; Compesi, 1980; Rubin, 1981, 1985), and television in general (e.g., Eastman, 1979; Kippax

& Murray, 1980; Rubin, 1983, 1984; Rubin & Rubin, 1982) support Katz'
(1959) suggestion that "people's values, their interests, their associations,
their social roles, are pre-potent and that people selectively 'fashion' what
they see and hear to those interests" (p. 2). Unfortunately, they do not
necessarily shed light on how particular motives influence the processing of
information and the corresponding effects that might occur. Indeed, Swanson
(1987b) has suggested that "the most interesting and important single question
confronting gratifications research at present involves understanding how
audience members' motives guide their interpretation of media messages"
(p. 345). In particular, according to Garramone (1985):

> The impact of motives on the processing (i.e., encoding, storing, decoding) of
> political information has been virtually ignored, as has the influence of motives on
> the utilization of political information in candidate evaluation. . . . The focus of
> gratifications research on the acquisition of political information has inhibited the
> investigation of the *interaction* of motives and message characteristics. (p. 202)

In recent years, a growing body of research has addressed this issue and
confirms the interrelationship between viewing motivations, media exposure,
interpretive processing of information, and corresponding effects (e.g., Palmgreen, Weener, & Rosengren, 1985; Rosengren, Weener, & Palmgreen,
1985). According to this work, cognitive schemata, or interpretive frames,
are established as a result of our social experience and are instrumental in our
interpretations of future encounters. These schemata reflect the particular
motivations that lead audience members to attend to a message, feature a
central focus that organizes and gives coherence to the message, direct attention to specific aspects of content that seem relevant to those initial motives
while obscuring others, and subsequently describe how messages provide the
desired gratification.

To date, two motives for attending political information—to form an
impression of candidate personal qualities and to learn candidate issue positions—have been found to result in different information processing behavior.
According to investigations by Ebbesen, Cohen, and Lane (1975); Cohen
and Ebbesen (1979); Garramone (1983); and others, issue-motivated persons
would attend to, encode, and recall more issue information from political
messages than would impression-motivated persons. This motive would activate a schema of rather concrete and specific issue-relevant attributes and
their interrelationships. Impression-motivated persons, on the other hand,
would more likely attend and base their inferences on the candidate's general
traits and characteristics. Consequently, when exposed to the same media
information, viewers with divergent motives for consumption process this
information in demonstrably different ways. This, in turn, may lead to corres-

pondingly different reactions and highly diversified effects (Blumler, Gure-vitch, & Katz, 1985; Swanson, 1977, 1987a).

Regarding religious television viewers' perceptions of religious fare before the PTL scandal, it is possible that each of the three distinctive types of viewers that comprise "The 700 Club" audience would "fashion" their viewing according to their unique viewing motivations. It is expected that viewer perceptions of the credibility of TV preachers in general and Pat Robertson in particular, as well as the perceived importance of these individuals, are likely to be quite different, although no doubt supportive.

In addition, information regarding the PTL scandal is likely to be utilized by the three types of viewers of religious television in significantly different ways and, thus, have a different impact on their perceptions of televangelists and then-presidential candidate Robertson. According to Garramone (1985), all motives identified by gratifications researchers are relevant to political communication and may influence schema choice: "motives to form an impres-sion of candidate personal qualities, learn candidate issue stands, acquire information for political discussion, enjoy the excitement of an election, and satisfy personal identity motives may each activate a particular type of schema" (p. 205).

Regarding the information-seeking instrumental user of religious fare—the viewer most reflective of the issue-motivated person identified by Ebbesen and his colleagues (1975)—it is likely that they would attend to, encode, and recall more concrete and specific issue information from reports of the PTL scandal (e.g., economic and political ramifications). Consequently, it is ex-pected that the level of perceived personal importance, and credibility of televangelists in general and Robertson in particular, would decrease. Their viewership is largely dependent on religious television serving as a reliable source of accurate information. The scandal, which involved the withholding, distortion, and manufacturing of information by the Bakkers, the PTL organi-zation, and other members of the televangelical community (e.g., Falwell, Swaggart, Ankerberg), will likely diminish the instrumental viewers' belief that religious television can serve as a viable information source. Although Robertson had managed to stay fairly clear of the scandal and publicly insisted that he is not a televangelist, his participation and leadership in religious broadcasting is likely to trigger schema associated with the scandal. This, in turn, will generate a perception of guilt by association.

To the contrary, it is expected that ritualized viewers—those most closely aligned with the impression-motivated persons identified by Ebbesen and his colleagues (1975)—would reflect an increase in an already high level of perceived credibility and personal importance. This form of viewership is primarily motivated by a strong sense of religiosity; a form of religious convic-tion that has been classified as a composite of "blind faith and Christian Charity" (see Fore, 1987). Because these viewers are more likely to "base their inferences of the actor's traits on prior assumptions" rather than concrete aspects of his or her behavior (Garramone, 1985, p. 205), it is likely that religiosity will direct their attention to aspects of PTL scandal information most pertinent to religion rather than politics. General impressions of tele-vangelists and Pat Robertson will form accordingly.

In support of this assumption, and as an example of Christian Charity at work, it has been found that ritualized viewers have already forgiven many of those associated with the PTL scandal. Although they "have become more selective in regard to the recipients of their [donations]," ritualized viewers "are demonstrating their support through an increase in the size and frequency of contributions" (Abelman, 1988b, pp. 33–34). This also suggests that some televangelists have not been incriminated by this segment of the audience. Because Robertson was neither directly involved in the activities that resulted in the PTL scandal nor instrumental in the uncovering of the scandal, he stands a good chance of surfacing unscathed in the eyes of this viewership.

Reactionary users—those who watch largely out of curiosity and in search of an interesting viewing alternative—have not been identified in audience research outside of the confines of religious fare and the uses-and-gratifications approach. Consequently, there is little by which to base expectations of viewer reaction to the PTL scandal. However, if it is true that individuals attend to and encode the selected aspects of information that are particularly relevant to their goals (see Cohen & Ebbesen, 1979; Garramone, 1985; Jeffery & Mischel, 1979), then reactionary users will only show an increase in the perceived personal importance of televangelists in general. Their goal is *not* the fulfillment of religious conviction or the pursuit of accurate information but, rather, the satisfaction of curiosity in the form of interesting television fare. It is quite likely that the consumption of PTL scandal information will neither activate schema associated with religion nor politics, but those associated with the entertainment aspects of religious programming. The fact that these viewers possess a low level of affinity for "The 700 Club" and its host (Abelman, 1988a) further supports this expectation.

METHODS

The sample was randomly drawn from a population of cable subscribers ($N = 5,000$) in a midwestern community. Of these subscribers, those who had access to the Christian Broadcasting Network, were regular viewers (at least three times a week) of "The 700 Club," and who were identified through daily diaries as having religious television programming comprise 50% or more of their total television viewing diet, were selected. Questionnaires were administered by trained interviewers to 679 people in February 1987 (prior to reports leading to the PTL scandal)[3] and again in May 1987 (in the aftermath of the takeover of PTL by Jerry Falwell and ousting of the Bakkers).[4] Completing the first survey were 597 individuals (response rate = 87.9%), with 100% retention rate for the second survey.

This criterion for high consumers of religious fare is consistent with the research literature (Gerbner et al., 1984; Horsfield, 1984), as is the demographic composition of the sample. The number of different religious programs viewed by the sample ranged from two to seven ($M = 3.8$, $SD = 2.2$). Respondents ranged in age from 26 to 77 ($M = 57.87$, $SD = 11.61$), were primarily female (65.2%) and Black (53.9%). All of those in the sample had read, seen, or heard information pertaining to the PTL scandal at the time of the second data collection.

Television-user motivations (e.g., information, entertainment, faith, habit, escape) and viewing patterns (e.g., religious and secular program consumption levels, program and medium affinity levels) were assessed and interrelated,[5] resulting in the extraction of three significant canonical roots identifying instrumental (51.9%), ritualized (37.8%), and reactionary (10.3%) viewers of religious television.[6] Also included in the questionnaire were indi-

---

[3]Results from this first data collection, not included in this chapter, were reported in Abelman (1987) and Abelman and Hoover (1990). The research presented here is a comparison of this collective data set and that of the follow-up survey to the same sample (100% retention). Classification as ritualized, instrumental, and reactionary viewers of religious television did not change from data-collection points. In other words, the viewing patterns and motivations of the religious televiewing audience did not change; this investigation assesses changes in attitudes toward religious television and televangelists.

[4]The first wave of data occurred 5 months after Robertson's first public and official announcement of his intentions to run as a presidential candidate for the Republican Party (Robertson, 1986b). The second wave of data collection occurred 4 months prior to Robertson's formal declaration that he would seek the Presidency of the United States (Robertson, 1987).

[5]Many of the procedures and items used to access "types" of religious television viewers were modified versions of those employed by Rubin and Rubin (1982) and by Rubin (1983) in response to his encouragement that scholars "conduct modified replications or extensions of [uses-and-gratifications] studies, to refine methodology, to comparatively analyze the findings of separate investigations" (p. 38). Some items were altered to reflect the unique television content and viewing audience examined in this study. Research reporting the items and mean responses for the extraction of ritualized, reactionary, and instrumental viewers is reported in Abelman (1987).

[6]Patterns of viewing motives were determined by intercorrelating the items and conducting a principal factor analysis with oblique rotation. Oblique rotation was performed because viewing motives were interrelated. Eigenvalues of at least one and a minimum of three primary loadings of .40 or greater (and no secondary loadings above .30 on any other factors) served as the criteria. The factor solution, which identified six factors (reaction, information, entertainment, faith, habit, escape), explained 52.8% of the total variance. Pearson product-moment correlations were computed to examine the interrelationships among television viewing motives. The analytical tool utilized to examine the multivariate associations between viewing motives and viewing patterns was canonical correlation. To reduce possible misinterpretations that might result from multicollinearity, structure coefficients were computed by summing the product of canonical

ces of perceived credibility and personal importance of the televangelical community, and questions pertaining to the perceived credibility and personal importance of Pat Robertson in particular. The potential impact of the PTL scandal was assessed through a comparison of the first and second administration of the questionnaire to the sample.

Televangelist Credibility.   Six statements formed a summated televangelist credibility index. Statements included: "TV preachers' practice what they preach"; "TV preachers' interpretation of the Bible is consistent with the interpretation held by their particular denomination (e.g., Evangelical, Fundamentalist, Pentacostal, Charismatic)"; "TV preachers are doing God's work"; "TV preachers can talk directly to God and create miracles, if that is what they claim"; "TV preachers are good Christians"; and "When a TV preacher requests financial contributions from his audience for various causes/ missions, those requests are justified." Responses were coded so that a "5" indicated a high level and "1" a low level of credibility. The credibility index had a .72 Cronbach alpha reliability coefficient.

Robertson's Credibility.   The same six statements, with the substitution of "Pat Robertson" for "TV preachers," formed a summated Robertson credibility index. This index had a .78 Cronbach alpha reliability coefficient.

Personal Importance—Televangelists.   Five statements, representing respondents' perceptions of the importance of televangelists in their lives, formed a summated religious television personal importance index. Statements included: "Watching TV evangelists is one of the more important things I do each day"; "If religious television featuring evangelical leaders were no longer available, I would really miss it"; "Watching TV preachers is very important to me"; "I could easily do without watching televangelists on religious television programming for several days"; and "I would feel lost without televangelists on religious programming to watch." Responses were coded so that a "5" indicated a high level and "1" a low level of perceived importance. Items that comprise the personal importance index were highly reliable (.89 Cronbach alpha reliability coefficient).

Personal Importance—Pat Robertson.   The same five statements, with the substitution of "Pat Robertson" for "TV preacher," "televangelist" and "evangelical leader," formed a summated Robertson importance index. This index had a .82 Cronbach alpha reliability coefficient.

---

loadings and standardized scores of the variables for each set (Levine, 1977). The canonical correlation extracted three roots significant at .001—reactionary, ritualized, and instrumental.

TABLE 8.1
Pre-Scandal Perceptions by Type of Viewer

	n	M	F-value	p<
Evangelists' credibility			13.07	.001
Instrumental	310	3.91[a]		
Ritualized	226	4.37[a]		
Reactionary	61	3.09[a]		
Robertson's credibility			4.12	.05
Instrumental	310	4.27[a]		
Ritualized	226	4.41[b]		
Reactionary	61	3.93[ab]		
Personal importance			11.54	.001
Instrumental	310	3.88[a]		
Ritualized	226	4.26[a]		
Reactionary	61	3.51[a]		
Robertson's personal importance			3.09	.05
Instrumental	310	4.11[a]		
Ritualized	226	4.34[b]		
Reactionary	61	3.59[ab]		

Note: Means with common superscripts differ significantly at the .05 level. Possible scores ranged from 1 to 5 for each index.

RESULTS

The first expected outcome, which predicted a differential perception of the credibility and personal importance of televangelists and Pat Robertson in particular across the three types of religious television viewers, was supported (see Table 8.1). Three significant differences in viewers' perceptions of the credibility of televangelists were revealed, between instrumental and ritualized viewers, between ritualized and reactionary viewers, and between instrumental and reactionary viewers.[7] A significant difference in perceived credibility of Pat Robertson and type of viewer was also found, with two significant differences—between instrumental and reactionary viewers, and between ritualized and reactionary viewers.[8] As expected, a significant difference in perceived personal importance of televangelists and type of viewer was found as well, with three significant differences among the viewers. The differences were between instrumental and ritualized viewers, between ritualized and

---

[7]Analysis of variance revealed significant differences in perceived televangelist credibility and type of viewer [$F(3, 585) = 13.07, p < .001$].

[8]Analysis of variance revealed significant differences in the perceived credibility of Pat Robertson [$F(3, 589) = 4.12, p < .05$].

TABLE 8.2
Differences in Viewer's Pre- and Post-Scandal Perceptions
(Cross-Lagged Coefficients[a])

Dependent Variables	Instrumental Beta n=310	Ritualized Beta n=226	Reactionary Beta n=61
Evangelists' credibility	−.085	.042	−.012
Robertson's credibility	−.078	.017	.021
Personal importance	−.062	.063	.038
Robertson's importance	−.067	.021	−.003

[a]Note: All underlined coefficients are significant at .05 (one-tailed, corrected for design effect).

reactionary viewers, and between instrumental and reactionary viewers.[9] Finally, a significant difference in perceived personal importance of Pat Robertson and type of viewer was found, revealing significant differences between instrumental and reactionary viewers, and between ritualized and reactionary viewers.[10]

The remaining expected outcomes were concerned with the type and direction of change in perception of credibility and personal importance of televangelists and Pat Robertson, from before and after the PTL scandal. As Table 8.2 indicates, the cross-lagged, standardized partial regression coefficients provide partial support for these hypotheses.

A comparison of the three types of viewers indicates that instrumental viewing is negatively related to increased perceptions of credibility and importance of televangelists in general and Robertson in particular, as anticipated. Ritualized viewing is positively related to the expected increase in perceptions of the credibility and importance of televangelists; the difference between these viewers' perceptions of Robertson's credibility and his importance in their lives is not significant. Reactionary viewing is positively related to personal importance of televangelists only; the remaining coefficients are not statistically significant.

SUMMARY AND DISCUSSION

The results of this investigation lend further support for the interrelatedness of television-use motives and information processing, and offer a case study of the implications of the divergent forms of viewership that have been extracted from "The 700 Club" audience. Findings suggest that information

[9]Analysis of variance revealed significant differences in perceived personal importance of televangelists [$F(3, 585) = 11.54, p < .001$].

[10]Analysis of variance revealed significant differences in perceived personal importance of Pat Robertson [$F(3, 589) = 3.09, p < .05$].

regarding the PTL scandal was utilized, processed and, consequently, effected the different types of viewers in significantly different ways. The largest contingency of viewers, the instrumental users of religious fare, had apparently lost its faith in the entirety of the televangelical population, including Pat Robertson. Although its pre-scandal perceptions of the televangelical community was relatively indistinguishable from those held by the highly religious ritualized viewers, media coverage of the PTL scandal appears to have provided sufficient information to quench the primary motivation for watching religious fare for the instrumental viewer—the search for accurate information presented by a reliable source.

It should be noted that there was no direct measure of these viewers' involvement in the New Christian Right movement or the extent of their political activity. However, their demographic composition is most comparable to that identified as Robertson viewers and political supporters by Wills (1988). Their motivations for viewing suggest that they are also likely to be the most informed viewers of "The 700 Club," which further describes Robertson's core constituency (Martz, 1988). Consequently, the significant decrease in their perceived personal importance and credibility of Robertson could certainly not have helped his cause. If these viewers do constitute a portion of Robertson's "invisible army" of evangelical supporters, then the findings reported here suggest that they were also a silent army in the voting booth.

The highly religious ritualized users of "The 700 Club" demonstrated an increase in the perceived personal importance of televangelists and in their credibility, thus maintaining and strengthening their faith in religious broadcasting as a whole. In addition, there was no significant change in an already high level of perceived importance of Pat Robertson. Similarly, there was no change in these viewers' perceptions of his credibility from before to after the PTL scandal. It has also been suggested (Kalette, 1988, p. 1A) that the highly religious viewers of evangelical fare will "probably prove amazingly forgiving" of Swaggart's confessions of sin as well. If these viewers are politically active, then it can be assumed that their voting behavior will not be negatively influenced by the recent demise of Bakker and Swaggart. If they are not members of Robertson's "invisible army," there is no indication from the findings reported here that the PTL scandal has inspired them to join up.

Regarding the reactionary viewer, perceptions of low-to-moderate credibility of televangelists (including Robertson), as well as their perceptions of Robertson's limited personal importance, did not change significantly over the course of the PTL scandal. However, increased perceptions of the personal importance of televangelists as a whole were evident. It should be noted that there is ample evidence that the PTL scandal generated a perception of newfound importance among the secular audience as well. Overnight ratings from the A. C. Nielsen Company indicated that the April 28 airing of CNN's "Larry King Live" scored its highest rating ever—and the second highest of any CNN telecast—when it narrowcasted an interview with new PTL leader Jerry Falwell. On May 27, ABC's "Nightline" presented a 72-minute interview with the Bakkers, which drew the most viewers in the 8-year history of the program (Stilson, 1987). The increase in reactionary viewers' report of personal importance of televangelists is likely a ramification of the same curiosity that has generated boosted ratings of these secular informational programs. Indeed, it is quite clear that these viewers attended to and encoded the selected aspects of PTL scandal information that were particularly relevant to their goals—curiosity satisfaction and entertainment acquisition. Although this investigation did not ascertain the level of political activity of this segment of Robertson's viewing audience, it is most likely that the PTL scandal did nothing to alter their voting behavior or preferences.

According to Garry Wills (1988), Professor of American Culture and Public Policy at Northwestern University:

> The signs of moral revolt have been there for some time. The Equal Rights Amendment was defeated because its foes could portray it as weakening the family. The Democrats have their moralists of the family, Jesse Jackson making it part of his political program to stop "babies making babies." Edward Kennedy and Gary Hart have been rejected as political leaders because of their failure as family men. (p. 27)

This investigation suggests that the immoral behavior of religious television's most highly successful and popular televangelists, or rather the media's coverage of this behavior, has negatively influenced viewer perceptions of Pat Robertson's credibility and importance by over half of his televiewing audience. Although ritualized viewers' positive impressions and perceptions of Robertson have not changed in the wake of the PTL scandal, they represent little more than one third of Pat Robertson's followers. Consequently, it is clear that the "core group of about 20% of those eligible to vote that is highly receptive to Robertson's evangelical message and can be mobilized" (Wills, 1988, p. 28) has been significantly reduced.

REFERENCES

A. C. Nielsen. (1987). *Year-end report*. Chicago, IL: Author.

Abelman, R. (1987). Religious television uses and gratifications. *Journal of Broadcasting & Electronic Media, 31*(3), 293–307.

Abelman, R., (1988a). Motivations for viewing "The 700 Club." *Journalism Quarterly, 65*(1), 112–118, 164.

Abelman, R. (1988b). Financial support for religious television: The impact of the PTL scandal. *Journal of Media Economics, 1*(1), 23–38.

Abelman, R. (1988c). The allure of religious television. *Critical Studies in Mass Communication,* 5(3), 259–265.

Abelman, R. (1989). "PTL club" viewer uses and gratifications. *Communication Quarterly,* 37(1), 54–66.

Abelman, R., & Hoover, S. (Eds.). (1990). *Religious television: Controversies and conclusions.* Norwood, NJ: Ablex.

Abelman, R., & Neuendorf, K. (1985). How religious is religious television programming? *Journal of Communication,* 35(1), 98–110.

Abelman, R., & Pettey, G. (1988). How political is religious television programming? *Journalism Quarterly,* 65(2), 311–317.

Alter, J. (1988, February 22). Pat Robertson: The telepolitician. *Newsweek,* pp. 18–19.

American Broadcasting Company. (1987a). Transcripts of "Nightline" Show #1520 (March 23). New York: Journal Graphics.

American Broadcasting Company. (1987b). Transcripts of "Nightline" Show #1521 (March 24). New York: Journal Graphics.

American Broadcasting Company. (1987c). Transcripts of "Nightline" Show #1523 (March 26). New York: Journal Graphics.

Blumler, J. G., Gurevitch, M., & Katz, E. (1985). Reaching out: A future for gratification research. In K. E. Rosengren, L. A. Weener, & P. Palmgreen (Eds.), *Media gratifications research: Current perspectives* (pp. 255–273). Beverly Hills, CA: Sage.

Bromley, D., & Shupe, A. (1984). *New Christian politics.* Macon, GA: Mercer University Press.

Buddenbaum, J. (1981). Characteristics and media related needs of the audience of religious TV. *Journalism Quarterly,* 51, 266–272.

Carey, J. (1985). Christian right aims votes at new targets. *U.S. News & World Report,* 99, p. 70.

Carveth, R. A., & Alexander, A. (1985). Soap opera viewing motivations and the cultivation process. *Journal of Broadcasting & Electronic Media,* 29(3), 259–273.

Castelli, J. (1988, Spring). The Evangelical vote. *Forum: The Newsletter of People For The American Way Action Fund,* p. 8.

Cohen, C. E., & Ebbesen, E. B. (1979). Observational goals and schema activation: A theoretical framework for behavioral perception. *Journal of Experimental Social Psychology,* 15, 305–329.

Compesi, R. J. (1980). Gratifications of daytime TV serial viewers. *Journalism Quarterly,* 57, 155–158.

Dennis, J. L. (1962). *An analysis of the audience of religious radio and television programs in the Detroit metropolitan area.* Unpublished doctoral dissertation, University of Michigan, Ann Arbor, MI.

Detwiller, T. (1988). Viewing Robertson's rhetoric in an Augustinian mirror. *Journal of Communication and Religion,* 11(1), 22–31.

Eastman, S. (1979). Uses of television viewing and consumer life styles. *Journal of Broadcasting,* 23, 491–500.

Ebbesen, E. B., Cohen, C. E., & Lane, J. L. (1975, August). *Encoding and construction processes in person perception.* Paper presented at the American Psychological Association Convention, Chicago, IL.

Fore, W. F. (1987). *Television and religion: The shaping of faith, values and culture.* Minneapolis, MN: Augsburg Publishing.

Frankl, R. (1987). *Televangelism: The marketing of popular religion.* Carbondale, IL: Southern Illinois University Press.

Gaddy, G. D. (1984). The power of the religious media: Religious broadcast use and the role of religious organizations in public affairs. *Review of Religious Research,* 25(4), 289–301.

Garramone, G. M. (1983). Issues versus image orientation and effects on political advertising. *Communication Research,* 10, 59–76.

Garramone, G. M. (1985). Motivation and political information processing: Extending the gratifications approach. In S. Kraus & R. Perloff (Eds.), Mass media and political thought: An information-processing approach (pp. 201–219). Beverly Hills, CA: Sage.

Gerbner, G., Gross, L., Hoover, S., Morgan, M., & Signorielli, N. (1984). Religion and television. Philadelphia, PA: University of Pennsylvania Press.

Hackett, G. (1987, April 6). It isn't the first time. Newsweek, p. 23.

Hadden, J., & Shupe, A. (1988). Televangelism, power and politics. New York: Holt.

Hadden, J., & Swann, C. E. (1981). Prime time preachers. Reading, MA: Addison-Wesley.

Hoover, S. (1985). The "700 Club" as religion and as television: A study of reasons and effects. Unpublished doctoral dissertation, The University of Pennsylvania, University Park, PA.

Hoover, S. (1989). Mass media religion: The social sources of the electronic church. Beverly Hills, CA: Sage.

Horsfield, P. G. (1984). Religious television: An American experience. New York: Longman.

Jeffery, K. M., & Mischel, W. (1979). Effects of purpose on the organization and recall of information in person perception. Journal of Personality, 47, 397–419.

Johnson, S. D., & Tamney, J. B. (1985). The Christian right and the 1984 presidential election. Review of Religious Research, 27(2), 124–133.

Kalette, D. (1988, February 23). Swaggart's "repentance" key to revival. USA Today, pp. 1–2a.

Katz, E. (1959). Mass communication research and the study of culture. Studies in Public Communication, 2, 1–6.

Kippax, S., & Murray, J. P. (1980). Using the media: Need gratification and perceived reality. Communication Research, 7, 335–360.

Levine, M. S. (1977). Canonical analysis and factor comparison. Beverly Hills, CA: Sage.

Mann, J., & Petersen, S. (1980, September 15). Preachers in politics: Decisive force in 1980? U.S. News & World Report, pp. 24–26.

Mashsek, J. W. (1986, July 14). From pulpit to podium, a forceful presence. U.S. News & World Report, pp. 24–25.

Martz, L. (1987, April 6). God and money. Newsweek, pp. 16–22.

Martz, L. (1988, March 7). Day of the preachers. Newsweek, pp. 44–46.

Mayer, A. J. (1980, September 15). A tide of born again politics? Newsweek, pp. 28–36.

Newhouse News Service. (1987, March 26). "Dark days for church," leaders say. Plain Dealer, p. 2a.

Ostling, R. (1986, February 12). Power, glory—and politics. Time, pp. 62–69.

Ostling, R. (1987a, March 30). A really bad day at Fort Mill. Time, pp. 62–69.

Ostling, R. (1987b, April 6). TV's unholy row. Time, pp. 60–67.

Ostling, R. (1987c, June 8). Of God and greed. Time, pp. 70–74.

Ostling, R. (1988a, February 15). Cleaning up their act. Time, p. 95.

Ostling, R. (1988b, March 7). Day of the preachers. Time, pp. 46–48.

Ostling, R. (1988c, April 11). Worshippers on a holy roll. Time, p. 55.

Palmgreen, P., Weener, L. A., & Rosengren, K. E. (1985). Uses and gratifications research: The past ten years. In K. E. Rosengren, L. A. Weener, & P. Palmgreen (Eds.), Media gratifications research: Current perspectives (pp. 11–37). Beverly Hills, CA: Sage.

Parker, E. C., Barry, D. W., & Smyth, D. W. (1955). The television-radio audience and religion. New York: Harper & Row.

Pierand, R. V. (1985). Religion and the 1984 election campaign. Review of Religious Research, 27(2), 98–114.

Press, A. (1987, May 11). Will those cards and letters keep coming? Newsweek, p. 72.

Rifkin, J., & Howard, T. (1979). The emerging order. New York: G. P. Putnam's Sons.

Robertson, P. (1986a, June). "The 700 Club" (Recording no. 157–86). Virginia Beach, VA: CBN Center, The Christian Broadcasting Network.

Robertson, P. (1986b, September). New conference (Recording no. 86). Washington, DC: C-Span Network Inc.

Robertson, P. (1987, September). *Road to the White House: Pat Robertson* (Recording no. 86). Washington, DC: C-Span Network Inc.

Rosengren, K. E., Weener, L. A., & Palmgreen, P. (Eds.). (1985). *Media gratifications research: Current perspectives.* Beverly Hills, CA: Sage.

Rubin, A. M. (1981). A multivariate analysis of "60 Minutes" viewing motivations. *Journalism Quarterly, 58,* 529–534.

Rubin, A. M. (1983). Television uses and gratifications: The interactions of viewing patterns and motivations. *Journal of Broadcasting, 27,* 37–51.

Rubin, A. M. (1984). Ritualized and instrumental television viewing. *Journal of Communication, 34*(3), 67–77.

Rubin, A. M. (1985). Uses of daytime television soap operas by college students. *Journal of Broadcasting & Electronic Media, 29*(3), 241–258.

Rubin, A. M., & Rubin, R. B. (1982). Older persons' TV viewing patterns and motivations. *Communication Research, 9,* 287–313.

Shapiro, W. (1988, January 18). Bush bites back. *Time,* pp. 42–43.

Stacks, J. F. (1988, March 21). Dwarfs no more. *Time,* pp. 12–13.

Stilson, J. (1987, June 1). Ratings high: The Bakkers are a hot draw on TV interview programs. *Electronic Media, 6*(22), pp. 1, 39.

Swanson, D. L. (1977). The uses and misuses of uses and gratifications. *Human Communication Research, 3,* 214–211.

Swanson, D. L. (1987a). Gratification seeking, media exposure, and audience interpretations: Some directions for research. *Journal of Broadcasting & Electronic Media, 31*(3), 237–254.

Swanson, D. L. (1987b). Review of "Media gratifications research: Current perspectives." *Journal of Broadcasting & Electronic Media, 31*(3), 343–345.

Watson, R. (1987a, May 11). Fresh out of miracles. *Newsweek,* pp. 70–72.

Watson, R. (1987b, June 8). Heaven can wait. *Newsweek,* pp. 58–65.

Wills, G. (1988, February 22). Robertson and the Reagan gap. *Time,* pp. 27–28.

9 | Sex Differences in Political Information Processing: An MDS Approach to Lateralization Predictors

Gary R. Pettey
Diane Brigliadoro
Cleveland State University

As early as 1836, Marc Dax was speculating that individuals may store and process verbal information primarily in one hemisphere of the brain. By 1864, Paul Broca (cited in Critchley, 1970) elaborated the argument by providing evidence that the left hemisphere of the brain usually controlled the speech function. He also studied the relationship between brain asymmetry and hand preference. Evidence presented by modern medical researchers points to hemispheric preferences for information (Geschwind and Galaburda, 1984). Studies of brain injury, split brains, and differential stimulation of brain hemispheres point toward different preferences for the processing of information (LeDoux, Wilson, & Gazzaniga, 1977; Nebes, 1978).

In the realm of information processing, and especially schema theory, scholars have asked: "How do people select and process information for incorporation into their thinking and what kinds of patterns do they impose on the information so that it will fit into established belief structures?" (Graber, 1984, p. 5). The development of political schema (or arguably any schematic structure) can be thought of as a matter of selecting information for incorporation. Because all individuals do not hold or value the same information concerning any given subject, it seems likely that we must have preferences for certain types of information that can be most efficiently processed. Here we are concerned with nonexperimental evidence that what has been referred to as the individual's hemispheric brain dominance may be descriptive of the way he or she schematically structures and processes political information.

BACKGROUND

Lateralization

Halpern (1986) cited Geschwind's definition of what hemispheric dominance means: "One hemisphere may be said to be dominant for a given function when it is more important for the performance of that function than the other hemisphere" (1977, p. 9).[1] Halpern noted that dominance is not an either/ or division of tasks: "It means instead that one half of the brain is more or less specialized or proficient in its ability to process certain types of stimuli" (p. 78). The suggestion that a particular hemisphere of the brain may process information differently, or the limitation of a stimulus to only one hemisphere, is referred to as *lateralization*.

The scientific discussions over the anatomical distinctions and processing differences due to laterality are not conclusive. Whether or not they eventually prove to be the case, the conceptual notion of individuals having a predisposition toward preferences in the information they choose to process, or preferences in the manner in which they process, the information selected is germane to researchers concerned with questions of information processing. For purposes of this chapter, then, we assume the validity of lateralization.

Task Specialty in Lateralization

Broca's (1864) postmortem examinations in the early 19th century suggested that the left temporal lobe of the brain was crucial for language function. Broca's argument that "the hemisphere controlling speech is opposite to the preferred hand was influential well into the twentieth century" (Springer & Deutsch, 1985, p. 11). More recent studies disclosed that the right temporal lobe appears to be essential to one's ability to recognize faces, learn mazes, and succeed in other spacial tasks (Benton, 1980; Milner, 1965).

Damage to the left brain often results in speech difficulty. For most people, the left hemisphere is the seat of speech, and this region of the brain appears to be highly specialized for this function. Some people with extreme left brain damage cannot move any of the right side of their bodies and cannot speak,

---

[1]There are physical differences in the brain hemispheres. The brain is divided into two complete halves joined by a bridge called the *corpus callosum*. Even a crude examination of the two halves of the brain shows differences. The folds in the left half generally go more vertically, whereas folds in the right brain are more horizontal (Geschwind & Galaburda, 1984). Geschwind and Levitsky (1968) examined 100 postmortem brains. They found that 65% of the brains had longer temporal planes in the left hemisphere, 11% had longer right temporal planes and 24% showed no difference. The temporal plane forms the upper surface of the temporal lobe and is considered part of Wernicke's area, a region concerned with language (Springer & Deutsch, 1985).

but sometimes they can sing certain songs or hymns. Music is "located" in the right brain.

Damage to the right hemisphere is often less noticed. The functioning in the right side appears to be more diffuse, often resulting in problems of perception, attention and in speech intonation. Ronald Reagan's press secretary, James Brady, is a good example of a person who has suffered damage of the right side of the brain. Although the damage from Hinckley's bullet was extensive enough to affect his general motor skills and slur his speech, it had much less impact on his verbal abilities because Brady's center of speech is in his left brain.

The right hemisphere appears to be the preferred processing site for spatial skills. Right-lateralized people seem to be able to more easily mentally rotate images than left-dominant individuals. The sides of the body are controlled primarily by the other side of the brain, and left handedness is one indication of right brain dominance. The department of neurology at the Harvard Medical School and Boston University of Medicine reported that left handers disproportionately occur in certain occupations where spatial abilities such as depth perception, mental rotation of objects, and cognitive mapping are essential (e.g., artists, architects, engineers, and professional athletes) (Harshman, Hampson, & Berenbaum, 1983).

Springer and Deutsch (1983) remind us, however, that

> Attentional factors may play a role in producing asymmetry in behavior. It is also clear that difference between the hemispheres go beyond the kinds of stimuli they are best equipped to deal with . . . we see that basic differences lie in the *processing strategies* of each hemisphere. (p. 91, italics added)

Such preferences in using one hemisphere over the other may be descriptive of what researchers often refer to as *cognitive styles*. Such differences in cognitive preferences should predict differences in the manner in which information is processed and evaluated by individuals. Individuals with inductive, holistic preferences may process and store information with the "big picture" in mind. Individuals who prefer to process more deductively should tend to see more interconnections, and see discrepancies in the "big picture," finding it less useful.

Information Processing

Within cognitive psychology, information processing centering on schema formation and maintenance has offered new opportunities for considering how information is selected and stored. Fiske and Taylor (1984) define *schema* as "a cognitive structure that represents organized knowledge about a given concept or type of stimulus. A schema contains the attributes of the concept and the relationship among the attributes" (p. 140). These authors noted that schema are formed either deductively or inductively and that researchers are primarily concerned with top-down processing strategies (or organization of information based on prior conceptual understanding). This is the case, presumably, because the bottom-up strategies (or data-driven schema) are probably constructed largely as an analogy to some similar organization already present in the structure (Shapiro, 1986).

Taylor and Winkler (1980) outlined the schema formation process in four steps. The first is the introduction of specific concrete knowledge: the second orders the most representative attributes; the third, which few reach, is the awareness of incongruities in the data (i.e., words an understanding of where the conceptual model, upon which the schema was based, breaks down); finally, the schema becomes highly integrated with tightly linked internal paths or connections.

Most researchers agree that experts have more highly developed schemata in their expertise, and the more highly developed the schema the easier it is to activate information that was either schema consistent or inconsistent (Fiske, Kinder, & Larter, 1983; Lau & Sears, 1986). But the assumption of most researchers is that given similar environments similar schema will be developed. Graber (1984) argued that schema represent social learning, but she noted that one of the many contingencies that form schema may be something called *personality*. Those who know more about politics, then, should have more highly developed schema about political matters than those who know less.

If one combines this last notion with the view that differently lateralized individuals may process and structure information consistently with their hemispheric preference (right-inductively/holistically; left-deductively/linearly), then one would expect that more knowledgeable people with opposite hemispheric preferences will have different cognitive structures for political information.

METHODOLOGY

Sample

The sample was drawn by using a proportionate probability sample of residential telephone lines with random-digit dialing within exchanges. The 40 telephone exchanges in Dane County, Wisconsin yielded 823 completed interviews during the last 2 weeks of October 1983. The interviewers were trained upper classmen and graduate students in a research methods class. The data were originally collected to study a variety of political matters and media preferences.

Measures

Sex As an Indicator of Lateralization. Much of the credible discussion of the cognitive, affective, and behavioral differences between human females and males since Freud (and perhaps in reaction to him) have centered on the social–psychological distinctions of being raised as a little girl or boy.[2]

Although social–psychological models emphasize the environment of the organism, cognitive theories put more emphasis on the organism itself. The development of sexual identities in a developmental process (Kohlberg, 1966) or the individual's construction of a gender schema (Bem, 1981) both argued that the mental arrangement of concepts into "maleness" and "femaleness" structures provide the basis for the establishment of sex differences. Implicit in these approaches is the theory that mental differences between females and males are primarily "learned" differences. But, of late, neurologists, psychiatrists, and increasingly psychologists are wondering if the organic distinctions between men and women may not account for much of their differences in "mental approaches" to problems and information.

The degree of lateralization appears to have a genetic component. Halpern (1986) argued that the process of lateralization begins approximately 7 weeks after fertilization. Ounsted and Taylor (1972) proposed that the female X chromosome was sexually neutral, and its role in sexual differentiation was to maintain ovarian function in females. They argued that it is the male Y chromosome that determines the developing gonads of the zygote.[3] It is testosterone and its metabolites that are necessary for normal growth and development of genitalia, secondary sex characteristics, nervous system, and brain.[4]

Geschwind's (1974) assertion that males tend to be more lateralized in the right hemisphere and thus tend to process information spatially, nonverbally,

---

[2]Researchers have used theories such as Learning and Imitation and have argued that little boys receive more praise than little girls for excelling in math (Stage & Karplus, 1981). Others have used Social Modeling theory (Bandura & Walters, 1963) and argued that sex roles and sex-typed behavior are learned through observation as well as direct rewards and punishment.

[3]Although the X chromosome carries an abundant amount of genetic information, the Y chromosome bears few genes but contains an abundant amount of a protein called the H–Y *antigen*. According to medical researchers from the department of neurology at the Harvard Medical School, it is this H–Y antigen that is essential for the development of the testes, which in fetal life secretes "T" or testosterone (Geschwind & Galaburda, 1984).

[4]These changes within the brain, some believe, are not trivial. Moore (1967) suggested that exposure to testosterone slows the development of the left hemisphere of the brain consequently increasing the strength of the right hemisphere. Hier and Crowley (1982) found that congenitally hypogonadal males (those who lack testosterone) displayed superior verbal scores and scored low on tests of spatial function unlike "normal males" who on the average scored in the reverse. Further, those females who were exposed to diethylstilbestrol, which resembles testosterone, reported masculizing effects such as, difficulties in menstruation and infertility and an increase in aggressive behaviors.

and symbolically is consistent with other scientific reports that males tend to store information pictorially and nonlinearly, grasping the concept of the whole from just a part. Females on the other hand, exhibiting a left hemisphere dominance, tend to process information linguistically, linearly, and analytically.

Waber's Maturation Rate Hypothesis (1976) predicts that females rely more on both hemispheres when processing verbal stimuli and have less room for spatial abilities to develop in their less dominant hemisphere, whereas a male's more compartmentalized brain tends to specialize—spatial tasks assigned to one part, verbal tasks to another. Males tend to have more reading disabilities, dyslexia, stuttering, and autism (Geschwind & Galaburda, 1984).

Nature Plus Nature. To claim either environment or biology as the exclusive force in cognitive differences is to disregard large bodies of literature (Halpern, 1986). On the biological side Halpern suggests that tests of spatial abilities (Harris, 1975; Sanders, Soares, & D'Aquila, 1982; Witkin, Dyk, Faterson, Goodenough, & Kane, 1962), sex by left- or righthandedness interactions (Harshman, 1983), female infant verbal precociousness (McGuiness, 1976), as well as the medical/chemical findings discussed earlier, all point to differences that are hard to explain environmentally. On the social–psychological side, Halpern noted that scores on spatial tests can be improved with training (Connor, Schackman, & Serbin, 1978); the size of the effects of cognitive difference have been decreasing during the last 20 years (Rosenthal & Rubin, 1982); the average differences in math scores are small (Benbow & Stanley, 1980); and the number of women entering math and science fields have been increasing in the last 20 years.

Recognizing that this is a sensitive scientific and political area, it may be prudent to present a few basic assumptions. First, differences between women and men (or left and right lateralization) do not necessarily imply betterness. Second, lacking convincing evidence to the contrary, sex differences must be applied to the groups as a whole. Thus, it is mean differences with which we are concerned. Third, environmental factors probably directly affect organic predispositions. Last, using sex as an indicator of lateralization is probably not the best operationalization of the concept. However, given the unavailability of a tested instrument for use in survey research of the general population, it serves our purpose in this initial project.

Schema Complexity. To determine which individuals were more or less knowledgeable about political matters, respondents were asked questions in three conceptual areas. They were asked to identify (a) some specific political actors and their parties, (b) some international actors and countries in the news at that time, and (c) the announced Democratic presidential candidates (see Appendix). The answers were summed ($\alpha = .82$) and divided on the mean to provide high and low levels of knowledge. These groups provide the measure of schema complexity—the higher knowledge group being more complex than the lower knowledge group.

Schema Structure. Political information in the form of national and international political issues were scaled multidimensionally within each cell of the sex/political knowledge typology. Each respondent was asked to describe how related two issues were by assigning to each dyad a score from 0 to 100. The larger the number of units the less related the respondent saw the two issues (dissimilarity measure). Each respondent was randomly asked to respond to either 16 or 17 of the potential 66 pairings of the 12 concepts (11 issues and "me"). Four respondents would make one complete matrix of distances. Each respondent was assigned a random starting point for his or her list of questions to minimize order effects.[5]

Controls. In order to try to isolate predispositions, we attempted to identify and remove the effects of several environmental factors. Five demographic variables, 1 psychographic, and 17 media variables were considered as controls. The individual's education and age often are related to the complexity of the individual's cognitive structure, and to the extent of one's socialization, an important concern in this study. The education of the individual's mother and father were also used as controls. These variables were controlled to help reduce the effects of social group socialization. Finally, the media are often considered important sources of socialization. Measures of the individual's overall exposure to media, the specific exposure to public affairs content, and the self-reported amount of attention to public affairs content were entered as controls. Because of the sheer number of media variables, factor analysis were employed to identify the latent dimensions of media.

Analysis

Using a MANOVA technique, the variance due to the control variables was then regressed out of the variables of interest. The means of the pairings, adjusted by the control variables, were then used as in the subsequent analysis. The means for each sex by political knowledge group were entered into a multidimensional scaling (MDS) program to provide the primary analysis. GALILEO was used to produce the coordinates for analysis. The use of MDS

---

[5]A two-way ANOVA was run for each of the 66 respondent pairings that makes up the positioning of the 12 concepts. The differences for each pairing was run with sex and high and low political knowledge as the independent variables. Of the 66 tests, 16 showed sex differences; 4 others showed political differences. Finally, 5 of the ANOVAs had significant interactions between sex and political knowledge.

to examine "space" has been well documented (Carroll & Chang, 1975; Shepard, Romney, & Nerlove, 1972; Wish, 1975; Woelfel & Danes, 1980; Woelfel & Fin, 1980).

It should be noted that the analysis employed here do not yield conventional tests of significance. Just as factor analysis is a descriptive technique used to reduce data and aid in its interpretation, so multidimensional scaling should not be expected to produce conclusions with directly testable probabilities.

We expect that men who hold higher amounts of information will have an MDS space that is more proportioned than will women who hold higher amounts of information. That is, given men's tendency toward holistic, inductive approaches they will tend to more easily find patterns in the concepts than will women. This tendency will facilitate their organization of concepts along a few dimensions. Given women's more linear, deductive approaches, they will have the tendency to force fit issues into dimensions, and will have more problems doing so. Although they may see similarities they will also see the differences. Their tendency to work in a top-down manner will result in a wider spread of concepts in the cognitive space. Thus, the MDS space of more knowledgeable men will fit more tightly across dimensions, whereas more knowledgeable women will use more of the space to try to represent more of what they see as subtle distinctions among the concepts.

Hyde (1981) reported that among the gifted, the lateralized differences between men and women are more acute. Other studies as well have demonstrated that, although some lateral differences are diminished by education, some differences remain constant regardless of training (Hyde, Geiringer, & Yen, 1975; Sherman, 1967). These differences are not large, but they are consistent across studies and time. Halpern (1986) noted that:

> it is possible that experimenters are unwittingly biasing the results so that they conform to their expectations, but given the fact that these results have been replicated many times by psychologists with strong feminine orientations, this explanation seems unlikely. (p. 152)

Thus, cerebral dominance results in a capability or propensity for a particular cognitive processing style or skill. This concept of lateralization is not meant to imply that each hemisphere presides over a mutually exclusive set of operations but, as Kinsbourne (1982) reported "all parts of the normal brain are at all times available for use, but people differ in their habitual patterns of thought" (p. 412).

RESULTS

Men and women held differing amounts of political information (see Table 9.1). Although there was no significant difference between men and women with lesser amounts of political information, there was a statistical difference between men and women at higher levels of political information. Given that

TABLE 9.1
Differences in Political Knowledge Among the
Sex/Knowledge Typology

| | Political Knowledge Groups | |
	Low	High
Men	$\overline{X}$=2.8	9.3
———	SD=1.6	2.0
	n=135	213
	Cell=(1)	(3)
Women	$\overline{X}$=2.4	8.1
———	SD=1.7	1.8
	n=304	161
	Cell=(2)	(4)

Scheffe Tests Among Cells

	Cell	1	2	3	4
Mean	Group				
2.8	1	—			
2.4	2	—	—		
9.3	3	a	a	—	
8.1	4	a	a	a	—

a=$p \leq .05$

both higher groups knew more than 60% of the questions (12 was the maximum score), and that the difference in means between sexes is slight, the two high knowledge groups were treated as practically, rather than statistically, equal.

To obtain a manageable number of media variables, they were subjected to a Principal Components factor analysis. The VARIMAX rotation produced five factors. The data presented in Table 9.2 show two attention factors (state/local and national/international), two public affairs content factors (television and newspaper), and a factor of television exposure.

The results of the MDS analyses are presented in four diagrams in two figures. Figure 9.1 compared the MDS spaces for men and women who had lower levels of political knowledge.

Figure 9.1 presents a three-dimensional representations of the 12 concepts in space. Dimension 1 is the horizontal x axis; Dimension 2 is the y axis, and the third dimension is the altitudinal z axis. Notice that the men tend to use the first and second dimension, whereas the women tend to use the first and third. But overall neither groups tends to see three-dimensional arrangements of concepts. The domestic economic issues tend to group along the left on

TABLE 9.2
Principal Component/VARIMAX Rotation Factor Analysis

	State/ Local Atten.	Nat/ Int. Atten.	TV Public Affairs	NP Public Affairs	TV Freq.
Television attention to local news	.81	.10	.23	.04	−.09
Newspaper attention to state news	.81	.10	.04	.22	.09
Television attention to state news	.77	.30	.22	−.02	−.11
Newspaper attention to state news	.76	.29	−.00	.18	.05
Newspaper attention to national news	.32	.73	.07	−.01	.03
Newspaper reading of international news	.01	.70	.16	.40	−.05
Newspaper reading of national news	.14	.70	.02	.46	.03
Television attention to national news	.38	.69	.22	−.13	−.07
TV/frequency/usage					
Television nat'l news	.08	.19	.74	−.01	−.00
Television local news	.28	−.22	.70	.07	.00
Television documentaries	.05	.23	.66	.13	.02
Television magazines	.02	.07	.59	.17	.06
Weekly newspaper use	.00	.06	.14	.64	.05
Local news	.53	.11	.02	.62	.07
State news	.47	.30	−.00	.59	.89
Editorials	.09	.05	.19	.53	−.22
Weekly TV frequency	.00	−.02	.10	−.04	.95
Eigenvalue	5.35	1.69	1.52	1.27	1.01
Pct of Variance	31.5	9.9	8.9	7.5	5.9

dimension one, the international issues tend to group to the right on the same dimension.

Figure 9.2 shows that for the men, there is only a small difference between the arrangements of concepts between the high and low groups. The primary difference is the accentuation of the concepts along the first and second dimension. The third dimension may actually be used slightly less. For the women, Fig. 9.2 shows an increased use of all the dimensions. Concept positions in space for the high group are further from the dimension axes. Men in the high political knowledge group tend to move toward the axes (when compared with the low political knowledge group), women tend to move away.

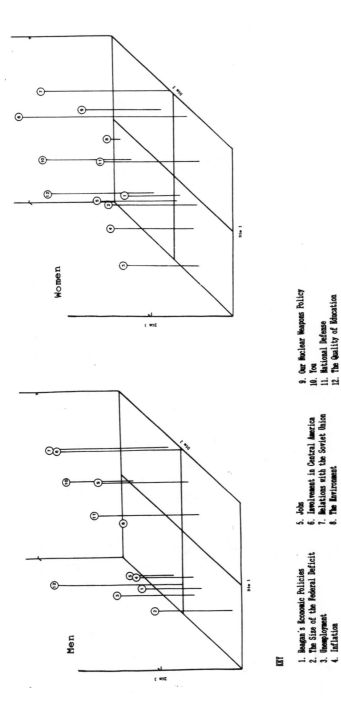

KEY

1. Reagan's Economic Policies
2. The Size of the Federal Deficit
3. Unemployment
4. Inflation

5. Jobs
6. Involvement in Central America
7. Relations with the Soviet Union
8. The Environment

9. Our Nuclear Weapons Policy
10. You
11. National Defense
12. The Quality of Education

FIG. 9.1.   The three-dimensional arrangement of issues for men and women who hold lower amounts of knowledge.

141

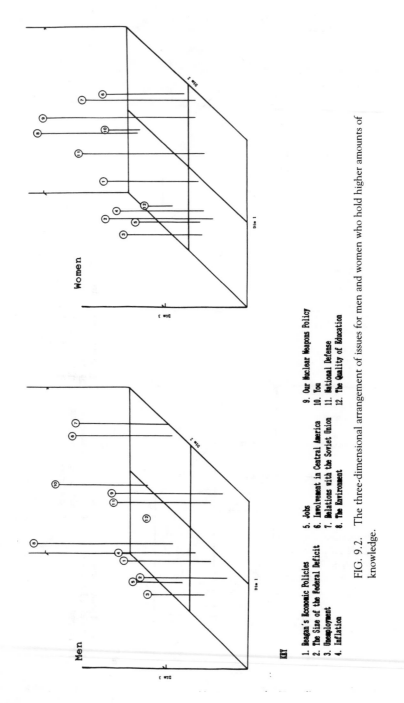

KEY

1. Reagan's Economic Policies
2. The Size of the Federal Deficit
3. Unemployment
4. Inflation

5. Jobs
6. Involvement in Central America
7. Relations with the Soviet Union
8. The Environment

9. Our Nuclear Weapons Policy
10. You
11. National Defense
12. The Quality of Education

FIG. 9.2.   The three-dimensional arrangement of issues for men and women who hold higher amounts of knowledge.

142

Notice also that women's use of the third dimension increases among the high political knowledge group. When compared with the men's space, this may signify that women see more connections between items. How schema are constructed may have consequences in how they are activated. If women and men do have the tendency to process information differently (men inductively, women deductively), a difference in the structure of the schema and, consequently, the schema's reactivation may occur.

It would appear that there is some support for our general expectations about the differences in the spread of the issues between men and women.

DISCUSSION

This study attempted to contribute to the political information-processing literature in three areas: They were (a) examining possible inherent processes of schema formation, (b) exploring alternatives to experimental and small group methodologies in studying schema formation, and (c) examining sex differences in the processing of political information.

The evidence presented here is consistent with the notion that individuals may prefer to process information in different ways. Future studies may find it useful to examine differences in processing preferences among individuals, such as whether the information is presented inductively or deductively, or is presented linearly or holistically. Further, whether or not individuals are physically lateralized, the distinctions commonly used to describe cerebral dominance bear further examination. Their elaboration could be fruitful in understanding information processing.

Using MDS may prove to be a useful technique to examine cognitive schema. Magnitude scaling rather than using differences between scores or sets of scores allows flexibility in comparing complete structures of particular information. The further use of such techniques in sample survey methodology may increase the generalizability of information-processing studies. In addition, most research examining schema usually try to induce certain schema, rather than attempting to ascertain what schema the individuals decide on their own to use. Further, the formation of schema is often taken to be primarily deductive, but the use of MDS could help clarify the induction processes as well.

We have at least added to the controversy of the differences between men and women. Finding small, regular differences between such large heterogeneous groups should bode well for elaborating processing differences of political information in more homogenous groups such as political activists or non-voters.

APPENDIX

Positions on Issues

Reagan:	Mondale:
ERA	ERA
Deficit	Deficit
Taxes	Taxes
Abortion	Abortion
School Prayer	School Prayer
Nuclear Weapons	Nuclear Weapons

Naming

Senator	Party
Senator	Party
Representative	Party
Representative's	Party
Opponent	

Length of Term

Senator
Representative

Naming

President of Soviet Union
Capital of Nicaragua
Two countries that border Lebanon

REFERENCES

Bandura, A., & Walters, R. H. (1963). *Social learning and personality development*. New York: Holt, Rinehart & Winston.

Bem, S. L. (1981). Gender schema theory: A cognitive account of sex typing. *Psychological Review, 88*, 354–364.

Benbow, C., & Stanley, J. C. (1980). Sex differences in mathematical ability: Factor or artifact? *Science, 210*, 1262–1264.

Benton, A. (1980). The neuropsychology of facial recognition. *American Psychologist, 35*, 176–186.

Carroll, J., & Chang. J. (1975). Analysis of individual difference in multidimensional scaling via N-way generalization of "Eckart Young" composition. *Psychometrika, 35,* 283–319.

Connor, J. M., Schackman, M., & Serbin, L. A. (1978). Sex-related differences in response to practice on a visual-spatial test and generalization to a related test. *Child Development, 49,* 24–29.

Critchley, M. (1970). *A phasiology and other aspects of language.* London: Edward Arnold.

Fiske, S., Kinder, D., & Larter, W. (1983). The novice and the expert knowledge based on strategies in political cognition. *Journal of Experimental Social Psychology, 19,* 381–400.

Fiske, S., & Taylor, S. E. (1984). *Social cognition.* New York: Random House Press.

Geschwind, N. (1974). The anatomical basis of brain hemisphere differentiation. In S. J. Dimond & J. G. Beaumond (Eds.), *Hemisphere function in the human brain* (pp. 9–18). New York: Wiley.

Geschwind, N., & Galaburda, A. (1984). *Biological foundations of cerebral dominance.* Boston, MA: Harvard University Press.

Geschwind, N., & Levitsky, W. (1968). Human brain: Left–right asymmetrys in the temporal speech region. *Science, 161,* 186–187.

Graber, D. (1984). *Processing the news.* New York: Longman.

Halpern, D. (1986). *Sex differences in cognitive abilities.* Hillsdale, NJ: Lawrence Erlbaum Associates.

Harshman, R. A., Hampson, E., & Berenbaum, S. A. (1983). Individual differences in cognitive abilities and brain organization: Part I: Sex and handedness differences in ability. *Canadian Journal of Psychology, 37,* 144–192.

Harris, L. J. (1975). Neurophysical factors in the development of spatial skills. In J. Eliot & N. J. Salkind (Eds.), *Children's spatial development.* Springfield, IL: Charles C. Thomas.

Hier, D., & Crowley, D. (1982). Spatial ability in androgen-deficient men. *New England Journal of Medicine, 306,* 1202–1205.

Hyde, J. S. (1981). How large are cognitive gender differences? *American Psychologist, 36,* 892–901.

Hyde, J. S., Geiringer, E. R., & Yen, W. M. (1975). On the empirical relation between spatial ability and sex difference in other aspects of cognitive performance. *Multivariate Behavioral Research, 10,* 289–309.

Kinsbourne, M. (1982). The mechanism of hemisphere asymmetry in man. *American Psychologist, 37,* 411–420.

Kohlberg, L. (1966). A cognitive-developmental analysis of children's sex role concepts and attitudes. In E. E. Maccoby (Ed.), *The development of sex differences.* Stanford, CA: Stanford University Press.

Lau, R., & Sears, D. O. (1986). *Political cognition.* Hillsdale, NJ: Lawrence Erlbaum Associates.

LeDoux, D., Wilson, H., & Gazzaniga, M. (1977). Manipulo-Spatial aspects of cerebral lateralization: Clues to the origin of lateralization. *Neuropsychologia, 15,* 743–750.

McGuinness, D. (1976). Sex difference in the organization of perception and cognition. In B. Lloyd & J. Archer (Eds.), *Exploring sex differences.* New York: Academic Press.

Milner, B. (1965). Visually guided maze learning in man: Effects of bilateral hippocampal, bilateral frontal and unilateral cerebral lesions. *Neuropsychologia, 3,* 317–338.

Moore, T. (1967). Language and intelligence: A longitudinal study of the first eight years. *Human Development, 10,* 88–106.

Nebes, D. (1978). Direct examination of cognitive function in the right and left hemisphere. In M. Kinsbourne (Ed.), *Asymmetrical functions of the brain.* London: Cambridge University Press.

Ounsted, D., & Taylor, D. (1972). The Y chromosome message: A point of view. In C. Ounsted & D. Taylor (Eds.), *Their ontogeny and significance.* London: Churchill.

Rosenthal, R., & Rubin, D. B. (1982). Further meta-analytic procedures for assessing cognitive gender differences. *Journal of Educational Psychology, 74,* 708–712.

Sanders, B., Soares, M., & D'Aquila, J. M. (1982). The sex differences on one test of spatial visualization: A nontrivial difference. *Child Development, 53,* 1106–1110.

Shapiro, M. (1986). Analogies, visualization, and mental processing of science stories. In M. McLaughlin (Ed.), *Communication yearbook 9.* Beverly Hills, CA: Sage.

Shepard, R., Romney, A., & Nerlove, S. (1972). *Multidimensional scaling: Theory and applications in the behavioral sciences* (Vol. 1). New York: Seminar Press.

Sherman, J. A. (1967). Problems of sex differences in space perception and aspects of intellectual functioning. *Psychological Review, 74,* 290–299.

Springer, S., & Deutsch, G. (1985). *Left brain, right brain.* New York: Freeman.

Stage, E. K., & Karlpus, R. (1981). Mathematical ability: Is sex a factor? *Science, 212,* 114.

Taylor, S., & Winkler, J. (1980). *The development of schemas.* Paper presented at the annual meeting of American Psychological Association, Montreal, Canada.

Waber, D. (1976). Sex differences in cognition: A function of maturation rates. *Science, 192,* 572–574.

Wish, M. (1976). Comparisons among multidimensional structures of interpersonal relations. *Multivariate Behavioral Research, 11,* 297–327.

Witkin, H. A., Dyk, R. B., Faterson, H. F., Goodenough, D. G., & Karp, S. A. (1962). *Psychological differentiation.* New York: Wiley.

Woelfel, J., & Danes, J. (1980). Multidimensional scaling models for communication research. In P. Monge & J. Capella (Eds.), *Multivariate techniques in communication research.* New York: Academic Press.

Woelfel, J., & Fink, E. (1980). *The measurement of communication processes: Galileo theory and method.* New York: Academic Press.

III | IMAGE-INFORMATION STIMULI

Changing Technologies, Mass Media, and Control of the Pictures in People's Heads: A Preliminary Look at U.S. Presidential Campaign Slogans, 1800–1984

James R. Beniger
Gary Jones
University of Southern California

Too often, ethnographers treat a society's shared symbols, metaphors, and images as an enduring part of human culture. Too often, cognitive scientists treat cognitive structures as enduring features of the human brain. Rarely is cognition studied in historical context broad enough to reveal the influences of technological change. But technological development and change—especially involving the mass media—can have a profound effect on cognition, in general, and on political information processing in particular.

One example of such an effect is the rise of broadcasting to replace mass newspapers (and hence transportation) as the dominant means of mass communication, with a resulting aggravation of the misfit between political boundaries and media markets. The result has been that increasingly we see news coverage and political commercials for supposedly local candidates for whom we cannot vote. The problem is especially aggravated by the new "superstations" for U.S. cable television that use satellites for national distribution of their programming, including local news coverage and commercials.

At the same time, many voters see less and less of their own officials and candidates among the many shown in news coverage and commercials. The effects on political cognition—on the pictures of politics in people's heads—might be predicted: Internalized political maps are increasingly impoverished, along with a blurring of the individual's sense of his or her own place among political boundaries. This is not to say that citizens know less than they once did—quite the contrary. It is rather to argue that what people do know is increasingly confused, misleading, or at least irrelevant.

For example, in public opinion polls in New Jersey, a state that until recently had no television station of its own, but that relied on broadcasts

149

from New York City or Philadelphia (or both), more people identified the governors of New York and Pennsylvania than their own governor, who received much less television coverage. Because no corresponding national poll has been taken (at least to our knowledge), we can only guess how many Americans know more about city government in Atlanta or Chicago or New York—thanks to the superstations based in those cities—than about the government in their own city or country. The effects on pictures of politics in people's heads is likely to be profound.

Another example of an effect of technological change on cognition, one that provides the focus of the preliminary investigation described here, involves the role of slogans in political campaigns. If our argument about technological change is correct, then we might expect changes in the form and impact of political slogans as mass media have evolved—at least in the United States—from penny to mass press and from radio to television.

JAKOBSON ON POLITICAL SLOGANS

Inspiration for such a study comes from Roman Jakobson's "Closing Statement" at the 1958 Conference on Style held at Indiana University and subsequently published in several different volumes under the title "Linguistics and Poetics" (Jakobson, 1960). In this 35-page paper, which still ranks among the most cited works in the arts and humanities (Garfield, 1987), Jakobson devoted one paragraph to a political slogan, "I like Ike," used in Dwight Eisenhower's successful campaign for the White House in 1952. After analyzing the linguistic structure of the three-word, three-syllable slogan in some detail, Jakobson concluded: "The secondary, poetic function of this electional catch phrase reinforces its impressiveness and efficacy" (p. 357).

What Jakobson called the "poetic function of language," which he defined as "the set (*Einstellung*) toward the *message* as such, focus on the message for its own sake" (p. 356), has important implications for the field of communication and cognition, and especially for the study of political information processing. When we ask Americans about presidential campaign slogans that they can remember (we are continuing to conduct just such informal surveys), for example, the most frequent response is "Tippecanoe and Tyler too," the slogan that helped Whig candidate William Henry Harrison to win the White House from incumbent President Martin Van Buren in 1840, nearly 150 years ago.

Many who cite this slogan remember little else about 19th-century American political history and most do not know the meaning of "Tippecanoe," the site of Harrison's victory over the Indians of Indiana Territory in 1811, and cannot identify "Tyler" as John Tyler, Harrison's vice presidential running-mate (soon to become president himself upon Harrison's death). Of all the trivia in U.S. history textbooks, "Tippecanoe and Tyler too" is remembered by even the more reluctant students for its poetic qualities, as is the second most frequent response in the survey, "Fifty-four forty or fight," a militaristic demand for a favorable boundary line between Oregon and Canada from James Polk's successful 1844 campaign.

For modern mass media politics in which name recognition seems to have superseded party affiliation in importance, the significance of the poetic function—focus on the message for its own sake—for control of cognition and hold on memory should be obvious. As Jakobson stated:

> The scrutiny of language requires a thorough consideration of its poetic function. Any attempt to reduce the sphere of poetic function to poetry . . . would be a delusive oversimplification. Poetic function is not the sole function of verbal art but only its dominant, determining function, whereas in all other verbal activities it acts as a subsidiary, accessory constituent. This function, by promoting the palpability of signs, deepens the fundamental dichotomy of signs and objects.

In analyzing the power of this effect for the slogan "I like Ike," Jakobson noted:

> Both cola of the trisyllabic formula . . . rhyme with each other, and the second of the two rhyming words is fully included in the first one (echo rhyme), /layk/-/ayk/, a paronomastic (word-playful) image of a feeling which totally envelops its object. Both cola alliterate with each other, and the first of the two alliterating words is included in the second: /ay/-/ayk/, a paronomastic image of the loving subject enveloped by the beloved object.

Perhaps the fastest way to share Jakobson's enthusiasm for the slogan is to attempt to coin alternatives for a candidate named "Dwight Eisenhower," nicknamed "Ike," who was an internationally known war hero with no previous political record. Whatever its impact on cognition and memory, the slogan singled out by Jakobson prompted the Democratic opposition to counter with its own variant, "I like Ike but I am going to vote for Stevenson," the only example in more than 1,200 presidential campaign slogans since 1800 in which one party faithfully repeated the slogan of another without disagreement.

Four years later, the Republicans campaigned for Eisenhower's second term in the White House with the slogan "We still like Ike," a rewording that destroyed most of the poetic functions noted by Jakobson. The Democrats countered with "Adlai likes me" (a reference to Adlai Stevenson, the Democratic nominee), proof enough of the power of three monosyllabic words to dominate the public discourse of two major parties over two successive campaigns.

BRINGING DISCOURSE BACK IN

Despite the obvious importance of discourse for the control of cognition and memory, the subject has been all but ignored by political scientists, and indeed by empirical researchers across the entire range of social science disciplines and specialties. To illustrate, the remainder of this section is taken virtually verbatim from the opening paragraphs of a recent review essay by Robert Wuthnow (1988) on religious discourse with only words like "religion" and "religious" replaced by the corresponding "politics" and "political." Despite these relatively few purely mechanical changes, Wuthnow's words should ring just as true to students of politics as they do to students of religion.

Social scientists have in recent decades developed a fairly standard way of studying politics. Survey research and public opinion polls are the methods of choice, supplemented by occasional applications of content analysis, in-depth interviews, and discussion of broader social developments to provide context. As a result of this often valuable research, we have a good sense of the public's tolerance for political leaders making statements about various kinds of social issues. We also have some evidence on the issues politicians speak about. And we have many studies of the ways in which political beliefs and attitudes toward social issues correlate. We even have frequency counts of the kinds of themes that are expressed on political talk shows or in political books.

But on political discourse *as discourse* we have virtually nothing. It is as if our standard methods have trained us to think of political communities (and not just political communities) as silent worlds. People have political beliefs, convictions, and sentiments. They harbor predispositions, orientations, and commitments. They behold political symbols that give meaning to their lives, help them to construct reality, and provide them with security and a sense of belonging. But they do not speak (for epistemological underpinnings of this and alternative approaches to cultural meaning in general, see Wuthnow 1987, especially chapter 2).

Or if they do speak, our standard methods register only the surface features of their discourse. For instance, we may cull through the transcripts of political broadcasts to see how many of them touched on abortion, school prayer, the Supreme Court, or politics in general. We may scan the titles of political books to see how many fall into various preconceived categories. But none of this gives us any indication of the ways in which political discourse is actually put together.

Of course, it may require more than a leap of political faith to argue that the actual composition of political discourse is itself important. To someone trained in the social psychology of opinion research, discourse is likely to be relevant only as a means of tapping into the deeper attitudinal predispositions that supposedly govern behavior. Discourse is in this view ephemeral, unpredictable, and superficial—only the underlying mindsets are meaningful. We want to discover how personalities are put together, not to invest time in the study of meaningless chatter (as political slogans are often viewed).

There has for some time been a movement in the social sciences to bring discourse back in. Besides the small coteries of ethnomethodologists and conversation analysts who have always studied discourse, we now have the formidable (and often forbidding) legacy of Foucault's decentered poststructuralism, Habermas's borrowings from speech–act theory, Derrida's language-focused deconstructionism, and a more scattered array of empirical investigations focusing on public discourse.

We need not become camp-followers of esoteric theoreticians, however, to appreciate the importance of understanding political discourse. Much of it is highly codified in political traditions. Its practitioners gain competence through long years of training and experience, and any competent practitioner could testify to the importance of discourse. But when political discourse becomes public rhetoric (as in political slogans), we confront another compelling reason for trying to understand it: Some of it seems to affront common sensibilities so deeply that we find it difficult even to focus on what is being said.

THE COGNITIVE REVOLUTION

The recent changes alluded to by Wuthnow as involving poststructuralism, speech–act theory, and deconstructionism (see also Beniger, 1988) are now manifest in political communication as a much more comprehensive paradigm shift—already the most far-reaching change in the field since the widespread acceptance of the minimal effects model in the late 1950s and early 1960s. The new shift is perhaps most succinctly summarized as a change in dependent variables from attitudes to cognitions, as a shift in independent variables from persuasive communication to less-directed media processes (like political slogans) ranging from "framing" through "discourse" to the social construction of reality, or as a refocusing of interest from simple change (like political conversion) to the structuring or restructuring ("structuration") of cognitions and meaning, with stability now no less interesting than change (Beniger, 1987).

Although most often identified as the *cognitive revolution*, the new paradigm transcends cognitive psychology to include political information processing, macrosociology, and much of the traditional subject matter of the humanities. New interest focuses on process, not only on the processing of information inside the citizen's head (the "black box" of survey research dedicated to static models that account for opinions using socioeconomic variables), but also on processes involving the "public" aspects of public opinion formation and change: news coverage and dissemination, public opinion measurement and reporting, interest group advertising and public relations (including slogans), and public policy debates—all conducted in public, mostly via the mass media, and all affecting political cognition in often complex ways. This new model of political cognition as a continuous public process has led researchers to supplement attitudinal survey methods with other data-collection techniques, including content analysis, focus groups, and quasi-experiments (Gamson, 1984, 1987; Modigliani & Gamson, 1979).

Although the new paradigm did not emerge in political communication until the mid-1970s, the development of its separate components has played an important role in the history of the social and behavioral sciences more generally. The idea of mental "schemata" was first devised—following Aristotle's "categories of thought"—by Immanuel Kant (1781/1929), who sought to explain what he called the *synthetic a priori*, the means by which knowledge might begin with experience (and thus be at least partly synthetic rather than purely analytic) and yet not derive from experience (be at least partly a priori rather than wholly a posteriori). Introduced into psychology by the British neurologist Henry Head (1926), the concept of schemata helped Frederic Bartlett (1932) to explain social and cultural components of memory.

Because behaviorism, which rejects all mentalistic terms to focus exclusively on the study of overt behavior, dominated psychology from the 1910s until the 1950s (inspiring the stimulus–response or "hypodermic needle" model of media effects), cognitive concerns survived in the work of only a few psychologists: Piaget's lifelong investigations of the development of the Kantian categories in children, for example, and the "cognitive maps" posited by Tolman (1932) to explain the ability of animals to navigate altered mazes.

In the development of American social and behavioral science, the new paradigm might claim several origins: the "enlisted interest" of Lippmann, which he illustrated with the same story-relaying parlor game—attributed to Jung (1916)—that inspired the adoption by Bartlett (1932) of the schemata idea (Lippmann, 1922); the conformity experiments of Sherif (1935) and Asch (1951/1963); the reference group theory of Sherif (1936) and Newcomb (1943); the work of Hovland, Janis, and Kelley (1953) on clues audiences use to judge the veracity of speakers; and the analysis of cognitive dissonance by Festinger (1957). Although dissonance theory suggested that people do not like inconsistency, cognitive balance theories—the first advanced by Heider (1946)—assumed the compatible idea that people prefer consistency, a model generalized from interpersonal relationships (Newcomb, 1953) to triadic sets of relationships among attitudes of all kinds by Cartwright and Harary (1956).

Other early contributions to the process model came from new research on mass media and political cognition in the 1950s: Berelson, Lazarsfeld, and McPhee (1954) and Campbell, Converse, Miller, and Stokes (1960) demonstrated that party labels provide a critical cue for the cognitive filtering of political information. Pioneering work on television's celebration of General Douglas MacArthur (Lang & Lang, 1953) and on McCarthy era journalism (Breed, 1955) showed the mass media to be active "framers" of social reality, even as they are constrained by larger political processes that frame expectations of both journalists and their audiences. Anthony Downs (1957) argued that people learn and use information only if their anticipated benefits exceed the costs of acquisition, thereby actively keeping exposure to political communication to a minimum—a model with obvious implications for the role of political campaign slogans.

By 1960, as the emergence of the new cognitive science began "picking up steam" in several academic disciplines (Gardner, 1985), the field of political communication had already been assimilating the essential ideas for several decades. Klapper (1960) reviewed 22 studies completed between 1936 and 1959—including the still frequently cited Hyman and Sheatsley (1947) study—that found audiences actively processing mass media messages through selective exposure, perception, and retention, with each individual thereby maintaining "a protective net in the service of existing predispositions" (Klapper, 1960, p. 25).

THE NEW MODEL OF POLITICAL COMMUNICATION

Although the cognitive revolution had transformed psychology and related disciplines by the late 1960s and the early 1970s (Gardner, 1985), the new paradigm did not emerge until the late 1970s in political science and public opinion research, then lagging psychology and other cognitive fields by a decade or more. In *Public Opinion Quarterly*, for example, the number of full-length articles on cognition, perception, knowledge and information, and dissonance actually fell by 50% during 1966–1976, when 23 articles appeared, only 4 on cognition and dissonance. The peak for such publications had come during the preceding 7 years, 1959–1965, when 24 relevant articles appeared (4 more than in the previous 22 years since the journal's founding)—13 on cognition and dissonance alone (compiled from Meyer & Spaeth, 1984; see Beniger, 1987).

The 1960s did bring the first major papers by political scientist Philip Converse, including "Information Flow and the Stability of Partisan Attitudes" (1962) and "The Nature of Belief Systems in Mass Politics" (1964). In addition to their immediate impact on macroanalysis, these papers stimulated the interest of political scientists in microanalysis and cognition over the 25 years that followed. As Kenneth Rasinski (personal communication, May 3, 1987), a cognitive social psychologist, stated, Converse's work on nonattitudes

has been very important in two respects: First, it has challenged our conception of the average citizen as a politically astute entity. This has forced us to think hard about the psychology of the survey respondent, and about the psychology of public opinion and political attitudes. Second, it has challenged our methodology, making us aware of the important role of survey context on responses. This has laid the foundation for recent work . . . on cognitive aspects of survey responding which attempts to specify under what conditions respondents will or will not have "real" attitudes and when they will exhibit "non-attitudes.". . . Without Converse's work as a stimulus, followed, of course, by the important books on survey responding by Sudman and Bradburn (1974) and by Schuman and Presser (1981), this present work would probably not have taken place.

The impact of Converse's 1960s papers on macroanalysis also led—indirectly via the agenda setting literature—to new models of political cognition. By suggesting that most citizens are not politically astute and have no specific policy agenda, Converse suggested a new way to transcend the minimal effects model still ascendant in the 1960s and early 1970s. Minimal-effects findings might simply be artifacts of improper measurement, or of measuring the wrong effects, Converse's work implied—certainly more likely if belief systems prevail and survey researchers concentrate on what he termed *non-attitudes* (for a review, see Smith, 1984).

One major effect to circumvent the findings of minimal effects in the early 1970s was agenda setting (McCombs & Shaw, 1972). Inspired in part by Converse's work, the agenda-setting literature argued that mass media might have minimal effects on public opinion, but they do influence what the public has opinions about—possibly an even stronger form of media influence. Major components of the agenda-setting model can be found in Lippmann's "pictures in our heads" and "enlisting of interest" (1922, chapters 1 and 11), in Merton's "frame of reference" (1945; Merton & Kitt, 1950, based on Stouffer 1949–1950), in the "status conferral" mechanism of Lazarsfeld and Merton (1948), in Festinger's "social reality" (1950), and in the long tradition of work in psychology on attention and salience in communication (Broadbent, 1958). Evidence for agenda setting had been presented in Berelson et al. (1954), and Lang and Lang (1959) had explicitly described the agenda-setting model: "The mass media force attention to certain issues by suggesting what individuals in the mass should think about, know about, and have feelings about" (p. 232).

A half-century after Lippmann's initial observations, however, little progress had been made on the empirical study of agenda setting. As Shanto Iyengar and Donald R. Kinder (1987) noted:

Even forty years later, Klapper's encyclopedic summary of findings on the effects of mass communication could develop just two pages to agenda-setting; moreover, that discussion was dotted with such disheartening phrases as "it is a matter of common observation" or "some writers believe" (1960: 104–5). Although research on agenda-setting has proliferated over the last decade, so far, unfortunately, the results add up to rather little. Even exponents of the agenda-setting idea acknowl-

edge the literature's fragmented and haphazard condition (e.g., McCombs, 1981).
Agenda-setting may be an apt metaphor, but it is no theory. (pp. 2–3)

The problem proved to be that the metaphor, which described individual cognition, had through the 1970s inspired mostly research at the macro-societal level. Origins of the agenda-setting model in social psychological phenomena like "social reality," attention, and salience, however, proved more fruitful in the end. Eventually the agenda-setting model, in the words of Lee Becker (personal communication, May 9, 1987), "led to further examination of cognitive effects and increased confidence on the part of researchers interested in studying media effects." Rapidly assimilating results from cognitive social psychology by the late 1970s, work on agenda setting produced much of the decade's most impressive research on political cognition and media effects, including Erbring, Goldenberg, and Miller (1980); Iyengar, Peters, and Kinder (1982); Behr and Iyengar (1985); and Iyengar and Kinder (1987).

Led by the initial flurry of interest in agenda setting during the 1970s, the new process model of political communication began to emerge during the same decade. No fewer than nine separate efforts to circumvent the findings of minimal effects—in addition to that of agenda setting—fed directly into the new paradigm: uses-and-gratifications research (Blumler & Katz, 1974; Blumler & McQuail, 1969; Katz, Gurevitch, & Haas, 1973), studies of the knowledge gap (Tichenor, Donohue, & Olien, 1970; Tichenor, Roden Kirchen, Olien, & Donohue, 1973), convergence and co-orientation models (Chaffee & Choe, 1980; McLeod & Chaffee, 1973), work on political cognition (Axelrod, 1973, 1976; Becker, McCombs, & McLeod, 1975; Bennett, 1981; Fiske & Kinder, 1981; Lau, Sears, & Centers, 1979; Modigliani & Gamson, 1979; Sears, Lau, Tyler, & Allen, 1980), and on the spiral of silence (Noelle-Neumann, 1974, 1980), diverse approaches to audience decoding (Bourdieu, 1980; Csikszentmihalyi & Kubey, 1981; Hall, 1974; Turner, 1977; Worth & Gross, 1974), hegemonic models (Hall, 1977; Hall, Critcher, Jefferson, Clarke, & Roberts, 1978; Gitlin, 1979, 1980; but see Kinder, 1982), and studies of "media events" (Katz, 1980; Katz, Dayan, & Motyl, 1981).

These 10 distinct currents of theory and research had by the early 1980s coalesced in what could justifiably be called a new paradigm of cognitive processing, media framing, and active audience engagement in mass communication. Although the many obvious differences within and among the separate approaches—often exaggerated by stereotyped distinctions like "empirical versus critical"—have obscured their similarities and convergence, they look surprisingly similar when collectively compared to the older tradition of mass society and minimal effects imagery. In sharp contrast to this tradition, all the new approaches sidestep questions of persuasion and conversion to concentrate on more complex processes involving information, whether on the individual level as cognitions or on the societal level as ideology or culture. As Chaffee (personal communication, May 14, 1987) stated, "I see most of the important research concepts of the past two decades as outgrowths of two themes: dynamic processes and the role of information."

SLOGANS IN POLITICAL COMMUNICATION

Political slogans provide an ideal means to study processes involving information. Consider just four of many possible areas, ranging from micro to macro, in which studies of slogans would seem likely to expose interrelationships among various components of the new process paradigm of political communication:

1. Uses-and-gratifications research establishes the audience of mass communication as an active processor of information in pursuit of individual needs, so that the media might be said to supply information "to think with" (Katz, 1987). What more economical vehicle than the slogan for supplying information with which to think?

2. Work on the knowledge gap shows that people who acquire information are the most likely to acquire still more, presumably because information creates cognitive structures that require what Gamson (1987) called "fleshing out." What type of information is more likely than the slogan—short of poetry (which Jakobson suggested may function similarly)—to create a cognitive structure that requires "fleshing out"?

3. Interpersonal-level convergence and coorientation models emphasize that individuals exchange even mass media information among themselves, thereby converging at least partially on shared schemata. Does it not seem likely that such discourse would converge on the sparser and more readily assimilated cognitive structures, much like those supplied by slogans?

4. Work on audience decoding, which focuses on individual "negotiations" within the constraints of message and text, supplies the microdynamics of the process paradigm. At the same time, several approaches to audience decoding generalize that process to the information exchange within "interpretive communities," which in turn exercise the control of public opinion and culture that plays a central role in hegemonic models (and which may be fed back to large audiences through the "framings" of media elite). What might afford a more tractable constraint of message and text than the slogan, or a cognitive and linguistic structure more likely to serve the elite "framings" of the hegemonic model?

Because the process paradigm can be construed as an accommodation to the disappointments of minimal effects, it has often been criticized for abandoning the study of public opinion altogether in favor of less-compelling dependent variables like public education, information, knowledge, or learning. If attitudes can be allowed to depend on cognition (knowledge and schemata) as well as affect, however, and possibly also on behavioral predispositions, then communication that provides or changes "only" cognitions might be just as important to attitudinal change as communication with affective components. Indeed, public opinion research has a venerable literature suggesting that credible information—or the more subliminal information like that of slogans—can have a more lasting impact on public opinion than mere persuasive appeals (Kelman, 1961; McGuire, 1969).

Doris Graber (1984), who stated her own slant on the process paradigm in the title of her book, *Processing the New: How People Tame the Information Tide,* concluded from her study: "Political communication is very much a transactional process. Mass media messages are not imprinted on the minds of media audiences in the precise manner in which they are offered. Rather, audience members condense the offerings in their own ways, select aspects of interest, and integrate them into their own thinking" (p. 209). What form of human communication might better facilitate the cognitive process captured by Graber's three verbs—condense, select, integrate—than the political slogan?

THE DATA SET

The data set for our study of political slogans includes 1,226 slogans used in U.S. presidential election campaigns between 1800–1980. These slogans come from two published compilations (Blake & Newman, 1984; Urdang & Robbins, 1984) representing at least 26 other published sources (Blake & Newman, 1984). All election years since 1828 are represented by 10 or more slogans; earlier years range from one slogan (1804) to 11 (1800). Election years with the most slogans include 1940 (61 slogans), 1860 (53), and 1864 (52). Apart from these 10 low and high extremes, the other 36 of the 46 election years in the data set are represented by between 16 and 44 slogans per year (see Table 10.1).

Length of the presidential campaign slogans ranges from two words (14 cases or 1.1%) to 28 words (1 case); only 42 (3.4%) of the slogans contain more than 13 words. The 1,226 slogans contain 7,114 words, a mean of 5.80 words per slogan (median of 5, mode of 4); 17.1% of all slogans have the modal length of 4 words. Election years with slogans of greatest mean length include 1800 (8.27 words), 1840 (7.26), and 1900 (6.87); years with the shortest slogans include 1816 (2.75 words), 1820 (3.33), and

TABLE 10.1
Words Per Slogan
U.S. Presidential Campaign Slogans, 1800–1980

Election Year	Number of Words Per Slogan														Total Slogans	Total Words	Words/ Slogan
	1	2	3	4	5	6	7	8	9	10	11	12	13	+			
1800		1		2	2					1	2	2		1	11	91	8.27
4					1										1	5	5.00
8	1	1		1											4	14	3.50
12	1	1	1		1			1							5	20	4.00
16		2	1	1											4	11	2.75
1820		1		2											3	10	3.33
4		3		1	2	1	1								8	33	4.12
8		4	2	6	4	1	2	1	1						21	95	4.52
32	2	2	3	3	1	4	2	3		1					21	140	4.95
6	2	3	2	2	3		2								16	72	4.50
1840		2	1	7	3	5	6	6	1	3	1		1	3	39	283	7.26
4		2	4	7	6	6	3	3	5	2			2	1	41	260	6.34
8	2	4	3	5	2	3	3	1	2	2	1			1	29	159	5.48
52		2	2	2	1	2	2	1	2	1		1			16	97	6.06
6		6	5	7	3	3	4	2	1	3	1		1		36	195	5.42
1860		6	5	6	8	5	9	3	2		1	3	1	4	53	356	6.72
4		3	3	5	5	6	9	9	6	3			2	1	52	355	6.83
8	2	4	6	5	2	4	4	1	7	1	2	1		2	41	256	6.24
72		2	5	5	9	2	2	3		2	1		1	1	28	151	5.39
6		7	5	2	3	7	1	3	1	1	2			2	34	201	5.91
1880		5	3		2	1	1	4		1	1			2	20	134	6.70
4	1	3	4	4	2	1	1	1	1		1	1	2	2	24	155	6.46
8		5	4	7	5	1	2		1		1	1		1	28	144	5.14
92	1	1	3	2	3	3		2	1					1	17	96	5.65
6		4	5	4	1	4	1	3		1				1	24	134	5.58
1900		1	6	6	3	2	1	5	1	1	2	1		2	31	213	6.87
4		5	2	3	6	1	3	1	1						22	102	4.64
8		2	4	6	1	3						1	1		19	101	5.32
12	1	4	5	4	4	2	4	2	2	2	2				32	176	5.50
6		4	1	1	4	2	3	3	1		3	1			23	146	6.35
1920		3	5	3	1	3	1							2	18	108	6.00
4		1	5	6	3	3	1	1	2				1	1	24	139	5.79
8		1	7	4	2	3	2	1	1	1	2	1		1	26	157	6.04
32		3	8	9	5	10	3	3	1	2					44	225	5.11
6		2	4	5	9	7	3	3		1	1	1			36	201	5.58
1940		1	11	13	9	8	6	4	4		1	1	1	2	61	358	5.87
4			4	6	6	2		1	1	2		2		1	25	153	6.12
8	1	2	4	5	9	8	1		1	2				1	34	180	5.29
52		4	8	8	10	3	5	1	1		3			1	44	233	5.30
6		1	4	6	1	3	1	1		3				1	21	122	5.81
1960		2	3	5	4	3	1	1	2		1				22	115	5.23
4		1	10	7	7	2	5							2	35	187	5.34
8		3	6	6	2	3	4	3	1	4	1	1	1	1	36	229	6.36
72		2	8	6	4	4	2	1		2	1	1		1	32	176	5.50
6		2	5	3	2	3	2	2	2					1	22	123	5.59
1980		3	10	8	5	6	4	2	1		1	1		2	43	239	5.56
	14	121	187	210	159	140	109	79	56	41	33	22	13	42	1226	7114	5.80

1808 (3.50). For the 19 elections since 1908, the mean number of words per slogan in each year has stayed within the narrow range of 5.11 to 6.36 words (Table 10.1).

The mean length of political slogans recalls cognitive psychologist George A. Miller's (1956) famous paper, "The Magical Number Seven, Plus or Minus Two: Some Limits on Our Capacity for Processing Information." In this paper, Miller showed that the individual's abilities to distinguish phonemes or other stimuli absolutely, to estimate numbers accurately, or to remember discrete items all begin to break down at about the level of seven items. A total of 543 slogans (44.3%) in the data set contain 5 to 9 words, although the distribution centers just below the lower end of Miller's interval (at mode 4): 926 or 75.5% of the slogans contain 2 to 7 words (Table 10.1).

It might appear tautological to conclude that political slogans are short— does not the definition of *slogan* demand precisely this criterion? The point is of course correct in theory but often overlooked in practice. One of the 10 longest slogans in the data set of 19 words, for example, is one from Barry Goldwater's unsuccessful 1964 campaign: "Extremism in the defense of liberty is no vice and moderation in the pursuit of justice is no virtue." Although this slogan has often been criticized for its content (taken from Goldwater's acceptance speech at the Republican Party convention), perhaps its greater shortcoming as a slogan proved to be its unwieldy length; 61.5% of the 13 slogans with 18 or more words belonged to losing campaigns.

TRENDS IN SLOGAN LENGTH

If technological development and change do indeed affect political informa- tion processing and cognition, as argued in the first section of this chapter, then we might expect changes in the form and impact of political campaign slogans—including their length of words—as mass media evolved from penny press to mass-circulation dailies and then to radio and television. Figure 10.1 plots the mean number of words per slogan for each of the 46 presidential election campaigns, 1800–1980, along with a 3-year moving average smooth of the time-series line.

As shown by Fig. 10.1, slogan length dropped below 5 during the period 1808–1836, but rose sharply and steadily—during the years 1816–1840—to well above 6 and as high as 7.26 (in 1840). Slogan length then remained generally above 6—and always above 5—until 1888, when it began a slow, century-long drop to the recent level of about 5.5 to 5.6 (slightly below the overall mean for the 180-year period of 5.80).

Table 10.2 groups the same 46 presidential election campaigns into six distinct technological eras according to the dominant mass medium of each

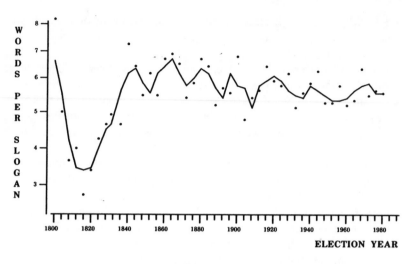

FIG. 10.1.

period: pre-mass (to 1832), penny press (1836–1848), telegraphic press (1852–1884), mass dailies (1888–1920), radio (1924–1948), and television (1952–1980). Each period includes four to nine presidential elections.

As shown by the mean number of words per slogan for the elections in each of the six periods in Table 10.2, slogans were much shorter in the pre-mass period than in any subsequent one—what might be expected for an era in which print played a relatively lesser role in campaigning and illiteracy may have risen. Also as expected, slogan length increased most sharply between this period and the era of the penny press, rising 1.41 words per slogan to 5.9. Longest slogans—a mean of 6.19 words—prevailed during the era of the telegraphic press, 1852–1884, falling most sharply into the next technological era, that of the mass dailies (1888–1920). This sharp drop in

TABLE 10.2
Mean Words Per Slogan, Major Mass Media Eras, 1800–1980

Years	Dominant Mass Medium	No. of Elections	No. of Slogans	Mean Words/Slogan
1800–1832	Pre-mass	9	78	4.49
1836–1848	Penny press	4	125	5.90
1852–1884	Telegraphic press	9	304	6.19
1888–1920	Mass dailies	9	214	5.67
1924–1948	Radio	7	250	5.69
1952–1980	Television	8	255	5.59
		46	1226	5.80

the length of campaign slogans corresponds closely in timing (mid-1880s) to the increased technological capacity for information processing and communication that has been called a *control revolution* (Beniger, 1986). Slogan length apparently dropped further with the most recent major innovation in political communications technology: television.

Word Frequencies in Campaign Slogans

Effects of these changes on political information processing and cognition are more likely to be reflected in the actual words used in campaign slogans. Table 10.3 lists the 53 words that have appeared most often (20 times or more) in U.S. presidential campaign slogans between 1800–1980. In addition to the articles, conjunctions, prepositions, and pronouns most commonly found in

TABLE 10.3
Most Frequently Used Words in Presidential Campaign Slogans,
1800–1980 (20 or more appearances, 1,226 slogans)

Rank	Word	Appearances	Rank	Word	Appearances
1 -	The	511	t27 -	I	30
2 -	And	322	t27 -	New	30
3 -	Of	240	t29 -	American	29
4 -	A	175	t29 -	It	29
5 -	For	167	t29 -	Liberty	29
6 -	To	119	t32 -	Let	28
7 -	With	85	t32 -	On	28
8 -	In	83	t34 -	Country	27
9 -	No	75	t34 -	Must	27
10 -	Is	71	36 -	Good	26
11 -	All	62	t37 -	Freedom	25
12 -	America	57	t37 -	Shall	25
13 -	Union	57	39 -	Will	24
14 -	Be	53	t40 -	His	23
15 -	Peace	52	t40 -	One	23
16 -	We	48	t40 -	President	23
t17 -	Our	47	t43 -	First	22
t17 -	People	47	t43 -	Old	22
t19 -	Not	43	t43 -	Or	22
t19 -	War	43	t43 -	Prosperity	22
21 -	Free	42	t47 -	Are	21
22 -	Right	41	t47 -	He	21
23 -	Man	39	t47 -	Out	21
t24 -	Roosevelt	38	t47 -	Party	21
t24 -	Vote	38	t47 -	Protection	21
26 -	You	34	t47 -	Us	21
			53 -	Work	20

TABLE 10.4
Over- and Under-utilized Words in Presidential Campaign Slogans,
1800–1980, Compared to Frequencies in Published American English

Rank	Word	Appearances of Word			Word	Appearances of Word		
		Actual	Expected	Difference		Actual	Expected	Difference
1	and	323	200.2	+122.8	in	83	148.2	−65.2
2	for	167	58.2	+108.2	to	119	181.4	−62.4
3	no	75	12.9	+ 62.1	was	2	61.2	−59.2
4	America('s)	60	2.1	+ 57.9	that	14	70.9	−56.9
5	union	57	0.7	+ 56.3	he	21	69.1	−48.1
6	peace	52	0.6	+ 51.4	the	511	557.8	−46.8
7	people(s)	60	12.4	+ 47.6	you	34	76.2	−42.2
8	man (men)	58	15.4	+ 42.6	it	29	70.7	−41.7
9	war(s)	44	2.3	+ 41.7	they	3	41.3	−38.3
10	free	42	1.2	+ 40.8	as	14	48.1	−34.1
11	with	85	45.6	+ 39.4	are	21	53.0	−32.0
12	Roosevelt('s)	39	0.2	+ 38.8	on	28	54.5	−26.5
13	vote(s)	39	0.4	+ 38.6	had	4	30.7	−26.7
14	our	47	8.8	+ 38.2	this	11	34.8	−23.8
15	all	62	25.5	+ 36.5	said	0	22.9	−22.9
16	American(s)	38	3.2	+ 34.8	each	0	21.4	−21.4
17	right	41	7.6	+ 33.4	by	9	30.2	−21.2
18	liberty	29	0.2	+ 28.8	when	3	23.7	−20.7
19	freedom(s)	28	0.6	+ 27.4	were	5	25.5	−20.5
20	shall	25	1.58	+ 23.42	she	0	20.4	−20.4
21	we	48	24.63	+ 23.37	is	71	91.0	−20.0
22	let	28	4.70	+ 23.30	from	15	34.1	−19.1
23	prosperity	22	0.04	+ 21.96	how	1	19.9	−18.9
24	country	27	5.11	+ 21.89	at	17	35.8	−18.8
25	of	240	218.26	+ 21.74	what	8	26.5	−18.5
26	president	23	1.4	+ 21.6	have	15	33.4	−18.4
27	party(ies)	22	1.1	+ 20.9	there	5	22.7	−17.7
28	new	30	9.17	+ 20.83	these	0	17.4	−17.4
29	protection	21	0.24	+ 20.76	which	4	21.0	−17.0
30	must	27	6.5	+ 20.5	words	0	16.8	−16.8

written English, the list in Table 10.3 also includes many potent symbols of American political history: union, peace, war, liberty, country, freedom, prosperity, party, protection, work. Table 10.4 lists the most over- and under-utilized words compared to frequencies in published American English; most over-utilized words include many of the same symbols: "America," "union," "peace," "people." Table 10.5 lists the relatively more utilized pairs of opposites; these also include potent rhetorical symbols of political struggle: "us–them," "our–their," "we–they."

TABLE 10.5
Relatively More Utilized Words in Pairs of Opposites,
U.S. Presidential Campaign Slogans, 1800–1980
(Word with More Appearances Listed First in Each Pair)

Opposite Word Pairs	Appearance of Words			Expected Pct. Former	Difference
	Former	Latter	Pct. Former		
Us–Them	21	2	91.30	24.67	66.63
Our–Their	47	5	90.38	30.35	60.03
We–They	48	3	94.12	37.33	56.79
Us–Me	21	3	87.50	38.87	48.63
White–Black	14	1	93.33	56.72	36.61
Win–Lose	9	1	90.00	55.92	34.08
Our–My	47	15	75.81	42.24	33.57
Down–Up	16	7	69.57	36.06	33.51
Give–Take	11	3	78.57	45.15	33.42
Day–Night	8	0	100.00	68.51	31.49
Peace–War	52	43	54.74	26.16	28.58
Work–Play	20	2	90.91	67.35	23.56
He–She	21	0	100.00	77.21	22.79
We–I	48	30	61.54	38.82	22.72
First–Last	22	2	91.67	71.64	20.03
Him/His–Her(s)	28	1	96.55	77.75	18.80
Brother–Sister	3	1	75.00	59.25	15.75
Full–Empty	9	1	90.00	74.87	15.13
No–Yes	75	0	100.00	86.56	13.44
West–East	7	3	70.00	56.62	13.38
Good–Bad	26	0	100.00	89.01	10.99
Man–Woman	39	1	97.50	87.97	9.53
More–Less	17	1	94.44	87.97	6.47
Freedom–Slavery	25	8	75.76	70.70	5.06
High–Low	3	1	75.00	72.30	2.70
With–Without	85	6	93.41	92.72	.69
Right–Wrong	41	5	89.13	88.82	.31
Little–Big	9	5	64.29	64.09	.20
On–Off	28	3	90.32	90.40	− .08
New–Old	30	22	57.69	58.32	− .63
North–South	7	7	50.00	51.22	− 1.22
Life–Death	9	2	81.82	83.45	− 1.63
There–Here	5	2	71.43	78.41	− 6.98
Can–Cannot	17	3	85.00	92.26	− 7.26
In–Out	83	21	79.81	89.00	− 9.19
All–None	62	9	87.32	97.67	−10.35
Just–Unjust	7	1	87.50	99.76	−12.26
Best–Worst	4	1	80.00	94.58	−14.58

REFERENCES

Asch, S. E. (1963). Effects of group pressure upon the modification and distortion of judgments. In H. S. Guetzkow (Ed.), Groups, leadership and men: Research in human relations (pp.177–190). New York: Russell & Russell. (Originally published 1951)

Axelrod, R. M. (1973). Schema theory: An information processing model of perception and cognition. American Political Science Review, 67(4), 1248–1266.

Axelrod, R. M. (Ed.). (1976). Structure of decision: The cognitive maps of political elites. Princeton, NJ: Princeton University Press.

Bartlett, F. C. (1932). Remembering: A study in experimental and social psychology. Cambridge, UK: Cambridge University Press.

Becker, L. B., McCombs, M. E., & McLeod, J. M. (1975). The development of political cognitions. In S. H. Chaffee (Ed.), Political communication: Issues and strategies for research (pp. 21–63). Beverly Hills, CA: Sage.

Behr, R. L., & Iyengar, S. (1985). Television news, real-world cues, and changes in the public agenda. Public Opinion Quarterly, 49(1) 38–57.

Beniger, J. R. (1986). The control revolution: Technological and economic origins of the information society. Cambridge, MA: Harvard University Press.

Beniger, J. R. (1987). Toward an old new paradigm: The half-century flirtation with mass society. Public Opinion Quarterly, 51(4), S46–S66.

Beniger, J. R. (1988). Information and communication: The new convergence. Communication Research, 15(2), 198–218.

Bennett, W. L. (1981). Perception and cognition: An information-processing framework for politics. In S. L. Long (Ed.), The handbook of political behavior (Vol. 1, pp. 69–193). New York: Plenum.

Berelson, B. R., Lazarsfeld, P. F., & McPhee, W. N. (1954). Voting: A study of opinion formation in a presidential campaign. Chicago: University of Chicago Press.

Blake, F. M., & Newman, H. M. (1984). Verbis non factis: Words meant to influence political choices in the United States, 1800–1980. Metuchen, NJ: Scarecrow.

Blumler, J. G., & Katz, E. (Eds.). (1974). The uses of mass communications: Current perspectives on gratifications research. Beverly Hills, CA: Sage.

Blumler, J. G., & McQuail, D. (1969). Television in politics: Its uses and influence. Chicago: University of Chicago Press.

Bourdieu, P. (1980). The production of belief (R. Nice, Trans.). Media, Culture and Society, 2(3).

Breed, W. (1955). Social control in the newsroom: A functional analysis. Social Forces, 33(4), 326–35.

Broadbent, D. E. (1958). Perception and communication. Oxford: Pergamon.

Campbell, A., Converse, P. E., Miller, W. E., & Stokes, D. E. (1960). The American voter. New York: Wiley.

Cartwright, D., & Harary, F. (1956). Structural balance: A generalization of Heider's theory. Psychological Review, 63(5), 277–293.

Chaffee, S. H., & Choe, S. Y. (1980). Time of decision and media use during the Ford–Carter campaign. Public Opinion Quarterly, 44(1), 53–69.

Converse, P. E. (1962). Information flow and the stability of partisan attitudes. Public Opinion Quarterly, 26(4), 578–599.

Converse, P. E. (1964). The nature of belief systems in mass publics. In D. E. Apter (Ed.), Ideology and discontent (pp. 206–261). New York: The Free Press.

Csikszentmihalyi, M., & Kubey, R. (1981). Television and the rest of life: A systematic comparison of subjective experience. Public Opinion Quarterly, 45(3), 317–328.

Downs, A. (1957). *An economic theory of democracy*. New York: Harper & Row.

Erbring, L., Goldenberg, E. N., & Miller, A. H. (1980). Front-page news and real-world cues: A new look at agenda-setting by the media. *American Journal of Political Science, 24*(1), 16–49.

Festinger, L. (1950). Informal social communication. *Psychological Review, 57*(5), 271–282.

Festinger, L. (1957). *A theory of cognitive dissonance*. Stanford, CA: Stanford University Press.

Fiske, S. T., & Kinder, D. R. (1981). Involvement, expertise, and schema use: Evidence from political cognition. In N. Cantor & J. F. Kihlstrom (Eds.), *Personality, cognition, and social interaction*. (pp. 171–190). Hillsdale, NJ: Lawrence Erlbaum Associates.

Gamson, W. A. (1984). *The changing culture of affirmative action*. Unpublished manuscript.

Gamson, W. A. (1987). *Media discourse and public opinion on nuclear power: A constructionist model*. Unpublished manuscript.

Gardner, H. (1985). *The mind's new science: A history of the cognitive revolution*. New York: Basic.

Garfield, E. (1987). A different sort of great-books list: The 50 twentieth-century works most cited in the arts & humanities citation index, 1976–1983. *Content Contents, 16*, 3–7.

Gitlin, T. (1979). Prime time ideology: The hegemonic process in television entertainment. *Social Problems, 26*(3), 251–266.

Gitlin, T. (1980). *The whole world is watching: Mass media in the making and unmaking of the new left*. Berkeley, CA: University of California Press.

Graber, D. A. (1984). *Processing the news: How people tame the information tide*. New York: Longman.

Hall, S. (1974). The television discourse: Encoding and decoding. *Education and Culture, 25*, 8–14.

Hall, S. (1977). Culture, the media, and the "Ideological effect." In J. Curran, M. Gurevitch, & J. Woollacott (Eds.), *Mass communication and society* (pp. 315–348). Beverly Hills, CA: Sage.

Hall, S., Critcher, C., Jefferson, T., Clarke, J., & Roberts, B. (1978). *Policing the crisis: Mugging, the state, and law and order*. New York: Holmes & Meier.

Head, H. (1926). Aphasia and kindred disorders of speech (2 vols.) New York: Macmillan.

Heider, F. (1946). Attitudes and cognitive organization. *Journal of Psychology, 21*(1), 107–112.

Hovland, C. I., Janis, I. L., & Kelley, H. H. (1953). *Communication and persuasion: Psychological studies of opinion change*. New Haven, CT: Yale University Press.

Hyman, H. H., & Sheatsley, P. B. (1947). Some reasons why information campaigns fail. *Public Opinion Quarterly, 11*(3), 412–423.

Iyengar, S., & Kinder, D. R. (1987). *News that matters: Television and American opinion*. Chicago: University of Chicago Press.

Iyengar, S., Peters, M. D., & Kinder, D. R. (1982). Experimental demonstration of the "not-so-minimal" consequences of television news programs. *American Political Science Review, 76*(4), 848–858.

Jakobson, R. (1960). Closing statement: Linguistics and poetics. In T. A. Sebeok (Ed.), *Style in language* (pp. 350–377). Cambridge: MIT Press and Wiley.

Jung, C. G. (1916). *Collected papers on analytical psychology* (C. E. Long, Trans.). London: Bailliere, Tindall & Cox.

Kant, I. (1929). *Critique of pure reason* (N. K. Smith, Trans.). London: Macmillan. (Originally published 1781)

Katz, E. (1980). Media events: The sense of occasion. *Studies in Visual Communication, 6*(3), 84–89.

Katz, E. (1987, April). *Communications research and the image of society (revisited)*. Paul F. Lazarsfeld Lecture, Columbia University, New York.

Katz, E., Dayan, D., & Motyl, P. (1981). In defense of media events. In R. W. Haigh, G.

Gerbner, & R. B. Byrne (Eds.), *Communications in the twenty-first century* (pp. 43–59). New York: Wiley-Interscience.

Katz, E., Gurevitch, M., & Haas, H. (1973). On the use of the mass media for important things. *American Sociological Review, 38*(2), 164–181.

Kelman, H. C. (1961). Processes of opinion change. *Public Opinion Quarterly, 25*(1), 57–78.

Kinder, D. R. (1982). *Enough already about ideology: The many bases of American public opinion.* Paper presented to the American Political Science Association, Chicago, IL.

Klapper, J. T. (1960). *The effects of mass communication.* Glencoe, IL: The Free Press.

Lang, K., & Lang, G. E. (1953). The unique perspective of television and its effect: A pilot study. *American Sociological Review, 18*(1), 3–12.

Lang, K., & Lang, G. E. (1959). The mass media and voting. In E. Burdick & A. J. Brodbeck (Eds.), *American voting behavior* (pp. 217–235). Glencoe, IL: The Free Press.

Lau, R. R., Sears, D. O., & Centers, R. (1979). The "Positivity Bias" in evaluations of public figures: Evidence against instrument artifacts. *Public Opinion Quarterly, 43*(3), 347–358.

Lazarsfeld, P. F., Merton, R. K. (1948). Mass communication, popular taste and organized social action. In L. Bryson (Ed.), *The communication of ideas: A series of addresses* (pp. 95–118). New York: Institute for Religious and Social Studies, Harper.

Lippmann, W. (1922). *Public opinion.* New York: Harcourt, Brace.

Lippmann, W. (1925). *The phantom public.* New York: Harcourt, Brace.

McGuire, W. J. (1969). The nature of attitudes and attitude change. In G. Lindzey & E. Aronson (Eds.), *The handbook of social psychology* (Vol. 3, 2nd ed., pp. 136–314). Reading, MA: Addison-Wesley.

McLeod, J. M., & Chaffee, S. H. (1973). Interpersonal approaches to communication research. *American Behavioral Scientist, 16*(4), 469–499.

Merton, R. K. (1945). The sociology of knowledge. In G. Gurvitch & W. E. Moore (Eds.), *Twentieth century sociology* (pp. 366–405). New York: Philosophical Library.

Merton, R. K., & Kitt, A. S., Contributions to the theory of reference group behavior. In R. K. Merton & P. F. Lazarsfeld (Eds.), *Continuities in social research: Studies in the scope and method of "The American soldier"* (pp. 40–105). Glencoe, IL: The Free Press.

Meyer, P., & Spaeth, M. A. (Eds.). (1984). A cumulative index of volumes 1–46, 1937–1982. *Public Opinion Quarterly, 48,* Part A.

Miller, G. A. (1956). The magical number seven, plus or minus two: Some limits on our capacity for processing information. *Psychological Review, 63*(2), 81–97.

Modigliani, A., & Gamson, W. A., (1979). Thinking about politics. *Political Behavior, 1*(1), 5–30.

Newcomb, T. M. (1943). *Personality and social change: Attitude formation in a student community.* New York: Holt, Rinehart & Winston.

Newcomb, T. M. (1953). An approach to the study of communicative acts. *Psychological Review, 60*(6), 393–404.

Noelle-Neumann, E. (1974). The spiral of silence: A theory of public opinion. *Journal of Communication, 24*(2), 43–51.

Noelle-Neumann, E. (1980). *The spiral of silence: Public opinion, our social skin.* Chicago: University of Chicago Press.

Schuman, H., & Presser, S. (1981). *Questions and answers in attitude surveys: Experiments on question form, wording, and context.* New York: Academic Press.

Sears, D. O., Lau, R. R., Tyler, T. R., & Allen, H. M., Jr. (1980). Self-interest vs. symbolic politics in policy attitudes and presidential voting. *American Political Science Review, 74*(3), 670–684.

Sherif, M. (1935). A study of some social factors in perception. *Archives of Psychology, 27*(187), 5–60.

Sherif, M. (1936). *The psychology of social norms.* New York: Harper.

Smith, T. W. (1984). Nonattitudes: A review and evaluation. In C. F. Turner & E. Martin (Eds.), *Surveying subjective phenomena* (Vol. 2, pp. 215–255). New York: Russell Sage.

Stouffer, S. A. (1949–1950). *The American soldier: Studies in social psychology in World War II* (4 vols). Princeton: Princeton University Press.

Sudman, S., & Bradburn, N. M. (1974). *Response effects in surveys: A review and synthesis.* Chicago: Aldine.

Tichenor, P. J., Donohue, G. A., & Olien, C. N. (1970). Mass media flow and differential growth in knowledge. *Public Opinion Quarterly, 34*(2), 159–170.

Tichenor, P. J., Rodenkirchen, J. M., Olien, C. N., & Donohue, G. A. (1973). Community issues, conflict, and public affairs knowledge. In P. Clarke (Ed.), *New models for mass communication research* (pp. 45–79). Beverly Hills, CA: Sage.

Tolman, E. C., (1932). *Purposive behavior in animals and men.* New York: Century.

Turner, V. (1977). Process, system, and symbol: A new anthropological synthesis. *Daedalus, 106*(3), 61–80.

Urdang, L., & Robbins, C. D., (Eds.). (1984). *Slogans.* Detroit: Gale Research.

Worth, S., & Gross, L. (1974). Symbolic strategies. *Journal of Communication, 24*(4), 27–39.

Wuthnow, R. (1987). *Meaning and moral order: Explorations in cultural analysis.* Berkeley, CA: University of California Press.

Wuthnow, R. (1988). Religious discourse as public rhetoric. *Communication Research, 15*(3), 352–371.

11

Corporate Image Advertising and the Federal Government: A Case Study of the Application of Information-Processing Models

Carl Camden
Steve Verba
George Sapin
Wyse Advertising

The role of the cognitive sciences (e.g., psycholinguistics and semiotics) on the theory and practice of marketing has been growing in importance in recent years.[1] An particularly important contribution has been an understanding of the role of schema[2] in advertising. An important impact of this understanding has been a shift away from a mechanistic sender-oriented perspective (see Fisher, 1978) to a receiver-oriented framework (e.g., Verba & Camden, 1985). Advertising professionals are becoming increasingly aware that they must understand the symbol sets of their critical audiences as well as the schema used by those audiences to interpret the symbolic messages (advertisements) directed at them (e.g., Yovovich, 1987).

However, the majority of studies and papers exploring this area have been written by individuals who were not involved in the planning, execution, and evaluation of the advertising campaigns (see for example many of the papers included in Umiker-Sebeok, 1987). Additionally, many of these studies have attempted to assess and explain the failure or success of a campaign without talking to the audiences for the advertisements. Although providing useful insights and hypotheses about cognitive processes and cultural symbology, such studies cannot (and generally do not claim to) serve as models for the development of effective advertising campaigns. This chapter presents a case study of the planning, execution, and evaluation of an advertising campaign developed by Wyse Advertising for General Dynamics. The develop-

---

[1] See for example Camden and Verba (1986) and Umiker-Sebeok (1987).

[2] For an overview of "schema" and information processing, see Hastie (1986).

ment of the campaign by the agency was specifically directed by the application of information processing theory.

BACKGROUND

In 1986, Wyse Advertising was retained by General Dynamics to develop a corporate image campaign.[3] General Dynamics is the country's second largest defense contractor and produces the M1 tank, the F-16 fighter, the Tomahawk cruise missile, and the Trident submarine. The company's revenues were approximately $8 billion in 1986.

In 1985 and 1986, General Dynamics, as was the case for the defense industry in general, found itself operating in a hostile, or at best a suspicious, environment. A corporate officer resigned in the face of criminal investigations. The media frequently reported seemingly exorbitant prices being charged to the government for spare parts or components (e.g., a wrench for $9,600). Congresspersons (especially John Dingell) spoke against the "waste" of taxpayers' money. The Pentagon temporarily suspended General Dynamics from bidding on new military contracts. *Forbes* ("Corporate cleaner-upper," 1988) magazine reported that in one weapon system alone, the Tomahawk missile program, the direct costs from the suspension were $24 million.

General Dynamics responded to the changing environment. A new chief executive officer and new corporate officers, committed to change, were installed. Strong ethics committees and procedures were instituted throughout the company. Accounting procedures were modified to eliminate any questionable cost. Finally, a corporate image campaign to develop a "reservoir of goodwill" for General Dynamics was authorized. The Wyse Advertising account services team for General Dynamics asked the Marketing Decisions Group (the agency's account planning group) and North Coast Behavioral Research Group (an independent market research firm in Cleveland, Ohio) to help identify potential advertising platforms for the corporate image campaign.[4]

North Coast Behavioral Research Group and Wyse Advertising use a multistaged research program to help determine appropriate advertising platforms for corporate image campaigns. Among the research techniques used are: market assessment focus groups, advertisement testing focus groups, and quantitative tracking surveys. Figure 11.1 displays a flow chart showing the

---

[3]Wyse Advertising is well-known for its corporate image advertising. Recent campaigns have included those for J. M. Smucker Co., TRW, Leaseway Transportation Corporation, and BP America.

[4]Worthy (1986) provided a good accounting of the troubles facing General Dynamics and other defense contractors, and the selection of Stan Pace as CEO of General Dynamics.

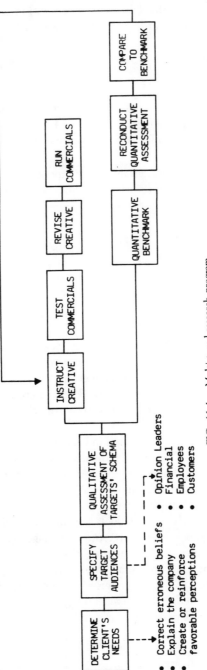

FIG. 11.1.   Multistaged research program.

research techniques used in the development, execution, and evaluation of a corporate image campaign that began with an assessment of the market.

MARKET ASSESSMENT STUDY

An assessment study was conducted to discover dominant schema for critical market segments in the perceptions of General Dynamics. A qualitative research program, based on eight focus groups, was used to make this assessment.[5]

Subjects. Focus groups (each group was comprised of 8–10 people) were conducted during January 1987 with individuals representing the following groups:

- formal opinion leaders,
- informal opinion leaders,
- investment officers,
- federal government bureaucracy, and
- military.

One focus group, held in New York City, was conducted with formal opinion leaders. These were individuals who were gatekeepers in the news media (i.e., editors, news directors, etc.) or elected local government officials. The news media representatives had to work for a publication or electronic medium that had the potential to print or air a story about a defense industry company.

Another focus group, also conducted in New York City, was comprised of informal opinion leaders. These were individuals who were board members of civic groups (i.e., political advocacy organizations, charitable foundations, etc.), appointed government officials, or recognized local community leaders.

Two groups were held in New York City with members of the financial investment community. These individuals were mutual fund executives (vice-presidents or directors), portfolio or investment managers of Fortune 500 firms or major brokerage houses, and major trust officers.

The federal government bureaucracy was represented by two groups conducted in Washington, DC. These groups were composed of individuals who were directors or assistant directors of federal regulatory agencies, department heads in federal cabinet departments, or members of congressional or senatorial staffs.

---

[5]Goldman and McDonald (1987) provided an excellent overview on focus group methodology and its application to marketing and advertising issues.

Finally, two groups, also held in Washington, DC, were conducted with U.S. military officers. The individuals were primarily associated with the procurement and evaluation of weapon systems. Additionally, two or three public affairs officers were recruited per group. Military officers cleared their participation with appropriate ethics and/or legal officers.

All respondents received $100 for participating. Many chose to have the fee donated to a charity in their name. Additionally, no person was selected for participation if they had been in a focus group in the preceding 6 months. Individuals from the same company or government department did not participate in the same groups.

Group Proceedings. The groups were led by a "moderator" with academic and applied experience in group dynamics. The moderator was instructed to be as unobtrusive as possible. The majority of comments by the moderator served to introduce new topics, to prevent the focus group participants from going off on tangents of little relevance to the purpose of the project (e.g., the quality of the snacks provided), or to encourage the subjects to delve more deeply into a particularly interesting observation or disagreement. For approximately 2 hours, each focus group explored the following discussion topics:

- perceptual categories used to differentiate among American industries;
- qualities of "good" and "bad" large American corporations;
- categorical differences between American business in general and the defense industry;
- the relationship of the defense industry to the government and the people; and
- current perceptions of specific defense industry companies.

Data Recording. Each focus group was videotaped. The camera was placed behind a two-way mirror and, therefore, was not visible to the participants. Participants were informed that they were being videotaped. There were no obvious reactions to the taping (as judged by the lack of respondents' comments) after a few minutes of group interaction. This lack of reaction to the taping is typical in an experimental setting (Wiemann, 1981).

Results. Four dominant schema that affected perceptions of defense contractors were discovered for the Washington military-government bureaucracy and those with significant influence on the bureaucracy (the financial-business community and opinion leaders).

1. *Defense companies are not "real" businesses.* When the focus group respondents were asked to categorize American businesses, the defense industry was never spontaneously identified as a "category" or "type" of business. Our analysis indicates that this lack of spontaneous mention is due to the fact that defense contractors are not seen as being within the "business world." Rather, defense contractors seem to be generally perceived as part of the government. There are three primary reasons for this perception.

First, the defense industry was generally recognized as having only one true customer, the U.S. defense establishment. (Foreign sales were dismissed as relatively insignificant or dependent upon support or approval by the U.S. military.) This solitary customer relationship was seen as reducing the normal "risks" experienced by business (e.g., "the government won't let them go out of business" or "if they don't get this contract, they'll get the next one"); removing accountability for mistakes (e.g., "either the government covers up the company's mistakes or allows them to bill the government for the costs of the mistakes"); contractually guaranteeing profit (e.g., "cost-plus billing"); and providing cloaks of secrecy (e.g., "able to conceal financial and operational information").

Second, like the government, defense contractors were seen as spending (and wasting) "taxpayers' money." When the defense contractor is perceived as being "inefficient, fat, and flabby," people perceive their tax dollars as being wasted. This often generates intense, negative emotional reactions and extensive news coverage. Contrast these perceptions to probable lack of reaction by the general public about similar inefficiency in a fast food company. Only stockholders in the fast food company would be outraged. The individuals in the focus groups considered themselves to be the equivalent of a stockholder in the defense industry.

Third, the federal government and defense contractors are perceived as having a "shared" work force. This relationship was often described as a "revolving door." Defense contractors were perceived as hiring many retired military officers or civilian managers from the Department of Defense. The top management of the Department of Defense was perceived as being heavily drawn from defense contractors. This revolving door relationship was frequently described as *incestuous*. The use of this term rather than other "in-bed together" relationships (e.g., prostitute) appears to be a significant sign of the perceptual relationship between defense contractors and the government. The term *incestuous* seems to have been specifically chosen because it implied a "kindred" relationship between the government and the defense industry. This perception of an incestuous relationship was a source of some of the strongest negative reactions to the defense industry by the respondents. The relationship was seen as removing the normal business "tension" between client and supplier.

2. *All defense companies are the same.* The focus group respondents could not easily differentiate among defense companies. Defense contractors were viewed as basically identical in nature, differentiated only by the product manufactured (e.g., airplanes vs. tanks). For example, a defense company that had never been accused of misconduct was assumed to be a company that merely had not yet been caught. Because of this general inability to significantly distinguish among defense companies, respondents' comments on specific defense contractors were generally vague, general, and/or inaccurate. Just as the first structure reported in this subsection prevents corporate image campaigns for a defense contractor from making a "we are a good business" claim, this structure renders ineffective the "we are different from the rest of them (defense contractors)" theme.

The strength of this belief structure is further revealed by reactions to "mixed" companies (i.e., companies with both defense and "consumer" divisions). When asked to identify defense contractors that were exceptions to the generally negative perceptions, the focus group respondents generally refused. Exceptional defense companies were viewed as nonexistent. The only companies judged to be "somewhat better" than the rest were those companies that also had large, easily recognizable consumer or commercial divisions (e.g., General Electric or Boeing).

Having a strong consumer or commercial component was perceived as having three mitigating influences on the negative consequences of being a defense company. First, technology transfer to consumer divisions was perceived as both making the defense work more "worthwhile" and as providing greater incentive to the company to do quality military work. Second, it was assumed that traditional (positively perceived) business values are transferred from the consumer divisions to the defense components. Managers who have successfully performed in the competitive consumer or commercial markets are believed to apply those same values and talents to their military business. Finally, the fact that mixed companies are less dependent on the single customer (government) for their success is perceived as making the company less susceptible to fraud and the like.

It is important to note that the image of the mixed companies improve the further they are perceptually distanced from the defense industry (i.e., the more they are known for the consumer or commercial business). The greater the percentage of defense business, the more undifferentiated the company is from other defense contractors. This understanding may have led many companies to emphasize their consumer operations in their corporate image advertising (e.g., Dow Chemical). This option is not available to companies whose business is primarily based on defense contracts (like General Dynamics). Additionally, if several companies adopt this advertising approach, its general effectiveness would be diminished.

3. *Defense versus social service spending is a zero-sum conflict.* Opinion leaders, the financial community, and major portions of the government and military groups view defense versus social service spending as a zero-sum conflict. Every dollar spent on defense expenditures is viewed as decreasing the amount that can be spent on social programs. Many of these respondents attached greater "social value" to spending on social programs. For these respondents, defense spending is at best tolerated and often resented. Advertising that is interpreted as asking for greater defense spending will be very negatively received.

4. *The U.S. military is not weak.* The military and government respondents were unanimous in their opinion that the U.S. military is not weak. Clear majorities of the financial and opinion leader groups also shared this perception. Many of the respondents believed that the military exaggerated the "Russian threat" in order to obtain approval for new weapon systems and increased defense spending. Advertisements that are perceived as claiming weaknesses in the U.S. military will be perceived as self-serving (asking for more money) by many and insulting by those who are a part of the defense establishment. This belief structure should, for example, inhibit advertisements based on strength comparisons between the United States and the Soviet Union.

The results of this analysis were then translated into instructions to the creative department at Wyse Advertising.

INSTRUCTIONS TO CREATIVE

The creative department was instructed to begin developing potential advertisements for General Dynamics' corporate image campaign. As part of the instructions, they were provided the following guidelines:

1. Although General Dynamics has a strong "good business" story to tell, they cannot use it as the platform for the advertising campaign. Claims that General Dynamics possesses traditionally valued attributes (e.g., efficient, innovative, etc.) will not be believed.

2. General Dynamics cannot claim to be an excellent defense contractor. The defense industry category is negatively perceived and most people cannot differentiate among defense contractors.

3. Advertisements for General Dynamics cannot be perceived as requesting a larger defense budget or as presenting the U.S. as militarily weak. Such advertisements will be perceived as self-serving.

4. General Dynamics should attempt to reduce the perceived distance

between themselves and their target audiences. They should "document" their beliefs in the same "superordinate" values as those believed in by most Americans. A list of potential values to consider for development was derived from Rokeach (1968).

The creative team developed 10 print advertisements (5 per execution format—one format featured quotations and the other format had substantially more text) and 3 television commercials. The print advertisements are included in Appendix I. These advertisements were then evaluated in creative testing focus groups.

CREATIVE TESTING FOCUS GROUPS

The creative executions were tested, and the following summarizes that research.

Subjects.   Four focus groups were conducted during May 1987 with individuals representing the following groups:

- formal opinion leaders,
- informal opinion leaders,
- federal government bureaucracy, and
- military.

The operationalizations, fees, and recruiting parameters were identical to those in the market assessment study.

Group Proceedings.   The general focus group proceedings parameters were the same as those discussed in the market assessment study. The following reactions to the creative executions and their anticipated impact were discussed:

- credibility of advertisement,
- changes in perceptions about General Dynamics,
- emotional reactions to the advertisements, and
- effectiveness of specific elements of the creative execution.

Data Recording.   Data was collected in the same manner as that identified in the market assessment study.

Results.   The advertisements tested in the focus groups appear in Appendix

I. They are in the following order (references in the results section are cited by the title abbreviations that are placed in parentheses) in the appendix:

- John F. Kennedy (JFK),
- General Douglas MacArthur (GDM),
- Lyndon B. Johnson (LBJ),
- Arthur M. Schlesinger, Jr. (AMS),
- Ralph Waldo Emerson (RWE),
- Lion and Lamb (LL),
- Soldier (SOL),
- Franklin Delano Roosevelt (FDR),
- Factory (FAC), and
- Old Car (CAR).

Reactions obtained to these 10 print advertisements confirmed and further refined the conclusions reached in the market assessment study. The following paragraphs identify the salient reactions to the individual advertisements and also provide any additional general understandings of the "category" that were revealed. However, the LBJ, AMS, and CAR advertisements are not discussed. They were disliked for specific execution problems that were independent of schema issues.

The JFK commercial generated more positive than negative reactions. Among the positive reactions were:

- quiet proclamation of strength,
- image of security (the lighthouse "symbol" was especially potent), and
- positive feelings about President Kennedy.

Negative comments can be attributed to specific execution problems and the limitations of the print medium (a television version of the advertisement tested much better). Reactions to this commercial confirmed the perception of America as being militarily strong. One additional insight was that proclamations of America's strength are more effective if done "quietly" rather than "aggressively."

Reactions to the GDM advertisement revealed another important dynamic. Focus group respondents commented that one factor in their resentment of defense contractors was that defense companies had a motive to promote war because they were perceived as "profiting from war." The GDM commercial clearly communicated that General Dynamics shared the respondents' revulsion for the "horrors of war." Aside from specific execution problems, the advertisement had a strong positive impact. The impact was greatest for the focus group participants who were veterans.

The RWE advertisement was rejected for two important reasons. First, many of the respondents perceived "productivity" and "quality" to be a central theme of the advertisement. Because productivity and quality are traditional business values, they were viewed as inappropriate for a defense contractor. Second, the focus on a blue-collar worker was perceived as counterproductive. Most of the focus group participants perceived the typical blue-collar worker as an extremely overpaid "weak link" in American industry. Additionally, blue-collar symbols were identified as incongruent with the "high technology" image of the defense industry.

The LL advertisement was the most negatively received advertisement of the 10 presented. It was interpreted by all audiences (except the military) as a self-serving plea for more spending on defense equipment. The delineation of differences in the military equipment levels of the U.S. and U.S.S.R. was perceived as a "sales pitch." Additionally, the military respondents rejected the advertisement because they interpreted it as portraying the U.S. military as a lamb. Although the negative reactions provided no new insights, the strength of the negative reactions to this advertisement, which appeared to violate the "instructions to creative," further validates the schema underlying the instructions.

The SOL advertisement was disliked by all audiences except the military. The soldier was perceived by many participants as being "too aggressive," "lacking humanity," and too blatant of a military symbol. The nonmilitary respondents stated they did not want to see "military symbols" in advertisements. This ban on the use of military symbols was specifically extended to cover military weapons, perceived as a typical aspect of advertising by defense contractors. Although some of the military respondents disliked the advertisement because it used the portrait of a Marine (the focus groups were held shortly after the U.S. Marine guard scandal at the U.S. embassy in Moscow), most approved of the advertisement because it represented a "strong" military.

The FDR advertisement received the most positive reactions of any of the print advertisements. The participants strongly approved of the programs that General Dynamics was supporting. None of the respondents were previously aware of the support General Dynamics provided to education and public television. The positive reactions to this advertisement clearly indicate that "education," "sense of history," and "public television" are effective symbols in communicating shared values between General Dynamics and their audiences.

The FAC advertisement also generated strong positive reactions. Participants indicated that defense companies are perceived as large, bureaucratic, and devoid of emotional links with their employees. However, the participants felt that the copy demonstrated how much General Dynamics cared about their employees and how much the employees cared about the company and their country. Therefore, the advertisement generated considerable surprise and positive impact on the corporate image of General Dynamics.

As a result of these results, five print advertisements were directed to production. A summary of these advertisements can be found in Appendix II.

QUANTITATIVE TRACKING SURVEY

The quantitative benchmark study had two major purposes. First, the study was designed to test the hypotheses formulated from the preceding qualitative focus group projects. Second, the study provides a "benchmark," against which changes resulting from the advertising campaign can be assessed. The following sections discuss the procedures and results of the benchmark study.

Subjects. The data for this study was gathered during July and August 1987. The sample consisted of 275 telephone surveys of executives and high-level executives from three distinct market segments. (The calls were placed to their place of employment and client identification was not provided to the respondents.) The following describes the parameters for each market segment.

Community Leaders ($N=100$)—Individuals who were considered formal or informal opinion leaders in Los Angeles, New York City, St. Louis, Providence, Dallas–Fort Worth, Detroit, Hartford–New Haven, San Diego, and Washington, DC. These cities represented either critical decision-making sites or locations of large General Dynamics operations (e.g., M1 tank plant in Detroit). Formal leaders consisted of editors, news directors, and reporters ($N=25$) from media capable of doing stories/articles about defense contractors, and elected local government officials ($N=25$). Informal leaders consisted of appointed officials (e.g., chief of police), board members of civic groups (e.g., charitable foundations), and local community leaders ($N=50$) (e.g., deans).

Financial Community ($N=75$)—Individuals responsible for controlling institutional investments. All respondents had influence on their company's stock management and worked at Fortune 500 firms (service and industrial) or in the top 100 mutual funds companies. Respondents were primarily employed as directors, vice presidents, treasurers, portfolio managers, or investment managers.

Government ($N=100$)—Individuals who were directors, assistant directors, or department heads at federal regulatory agencies and executive branch departments ($N=67$) or members of Congressional staffs ($N=33$).

The benchmark represented all segments from the market assessment study, with the exception of the military. The military was excluded due to concerns with sampling (i.e., nearly all relevant officers had been contacted in the market assessment study) and the lengthy time required for potential participants to obtain permission (from judicial or ethics officers) to answer such a survey.

Questionnaire. The questionnaire used in the study covered the following areas:

Unaided awareness of the companies that immediately come to mind as diversified suppliers of products in the defense industry;

Aided awareness of selected companies in the competitive set;

Respondents' evaluations of the desirability of 16 attributes identified as critical to corporate image in the market assessment study;

Perceived association of the attributes with the selected companies in the competitive set and selected "normal business" companies;

Respondents' evaluations of 10 value statements designed to reflect the superordinate values discussed earlier in this chapter;

Respondents' opinions concerning the major challenge(s) facing the defense industry in the next decade;

Respondents' cable television usage; and

Demographic questions related to the respondents' job titles, ages, and annual personal incomes.

Results. Results affirm the hypotheses formed in the market assessment study and indicate the criteria for the success of the campaign as it will be judged in the future.

1. *General Dynamics does not currently have a favorable corporate image.* Of the seven companies evaluated, General Dynamics was the company most associated with the following negative attributes:

- is too secretive (27%), and
- is unethical (28%).

Additionally, General Dynamics was the company least associated with the following positive characteristics:

- is a good corporate citizen (36%), and
- takes a position on social values (15%).

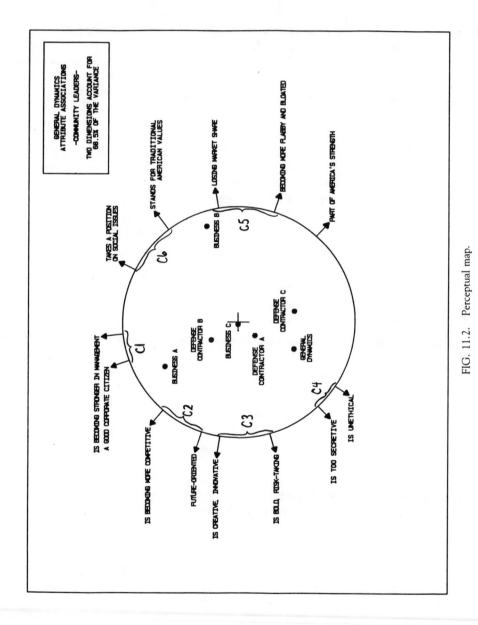

FIG. 11.2.   Perceptual map.

184

Finally, the company had only weak associations with the following desirable characteristics:

- has the courage to stand up for what they believe in (37%),
- is becoming more competitive (38%),
- is becoming stronger in management (29%), and
- is bold, risk-taking (38%).

2. *Defense companies are not perceived as "regular" businesses.* The relative perceptions of General Dynamics, other defense contractors, and selected businesses were examined via perceptual mapping.[6] The perceptual map in Fig. 11.2 clearly shows the clustering of defense companies A and C and General Dynamics distinctively apart from other regular business companies. Additionally, the position (located between business companies A and C) of Defense Company B (the defense company with the largest proportion of consumer/commercial business) demonstrates the ability of non-defense components to move the perception of a defense company closer to businesses in general. If the corporate image advertising campaign is successful, then the perceptual map from the 1988 tracking study should show General Dynamics beginning to move toward the "C6" cluster on the map.

3. *The values believed in by General Dynamics and expressed in the corporate image campaign reflect values shared by the critical audiences.* The three values (all reflected in the final advertisements) most agreed to by the respondents were:

Value Statement	$\overline{X}$
Our children's sense of history is crucial to our future	4.16
Our educational system is this country's asset	4.02
Future improvements in our quality of life will depend primarily on the free market	3.95
1 = Strongly Disagree 5 = Strongly Agree	

The values expressed in the advertisements are beliefs strongly felt by the respondents.

DISCUSSION

Beyond outlining a model for developing corporate image campaigns, the specifics of the study identify three critical decision-making rules in the preparation of advertising directed at the federal government (its members, employees, and those who influence the government's decisions).

---

[6]Coxon (1982) and Coxon and Davies (1982) provided a good overview of the perceptual mapping analysis technique and underlying theory.

It is worth noting that, in addition to this case study, the authors have conducted several studies and advertising campaigns targeted to the Washington community. The following decision criteria seem critical to the success of an advertisement targeted at this audience. (Although presented linearly, many of the decision rules probably function simultaneously.)

1. *Is the company perceived as within the "business world" or as a "part of government?"* As this case study has clearly demonstrated, companies are not always perceived as within the business world. Two factors seem critical to this placement of a company: the number of years with a visible government contract and the percentage of revenue derived from government contracts. In our example of General Dynamics, the company has had a highly visible contract with the federal government every year in the last 20 and currently derives approximately 90% of its revenue from such contracts. Obviously, General Dynamics would rate highly on a "government" index based on these two factors. In fact, analysis of the tracking study data indicates that such an index based on the following formula:

Government Index = (% of years in last 20 with visible contract) × (% of revenue from government contracts)

highly predicts the ability of a company to differentiate itself from the previously identified defense industry stereotypes. A company that scores above .80 on the government index seems to have little possibility of success utilizing a "traditional" business-oriented corporate image campaign.

2. *If perceived as part of government, identify advertising platforms that can successfully alter the "frame of reference" used to evaluate the company.* This research project indicates that the following advertising platforms are not available to a defense contractor:

- better than other defense companies,
- competitive and efficient,
- an ethical company,
- a good business,
- a reformed company, and
- responsible spending of taxpayers' money.

For this project, a "shared-values orientation" was chosen as the platform to alter the frame of reference used in the evaluation of General Dynamics. The values discussed in the final advertisements (see Appendix II) are:

- children's education,
- democracy,
- literary,
- patriotism,
- quiet strength,
- respect for history, and
- support for public broadcasting.

These values were not only highly respected by General Dynamics audiences, they also represented themes that General Dynamics had a long history of supporting.

3. *If perceived within the business world, do the advertisements use current business symbols or myths?* Over the last 6 years, we have traced the evolution of business symbols and myths. For example, consider the evolution to the current positive perception of "risk-taking" (the current business symbol for innovation):

Value: Innovation

1983   1985   1987

computerization→   high technology→   risk-taking

The value of "innovation" has been consistently identified as an important component of corporate image. However, the symbols accepted as valid expressions of that value have been constantly changing. Among the major values and myths, and their current "symbols," are the following:

Category Leader: New product introduction
Community Involvement: Contributions to PBS
Innovation: Risk-taking
Leadership: CEO as healer

Successful corporate image campaigns for companies perceived as businesses must be preceded by research that identifies critical values and current symbology for the audiences being addressed.

Although the case study discussed in this chapter is directly applicable only to companies advertising to the U.S. federal government, the methodologies have also proven successful for political and product campaigns. The recognition of companies, products, and candidates as "symbols," to be given meaning by their association with other symbols, is vital to the development of effective communication campaigns.

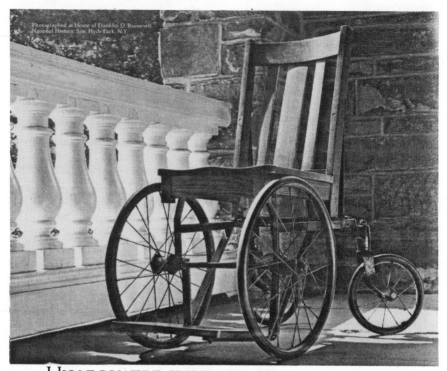

Photographed at Home of Franklin D. Roosevelt
National Historic Site, Hyde Park, N.Y.

HIS LEGS WERE CRIPPLED.
BUT HE CARRIED THE WEIGHT
OF THE FREE WORLD ON
HIS SHOULDERS.

He was used to carrying a heavier load than most. The braces on his legs weighed fourteen pounds.

But he not only campaigned for and won the Presidency despite his handicap, he won it four times. From his wheelchair, he steered the country through two of the most important events of the twentieth century — the Great Depression and World War II.

Yet in a survey of high school seniors, 52% could not identify Franklin Delano Roosevelt.

Many could not identify Churchill or Eisenhower, either.

That's shocking and sad, and we wanted to do something about it.

So General Dynamics has brought a series of dramatic profiles of twentieth century leaders to PBS. And in a mailing to America's high schools, we have offered free videocassettes of our PBS programs featuring Churchill, Eisenhower, LBJ, and Pope John XXIII.

Twenty-two million American students will see them and learn how individuals with courage and conviction can make a difference.

GENERAL DYNAMICS
A Strong Company For A Strong Country

188

THEY DIDN'T ASK
A DECORATOR FOR IDEAS.
THEY HAD THEIR OWN IDEAS.

Our aircraft factory in Ft. Worth, Texas is one of the largest production plants in the world. The factory floor is a mile long. B-24 Liberators rolled off the line here, then flew off to help roll back the Axis advance in World War II.

Today we build the F-16 Fighting Falcon here. The Air Force rates it the highest quality tactical fighter in the world.

We are proud of our plant.

We are proud of our plane.

But we are most proud of our people.

See those American flags? There's a full mile of them.

We didn't put them there. Our people did.

We didn't pay for them. Our people did.

We don't clean and care for them. Our people do. Spending their own time. And their own money to do it.

We guess that the flags help our people create the kind of environment they want to work in by reminding them what they are working for.

They are proud of our plant.

And are proud of our planes, too.

But they are most proud of our country.

GENERAL DYNAMICS
A Strong Company for A Strong Country

189

"We must be constantly prepared for the worst and constantly acting for the best— strong enough to win a war and wise enough to prevent one."

—Lyndon B. Johnson, State of the Union Message, Jan. 8, 1964.

GENERAL DYNAMICS
If we work hard enough for freedom, we won't have to fight for it.

190

"Leadership ignites the circuit between the individual and the mass and thereby alters history."

-Arthur M. Schlesinger, Jr., *Introductory Essay on Leadership.*

GENERAL DYNAMICS
If we work hard enough for freedom, we won't have to fight for it.

"The American workman who strikes ten blows with his hammer, while the foreign worker only strikes one, is really vanquishing that foreigner as if the blows were aimed at his person."

-Ralph Waldo Emerson, *Conduct of Life: Worship*

GENERAL DYNAMICS
If we work hard enough for freedom,
we won't have to fight for it.

"The United States is a peaceful nation. And where our strength and determination are clear, our words need merely to convey conviction, not belligerence. If we are strong, our strength will speak for itself. If we are weak, words will not help."

-John F. Kennedy, speech prepared for delivery in Dallas on Nov. 22, 1963, the day of his death.

GENERAL DYNAMICS
If we work hard enough for freedom, we won't have to fight for it.

193

"The soldier, above all other people, prays for peace, for he must suffer and bear the deepest wounds and scars of war."

—General Douglas MacArthur, Address at US Military Academy, West Point, N.Y., May 12, 1962

GENERAL DYNAMICS
If we work hard enough for freedom, we won't have to fight for it.

YOU CANT PRODUCE 1987 GOODS ON 1947 TOOLS.

The steel industry has proved it.

The auto industry has proved it.

The consumer electronics industry has proved it. They have proved it by losing much of their business to high-tech, low cost foreign manufacturers. And they have proved it most convincingly to the 3.5 million American workers whose jobs were shipped overseas last year.

Some see this industrial erosion as a natural transition to a service-based economy. We see it as an erosion of America's ability to protect herself.

Our armed forces depend on our defense industry to supply the best weapons systems in the world. And defense manufacturers like General Dynamics depend on American leadership in steel, machine tools, semi-conductors and other basic industries.

America needs new, more competitive tools. And new, more competitive thinking.

We can't protect 1776 ideals with 1947 ideas.

GENERAL DYNAMICS
A Strong Company for A Strong Country

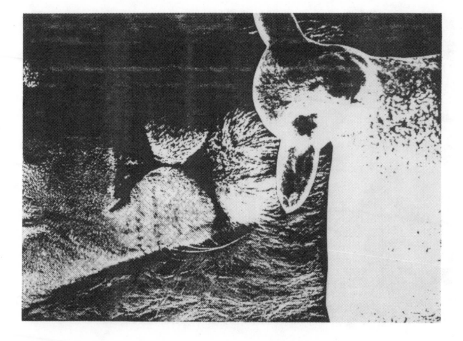

THE LION AND THE LAMB MAY LIE DOWN TOGETHER, BUT THE LAMB WON'T GET MUCH SLEEP.

Just suppose that in the last ten years Country A built 3000 ballistic missiles, while Country B built only 850.

Country A built 140,000 surface-to-air missiles, while Country B built 16,200.

Country A built 90 submarines. Country B built 43.

Is it any wonder that country B isn't getting much sleep?

At General Dynamics, we want peace... with peace of mind. And we are working for both.

Our people supply America's fighting men and women with the best weapon systems in the world.

We are dedicated to quality and to technological leadership because America's defense depends on it. Quantity is against us.

You see, we live in Country B.

And when it comes to protecting our freedom, it's smarter to sleep with one eye open.

GENERAL DYNAMICS
A Strong Company for A Strong Country

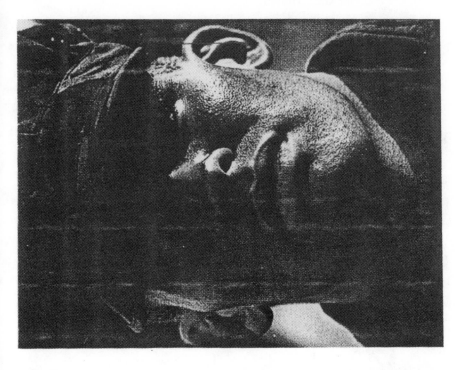

IF WE WORK HARD ENOUGH FOR FREEDOM, HE WON'T HAVE TO FIGHT FOR IT.

Today you will spend about one half hour of your work day defending your freedom.

That's how much the taxpaying American working person spends to support the American fighting man.

Isn't that a lot? Yes.

But it's only about half of the per capita cost the colonists paid to support our American revolution. And it's about 40% less than the average Soviet citizen is paying to oppose us.

Our country was founded upon the idea that freedom is worth fighting for. Even dying for. Certainly it's worth working for.

That's why every day more than 100,000 Americans come to work at General Dynamics to make products they hope will never be used in anger.

Our duty as working men and women is to supply America's fighting men with the best. And if the weapons we make are never used, our work will not be wasted.

GENERAL DYNAMICS
A Strong Company for A Strong Country

197

APPENDIX II:
FINAL CREATIVE EXECUTIONS

Headline and Message for Finished Ads

AD: Wheelchair

HEADLINE: His legs were crippled. But he carried the weight of the free world on his shoulders.

MESSAGE: General Dynamics is reminding America of its historical leaders through Public Broadcast and outreach programs to high schools.

AD: Literacy

HEADLINE: One out of five adult Americans is unable to read this sentence.

MESSAGE: General Dynamics is making a contribution to overcome illiteracy.

AD: Flag

HEADLINE: They didn't ask a decorator for ideas. They had their own ideas.

MESSAGE: Employees making F-16's decorated the plant with American flags to express their patriotism.

AD: Pins

HEADLINE: They all pinned their hopes on peace.

MESSAGE: America's political system is characterized by leaders who fought for their beliefs.

AD: Special Olympics

HEADLINE: We couldn't make it easy for him to reach the finish line. Just the starting line.

MESSAGE: General Dynamics and their customers donated their aircraft, manufactured by General Dynamics, to help the Special Olympics.

Photographed at Home of Franklin D. Roosevelt
National Historic Site, Hyde Park, N.Y.

HIS LEGS WERE CRIPPLED.
BUT HE CARRIED THE WEIGHT
OF THE FREE WORLD ON
HIS SHOULDERS.

He was used to carrying a heavier load than most.
The braces on his legs weighed fourteen pounds.

But he not only campaigned for and won the
Presidency despite his handicap, he won it four
times. From his wheelchair, he steered the country
through two of the most important events of
the twentieth century — the Great Depression and
World War II.

Yet in a survey of high school seniors,
52% could not identify Franklin Delano Roosevelt.

Many could not identify Churchill or
Eisenhower, either.

That's shocking and sad, and we
wanted to do something about it.

So General Dynamics has brought a series of
dramatic profiles of twentieth century leaders to PBS.

And in a mailing to America's high schools,
we have offered free videocassettes of our PBS
programs featuring Churchill, Eisenhower, LBJ,
and Pope John XXIII.

Twenty-two million American students will
see them and learn how individuals with courage
and conviction can make a difference.

GENERAL DYNAMICS
A Strong Company For A Strong Country

199

ONE OUT OF FIVE ADULT AMERICANS IS UNABLE TO READ THIS SENTENCE.

Or a warning label. Or a job application. Or a love letter.

You see, more than 27 million adult Americans are functionally illiterate. And their ranks are swelling by more than two million every year.

As a high-technology maker of America's defense systems, we find this trend more menacing than Soviet missiles.

In the year when all Americans celebrate the two hundredth birthday of the Constitution, millions of us can't even read it.

Experts say curing illiteracy will require the efforts of tens of thousands of us.

That's why General Dynamics has made a grant to help keep the Project Literacy U.S. Hotline operating, toll-free. Call the Hotline, 1-800-228-8813. Find out how you can help someone overcome this terrible handicap.

We think every American ought to be able to read this ad. Don't you?

GENERAL DYNAMICS
A Strong Company For A Strong Country

200

THEY DIDN'T ASK A DECORATOR FOR IDEAS. THEY HAD THEIR OWN IDEAS.

This factory floor in Ft. Worth, Texas, is almost a full mile long. B-24 Liberators rolled off the line here, then flew off to help roll back the Axis advance in World War II.

Today, we build the F-16 Fighting Falcon here. The Air Force rates it the highest-quality tactical fighter in the world.

We are proud of this plant.
We are proud of our plane.

But we are most proud of our people.
See those American flags? There's over a mile of them.

We didn't think of putting them there. Our people did.

They created their own fund—and donated their own money—to help do it.

Perhaps the flags help our people create the kind of environment they want to work *in* by reminding them what they are working *for.*

They are proud of the plant. And are proud of our planes, too.

But they are most proud of our country.

GENERAL DYNAMICS
A Strong Company For A Strong Country

THEY ALL PINNED THEIR HOPES ON PEACE.

They were all fighters.

The conservatives fought with the liberals. The Democrats fought with the Republicans. The Bull Moosers fought with everybody.

They fought for different policies. But for the same principles. For freedom. And the freedom to live in peace.

Americans are still fighting for those principles today.

And working for them too.

That's why every day more than 100,000 Americans work at General Dynamics to supply America's fighting men and women with the best weapon systems in the world.

They are working for peace. And for peace of mind.

GENERAL DYNAMICS
A Strong Company For A Strong Country

WE COULDN'T MAKE IT EASY FOR HIM TO REACH THE FINISH LINE. JUST THE STARTING LINE.

It isn't easy for many Special Olympians to run 100 yards. Much less fly 1,000 miles.

They have the spirit, the dedication, and the will needed for running. But flying takes something mentally retarded people may be short of. Money.

That's why this year some 130 companies donated their Cessna Citation jets and pilots for the Citation Special Olympics Airlift.

The airlift, organized by our Cessna Aircraft Company, flew more than 900 Special

Olympians and their coaches from 12 states to South Bend, Indiana, to compete in the Seventh International Summer Games. The Special Olympians competed there for a full week. Then the airlift fleet of Citations returned to pick them up and fly them home.

A Cessna Citation jet takes off on a business mission every minute of every day. That's testimony to the quality of our jets.

But 130 companies decided to set aside business missions in favor of one that is more important. Special Olympics.

And we think that's testimony to the quality of our customers.

GENERAL DYNAMICS
A Strong Company For A Strong Country

203

REFERENCES

Camden, C. T., & Verba, S. (1986). Communication and consciousness. *Western Journal of Speech Communication, 50,* 64–73.

Corporate cleaner-upper. (1988, January 11). *Forbes,* p. 70.

Coxon, A. P. M. (1982). *User's guide to multidimensional scaling.* Exeter, NH: Heinemann Educational Books.

Coxon, A. P. M., & Davies, P. M. (1982). *Key texts in multidimensional scaling.* Exeter, NH: Heinemann Educational Books.

Fisher, B. A. (1978). *Perspectives on human communication.* New York: Macmillan.

Goldman, A. E., & McDonald, S. S. (1987). *The group depth interview: Principles and practices.* Englewood Cliffs, NJ: Prentice-Hall.

Hastie, R. (1986). A primer of information processing theory. In R. R. Lau & D. O. Sears (Eds.), *Political cognition* (pp. 11–39). Hillsdale, NJ: Lawrence Erlbaum Associates.

Rokeach, M. (1968). *Beliefs, attitudes, and values.* San Francisco: Jossey-Bass.

Umiker-Sebeok, J. (1987). *Marketing and semiotics. New directions in the study of signs for sale.* Berlin: Mouton de Gruyter.

Verba, S., & Camden, C. T. (1985). Barthes' *The fashion system:* An exploration at the recipient level. In J. Deely (Ed.), *Semiotics 1984* (pp. 471–489). Champaign-Urbana, IL: University Press of America.

Wiemann, J. M. (1981). Effects of laboratory videotaping procedures on selected communication behaviors. *Human Communication Research, 7,* 302–311.

Worthy, F. S. (1986, April 28). Mr. Clean charts a new course at General Dynamics. *Fortune,* pp. 70–76.

Yovovich, B. G. (1987, June 1). Those heavy implications of light food marketing. *Adweek,* p. 17.

12 | Refocusing the Politician's Image: Political Consultants and Political Discourse in Belgium

E. De Bens
State University of Gent, Belgium
Gary R. Pettey
Cleveland State University

The modern science of campaign politics has an indisputable United States flavor. The marriage between Madison Avenue and Pennsylvania Avenue is not soon likely to be dissolved. U.S. citizens have for more than a generation suffered through presidential campaigns that begin almost before the last one officially ends. Americans have become accustomed to the deluge of campaign coverage, literature and advertisements all carefully devised to get out the vote and to address problems deemed to be important to voters. A new breed of political consultants make their campaign decisions based on hard data collected from samples of the targeted electorate. Today's consultant is concerned with political information processing: Getting inside a voter's mind by devising sophisticated ways of determining how people think about candidates and how to alter or reinforce preferred cognitive structures. As Graber (1988) noted, it is the how questions that are important. How do people select information? How do they process that information? How does that processing produce and affect people's belief structures? This approach to campaigning has spread from national to state races, and has even led to spending millions to secure a seat in a state assembly (Weiner, 1986).

Although any serious U.S. candidate must consider employing a political consultant, international politics is only now catching up with modern campaigning techniques. The current trend in such international consulting, although, is not novel. As early as 1969, U.S. consultant Joseph Napolitan aided President Ferdinand Marcos in becoming the first Philippine president ever to be re-elected (Sabato, 1981). More recently, President Carter's 1976 consultant managed to stage an upset victory in Panama (Stark, 1985). U.S.

strategists have played major roles in elections in Costa Rica, Venezuela, Colombia, Spain, Nigeria and even Nicaragua ("The Selling. . .," 1986).

Parliamentary governments such as Israel, Australia, and Canada have used U.S. campaign know-how, but only more lately have Western European candidates and parties sought the opinions of U.S.-style political consultants. Margaret Thatcher and the Conservatives employed Saatchi & Saatchi to develop a U.S.-style campaign in 1979 and 1983. Saatchi & Saatchi's advertisements made the company known throughout the United Kingdom by soundly defeating Labor, comparing it with Marxism and portraying the left as weak and ineffective, emphasizing images largely already present in the people's minds.

Although there is a ban on paid political ads on British television, Saatchi and Saatchi remodeled the traditional 10-minute prime-time political slots made available to the major parties. First, the company "slashed the broadcasts into a more viewable five minutes and crammed them with real people, quick cuts and heart-tugging emotion. They looked, in fact, just like TV commercials" (Cote & Wentz, 1987, p. 60). By 1987, Labor had commissioned its own 10-minute tear-jerker from *Chariots of Fire* director, Hugh Hudson, while the Conservatives countered with Andrew Lloyd Webber of *Cats*, *Jesus Christ Superstar*, and *Evita* fame (Knight, 1987). Modern consultants understand that exposure *and* attention to the message is the prerequisite to affecting individuals' belief structures. One country, Belgium, is a recent adopter of modern campaign communication techniques.

Belgium has no doubt lagged behind other European countries in modern techniques largely because of its relatively small size and language-divided population. Direct mail marketing has zoomed in the last 2 years. But Belgium's language division and highly politized press have made print campaigning difficult, "most of a potential audience is reached [only] after two or three insertions, leading to high costs-per-thousand" (Montgomery, 1987 p. S-22). Bilingual societies pose special problems for the media consultant. Influencing the associations between candidates and images and issues becomes even more complex when voters' belief structures are composed of different building blocks (i.e., language).

But Belgium would appear ripe for political/media consultation. Party loyalty is declining. When a national study asked respondents whether they would vote in the 1987 election for a different party then they had in 1981, 26% said they would. But in addition, 32% of the respondents were still undecided for whom they would vote only 2 weeks before the election, up from 15% undecided at a similar time in 1982 (De Bens & Van Malderen, 1982). This is especially important in the Belgium context where the campaign traditionally runs for only 3 weeks, and every adult is legally required to vote—a virtually consummate environment, it would seem, for the media consultant. Motivation is not an issue in such a system (Chaffee, 1981), as virtually everyone will vote. Instead, name recognition combined with a positive image evaluation of the candidate can greatly increase the likelihood of electoral success (Goldenberg & Traugott, 1984). Hence, consultants who understand the associations between Belgium audiences and Belgium candidates should be considerably effective in reshaping the public conception of their candidate *and* the opposition.

TELEVISION DOMINATES THE ELECTION CONTEXT

Television has become the major campaign medium in Belgium. A 1982 opinion poll reported that 80% of the 2,310 respondents named television as their primary source of information on the election issues perhaps even a stronger influence on the Belgium audience than other European countries (Blumler, 1983; De Bens & Van Malderen, 1982). A more recent survey revealed that 30% of the Flemish population never reads a newspaper. Although no recent data are available for the French-speaking Wallonia, circulation figures and penetration rates would imply a similar percentage of nonreaders among French speakers.

Although television is the primary source for issues, some studies have shown that even one day after viewing an event respondents could remember little about the issues. They were more likely to remember image information about the politicians, including a politicians hairstyle and clothes (Blumler, Cayrol, & Thoveron, 1986).

Some uninterested viewers will watch the election programs simply because they are on when they want to watch television, or because it is fun or entertaining. However, in a country such as Belgium with the greatest cable density in the world, there is a considerable probability that politically uninterested viewers will turn to one of the 17 foreign channels to escape some of the national political content. And indeed, it has been demonstrated that viewers' loyalty to their national channels has been waning in general (De Bens, 1986). It does not take a high-priced political consultant to see that in order to maintain audiences for televised political messages, the messages are bound to be increasingly conceived on the pattern of entertainment programs. Political discourses may well become more trivial—emphasizing personal qualities of the candidates and excluding polemic discussion in general.

TELEVISION AND POLITICAL STARDOM

Since the 1960s the emphasis on personal qualities of candidates in European elections has been on the upswing. Many researchers have named television as the primary agent of this shift (see Dewachter, 1987). With the advent of television, Belgium politicians were no longer just a party and a name. Now a human face, with all its strength and weakness, was beamed into living rooms across the country. A politician's image became his trademark. His charm, determination, humor, and physical appearance all combined into a charismatic figure that voters recognize as the candidate. And, of course, in a competitive world such an image cannot be left to chance. It must be carefully designed.

In Belgium, personal advertising has gradually gained considerable importance. Ubiquitous political posters on the street force the individual to confront the politician's image whenever one ventures out. In 1971, 68% of the political posters advertised the party over the candidate, and 32% of the posters advertised the candidate personally. Further, personal advertisements were the exclusive domain of senior-party leadership competition. But by 1981, the posters were candidate centered, and the party financed only 43% of the posters, whereas the politicians themselves financed 57% of all the posters (Hooghe, Verminck, & Dewachter, 1987). The candidates themselves were now the primary campaign financiers, and they had to be able to command substantial financial resources. Such situations raise the obvious questions of the relationship between campaign contributions and the contributors influence on the candidate and office holder, especially when the cost of a campaign surged from 218 million Belgium Francs in 1974 to 838 million in 1985.

POLITICAL CONSULTANTS IN BELGIUM ELECTIONS

It comes as no surprise, then, that political marketing has boomed in Belgium in the last few years. The candidates of the large parties leave nothing to chance. Consider, for example, the development of a candidate's image in the campaign of Mrs. Annemie Neyts. This young candidate of the Flemish Liberal Party (PVV) was virtually unknown by the general public before 1985, but, with a carefully managed campaign, on election day she did very well. The agency that conducted her campaign decided to present her as a "charming, seductive but self-assured woman." A fashion photographer was brought in for her poster pictures, a makeup expert hired for television appearances. Not only was Neyts elected president of the Flemish Liberal Party in 1985, but, through her advertising campaign, she became a well-known public figure. Her new role, however, demanded a new image. The fashion-model image was abandoned and Neyts' own character and image of a determined woman was allowed to emerge. A newspaper paraphrasing a popular song from the play Evita, "Don't cry for Annemie" ("Affiches en verkiezingsampagnes," 1987), described Neyts' new image "as a ceremonial portrait of the president of a developing country."

Top, Annemie Neyts in a news photo; Bottom left, the candidate poster "I Persevere," the Liberal Party slogan; Bottom right, "Annemie Thinks of You."

Neyts' posters were basically apolitical. The posters carried messages such as: "Annemie," "Annemie works for Brussels," "Annemie Decides" or "Annemie Thinks of You." Other parties' posters were equally vague and image based. The Flemish Christian Democrats' (CVP) posters simply read "Yes. For Security." The Flemish Socialists used "Let's progress together," the Nationalist Party, "Now. For a firm line," and the Flemish Liberals simply, "I Persevere."

Deputy Prime Minister Guy Verhofstadt had his poster pictures so carefully staged that some voters may have not even recognized him. One wonders if such "polish" might actually alienate some people who have a "stored" media pictorial image of a candidate and find the poster to significantly vary from that image.

Modern touch-up techniques, however, are not limited to print. Video techniques allow an editor to make "candidates' noses shrink and bald spots disappear, electronically" and even allow a technician to give candidates a angelic persona. "[E]very time the profile photo of [George] Bush appeared, a thin halo of light outlined the back of his head" (Skenzay, 1988, p. 3). Italy and France have already seen nudes on campaign posters ("Naked came. . .", 1987), and Belgium is not far behind. One female candidate in the 1987 election was photographed wearing a leather jacket without a blouse. Her poster read: "The Hart is Back," and "Going Red for Me."

A NEED FOR RESEARCH

Although the United States has led the way in election research, elections in Europe and especially Belgium have received much less scrutiny. During the 1985 election in Belgium, the Department of Communication Science at the University of Ghent conducted a small experiment using communication and political science students. The 60 students were in their final year at the university. Each student was given printed texts of television statements made by the four major Flemish political parties. The students were given no reference to the visual content that surrounded the television message. Neither were any cues given as to the politician or party presenting the message. Only 14% of the students could attribute the message to the party that espoused it. Although this was certainly a biased sample, it should be biased in favor of political awareness, knowledge, and interest. So one might reasonably wonder how well the general population could be expected to perform under similar circumstances.

This small study is hardly conclusive, but it might well be indicative of the trend in European politics in general and Belgium politics specifically. Where are the issues? What are the differences between the candidates and the parties? The question remains whether U.S.-style politics can be transplanted

Left, Deputy Prime Minister Guy Verhofstadt in a news photo; right, his Liberal Party poster.

211

"Go Red for Me," is the slogan for this district candidate.

to the European context, or what exactly politics will look like in Belgium in 20 years. Three issues are clear. First, is that politics in Europe is rapidly changing, and that it will probably never return to the largely issue-based and party-driven campaigns of even 15 years ago. Second, European elections are going to look more like their U.S. counterparts both in content and style. Finally, the changes, perhaps largely as a function of televised communication, might trivialize political discourse in general. Such concerns are important to the very roots of society. If political consultants can have such a dramatic effect on European political culture, how will the "new mass communication" affect European societies and cultures in general. Political consultants will continue to assess how individuals process political information, construct more effective messages, and attempt to better sell their political products.

REFERENCES

Affiches en verkiezingscampagnes [Posters and election campaigns]. (1987, Nov. 28). *De Standaard*, p. 3.

Blumler, J. (1983). *Communicating to voters*. London: Sage.

Blumler, J., Cayrol, R., & Thoveron, G. (1986). *Television and politics*.

Chaffee, S. (1981). Mass media in political campaigns: An expanding role. In R. Rice & W. Paisley (Eds.), *Public communication campaigns* (pp. 181–199). Beverly Hills, CA: Sage.

Cote, K., & Wentz, L. (1987, June 8). British ad duel heats up, *Advertising Age*, p. 60.

De Bens, E. (1986). Cable penetration and competition among Belgian and foreign channels. *European Journal of Communication, 2*, 377–492.

De Bens, E., & Van Malderen, R. (1982). *Results of the 1982 election research*. Brussels: UNIOP.

Dewachter, W. (1987). Changes in a particratie: The Belgian party system from 1944 to 1986. In H. Daalder (Ed.), *Party systems in Denmark, Austria, Switzerland, The Netherlands and Belgium* (pp. 283–363). London: Pintar.

Goldenberg, E., & Traugott, M. (1984). *Campaigning for Congress*. Washington, DC: Congressional Quarterly.

Graber, D. (1988). *Processing the news*. New York: Longman.

Hooghe, L., Verminck, M., & Dewachter, W. (1987). *Blikvangers. Of de partij in eigen persoon*. Belgium: Leuven.

Knight, R. (1987, June 15). In the telly's eye. *U.S. News & World Report*, p. 10.

Montgomery, P. (1987, January 12). Direct marketing makes international waves. *Advertising Age*, p. s-22.

Naked came the Socialist. (1987, December 21). *Time*, p. 51.

Sabato, L. (1981). *The rise of political consultants*. New York: Basic Books.

Skenzay, L. (1988, April 18). Political touch-ups. *Advertising Age*, p. 3.

Stark, S. (1985, March). Serving tv winners. *Atlantic*, p. 84.

The selling of the candidates. (1986, September 6). *U.S. News & World Report*, p. 19.

Weiner, J. (1986, November 29). Tom Hayden's new workout. *Nation*, p. 603.

Name Index

Subject Index